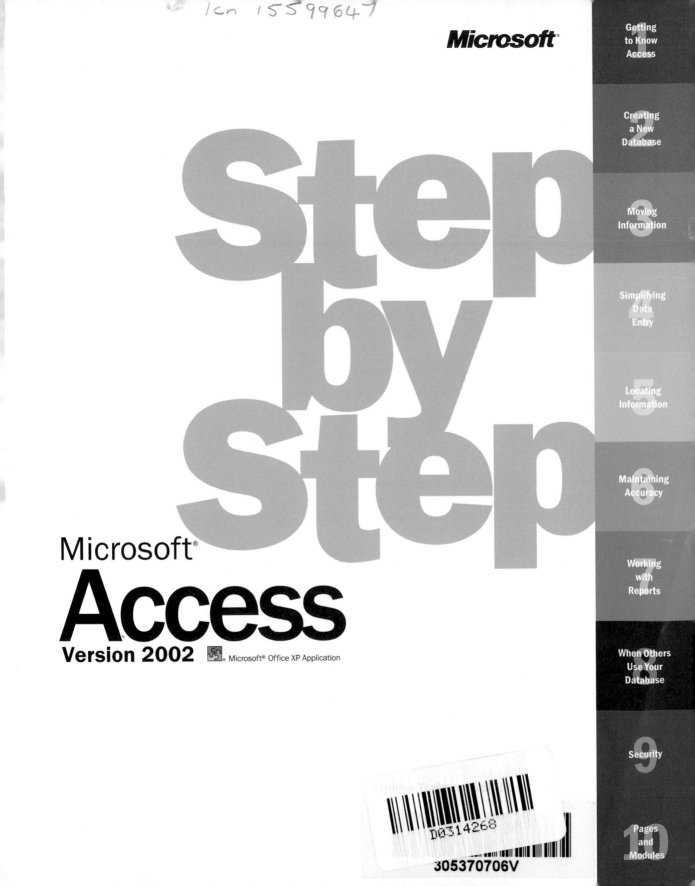

Microsoft

Step by Step

Microsoft®
Access
Version 2002 Microsoft® Office XP Application

Getting to Know Access

Creating a New Database 2

Moving Information 3

Simplifying Data Entry 4

Locating Information 5

Maintaining Accuracy 6

Working with Reports 7

When Others Use Your Database 8

Security 9

Pages and Modules 10

PUBLISHED BY
Microsoft Press
A Division of Microsoft Corporation
One Microsoft Way
Redmond, Washington 98052-6399

Library of Congress Cataloging-in-Publication Data
Microsoft Access Version 2002 Step by Step / Online Training Solutions, Inc.
        p. cm.
    ISBN 0-7356-1299-4
    1. Microsoft Access.   2. Database management.   I. Online Training Solutions (Firm).

    QA76.9.D3 M55698   2001
    005.75'65--dc21   2001030586

Printed and bound in the United States of America.

7 8 9 10   QWT   7 6 5 4 3

Distributed in Canada by H.B. Fenn and Company Ltd.

A CIP catalogue record for this book is available from the British Library.

Microsoft Press books are available through booksellers and distributors worldwide. For further information about international editions, contact your local Microsoft Corporation office or contact Microsoft Press International directly at fax (425) 936-7329. Visit our Web site at www.microsoft.com/mspress. Send comments to *mspinput@microsoft.com*.

FoxPro, FrontPage, IntelliMouse, Microsoft, Microsoft Press, Outlook, PivotChart, PivotTable, PowerPoint, VGA, Visual Basic, Windows, and Windows NT are either registered trademarks or trademarks of Microsoft Corporation in the United States and/or other countries. Other product and company names mentioned herein may be the trademarks of their respective owners.

The example companies, organizations, products, domain names, e-mail addresses, logos, people, places, and events depicted herein are fictitious. No association with any real company, organization, product, domain name, e-mail address, logo, person, place, or event is intended or should be inferred.

Acquisitions Editor: Kong Cheung
Project Editors: Wendy Zucker and Jenny Moss Benson

Body Part No. X08-06228

Contents

1   Getting to Know Microsoft Access 2002   1

2   Creating a New Database   24

3   Getting Information Into and Out of a Database   48

Contents

4 Simplifying Data Entry with Forms　72

5 Locating Specific Information　106

6 Keeping Your Information Accurate　132

7 Working with Reports 160

8 Making It Easy for Others to Use Your Database 186

9 Keeping Your Information Secure 210

10 Working with Pages and Modules 242

Quick Reference 279

Glossary 299

Index 309

What's New in Microsoft Access 2002

You'll notice some changes as soon as you start Microsoft Access 2002. The toolbars and menu bar have a new look, and there's a new task pane on the right side of your screen. But the features that are new or greatly improved in this version of Access go beyond just changes in appearance. Some changes won't be apparent to you until you start using the program.

The following table lists some of the new Access 2002 features. When you have some experience using Access, you might be interested in exploring some of the features not covered in this book to see whether they might be of use in your own databases.

Use this new feature	To do this
Speech recognition	Give commands and dictate text
Data Access Page Designer	Efficiently design data access pages
Save as data access pages	Save existing forms and reports as pages that can be viewed over the Web
Access 2002 file format	Gain faster access and processing of large databases
Conversion error logging	Log errors when converting Access 95, Access 97, and Access 2000 databases to Access 2002 file format
Multiple undo and redo	Undo or redo several actions instead of just the last one
PivotTables and PivotCharts	Analyze data by creating dynamic views of data
XML input and output	Import XML data and publish Access data to the Web by exporting it in XML format
Stored Procedure Designer	Create simple SQL Server stored procedures
Batch updating	Save updates to records on a local computer and send them to the server all at once
Script language support	Set preferences for complex script languages, including the reading direction

For more information about the Access product, see *http://www.microsoft.com/office/access*.

Getting Help

Every effort has been made to ensure the accuracy of this book and the contents of its CD-ROM. If you do run into problems, please contact the appropriate source for help and assistance.

Getting Help with This Book and Its CD-ROM

If your question or issue concerns the content of this book or its companion CD-ROM, please first search the online Microsoft Knowledge Base, which provides support information for known errors in or corrections to this book, at the following Web site:

http://mspress.microsoft.com/support/search.htm

If you do not find your answer at the online Knowledge Base, send your comments or questions to Microsoft Press Technical Support at:

mspinput@microsoft.com

Getting Help with Microsoft Access 2002

If your question is about a Microsoft software product, including Access 2002, and not about the content of this Microsoft Press book, please search the Microsoft Knowledge Base at:

http://support.microsoft.com/directory

In the United States, Microsoft software product support issues not covered by the Microsoft Knowledge Base are addressed by Microsoft Product Support Services. The Microsoft software support options available from Microsoft Product Support Services are listed at:

http://support.microsoft.com/directory

Outside the United States, for support information specific to your location, please refer to the Worldwide Support menu on the Microsoft Product Support Services Web site for the site specific to your country:

http://support.microsoft.com/directory

Using the Book's CD-ROM

The CD-ROM inside the back cover of this book contains all the practice files you'll use as you work through the exercises in this book. By using practice files, you won't waste time creating sample databases with which to experiment—instead, you can jump right in and concentrate on learning how to use Microsoft Access 2002.

Important

The CD-ROM for this book does not contain the Access 2002 software. You should purchase and install that program before using this book.

Minimum System Requirements

To use this book, your computer should meet the following requirements.

Computer/Processor

Computer with a Pentium 133-megahertz (MHz) or higher processor

Memory

RAM requirements depend on the operating system used:

- Microsoft Windows 98, or Windows 98 Second Edition

  24 MB of RAM plus an additional 8 MB of RAM for each Microsoft Office program (such as Microsoft Word) running simultaneously

- Microsoft Windows Millennium Edition (Windows Me), or Microsoft Windows NT

  32 MB of RAM plus an additional 8 MB of RAM for each Office program (such as Microsoft Word) running simultaneously

- Microsoft Windows 2000 Professional

  64 MB of RAM plus an additional 8 MB of RAM for each Office program (such as Microsoft Word) running simultaneously

Hard Disk

Hard disk space requirements will vary depending on configuration; custom installation choices may require more or less hard disk space.

- 245 MB of available hard disk space with 115 MB on the hard disk where the operating system is installed. (Users without Windows 2000, Windows Me, or

Office 2000 Service Release 1 require an extra 50 MB of hard disk space for System Files Update.)

■ An additional 94 MB of hard disk space is required for installing the practice files.

Operating System

Windows 98, Windows 98 Second Edition, Windows Me, Windows NT 4.0 with Service Pack 6 or later, or Windows 2000 or later. (On systems running Windows NT 4.0 with Service Pack 6, the version of Microsoft Internet Explorer must be upgraded to at least version 4.01 with Service Pack 1.)

Important

The exercises in this book were created on a computer running Windows 98. Other operating systems might display slightly different results than those in the book's graphics.

Drive

CD-ROM drive

Display

Super VGA (800 × 600) or higher-resolution monitor with 256 colors

Peripherals

Microsoft Mouse, Microsoft IntelliMouse, or compatible pointing device

Applications

Microsoft Access 2002

Microsoft Word 97 or later

Microsoft Excel 97 or later

Installing the Practice Files

You need to install the practice files on your hard disk before you use them in the chapters' exercises. Follow these steps to prepare the CD-ROM's files for your use:

1 Insert the CD-ROM into the CD-ROM drive of your computer.

A menu screen appears.

Important

If the menu screen does not appear, start Windows Explorer. In the left pane, locate the icon for your CD-ROM drive, and click this icon. In the right pane, double-click the file named *StartCD*.

2   Click **Install Practice Files**.

3   Click **OK** in the initial message box.

4   If you want to install the practice files to a location other than the default folder (*C:\SBS\Access*), click the **Change Folder** button, select the new drive and path, and then click **OK**.

Important

If you install the practice files to a location other than the default folder, the file location listed in some of the exercises will be incorrect.

5   Click the **Continue** button to install the selected practice files.

6   After the practice files have been installed, click **OK**.

Within the installation folder are subfolders for each chapter in the book.

7   Remove the CD-ROM from the CD-ROM drive, and return it to the envelope at the back of the book.

Using the Practice Files

Each chapter's introduction lists the folders where you will find the files that are needed for that chapter. Each topic in the chapter explains how and when to use any practice files. The majority of the topics use the GardenCo database, a sample database created for a fictitious garden and plant store called The Garden Company. However, the database varies from topic to topic, so be sure to use the one in the folder specified for the particular topic you are working on. The file or files that you'll need are indicated in the margin at the beginning of the procedure above the CD icon, like this:

GardenCo

The following table lists each chapter's practice files.

Chapter	Folder Name	Subfolder Name
Chapter 1: Getting to Know Microsoft Access 2002	KnowAccess	Open Tables Queries Forms Reports
Chapter 2: Creating a New Database	CreateDB	CreatingDB CheckingDB Refining Manipulate
Chapter 3: Getting Information Into and Out of a Database	Importing	ImportExcel ImportDText ImportFText ImportAccess ImportDbase ImportHTML ImportXML Export Link OfficeLink
Chapter 4: Simplifying Data Entry	Forms	FormByWiz Properties Layout Controls Events AutoForm Subform
Chapter 5: Locating Specific Information	Queries	Sort FilterDS FilterForm AdvFilter QueryDes QueryWiz Aggregate

Chapter	Folder Name	Subfolder Name
Chapter 6: Keeping Your Information Accurate	Accurate	DataType FieldSize InputMask ValRules Lookup QueryUp QueryDel
Chapter 7: Working with Reports	Reports	RepByWiz Modify ByDesign Subreport Print
Chapter 8: Making It Easy for Others to Use Your Database	Switchbrd	SBManager Splash Startup Health
Chapter 9: Keeping Your Information Secure	Secure	Encrypt Password Share Replicate Split Multi Maintain VBA MDE
Chapter 10: Working with Pages and Modules	PgsMods	Static VBA AutoPage Wizard Anaylze

Uninstalling the Practice Files

After you finish working through this book, you should uninstall the practice files to free up hard disk space.

Tip

If you saved any files outside the *SBS\Access* folder, they will not be deleted by the following uninstall process. You'll have to manually delete them in Windows Explorer.

1   On the Windows taskbar, click the **Start** button, point to **Settings**, and then click **Control Panel**.

2   Double-click the **Add/Remove Programs** icon.

3   Click **Microsoft Access 2002 SBS Files**, and click **Add/Remove**. (If you're using Windows 2000 Professional, click the **Remove** or **Change/Remove** button.)

4   Click **Yes** when the confirmation dialog box appears.

Important

If you need additional help installing or uninstalling the practice files, please see the section "Getting Help" earlier in this book. Microsoft's product support does not provide support for this book or its CD-ROM.

Conventions and Features

You can save time when you use this book by understanding how the *Step by Step* series shows special instructions, keys to press, buttons to click, and so on.

Convention	Meaning
1 **2**	Numbered steps guide you through hands-on exercises in each topic.
⊙	This icon at the beginning of a chapter indicates the list of folders that contain the files that the topics in the chapter will use.
FileName ⊙	At the beginning of an exercise, this icon appears preceded by a list of the practice files required to complete the exercise.
Ac2002-3-5 MICROSOFT OFFICE SPECIALIST Approved Courseware	This icon indicates a section that covers a Microsoft Office User Specialist (MOS) exam objective. The numbers above the icon refer to the specific MOS objective.
new for **Office**XP	This icon indicates a new or greatly improved feature in this version of Microsoft Access.
Tip	This section provides useful background information or a helpful hint or shortcut that makes working through a task easier.
Important	This section points out information that you need to know to complete the procedure.
Troubleshooting	This section shows you how to fix a common problem.
Save 💾	When a button is referenced in a topic, a picture of the button appears in the margin area, preceded by the name of the button.
Alt + Tab	A plus sign (+) between two key names means that you must press those keys at the same time. For example, "Press Alt + Tab" means that you hold down the Alt key while you press Tab.
Black boldface type	Program features that you click are shown in black boldface type.
Blue boldface type	Terms explained in the glossary are shown in blue boldface type.
Red boldface type	Text you are supposed to type appears in red boldface type in the procedures.
Italic type	Folder paths, URLs, and emphasized words appear in italic type.

MOS Objectives

Each Microsoft Office Specialist (MOS) certification level (core and expert) has a set of objectives. To prepare for the MOS certification exam, you should confirm that you can meet its respective objectives.

This book will prepare you fully for the MOS exam at either the core or the expert level because it addresses all the objectives for both exams. Throughout this book, topics that pertain to MOS objectives are identified with the MOS logo and objective number in the margin, like this:

Ac2002-3-5

Approved Courseware

Multiple MOS objectives may be covered within one topic.

Core MOS Objectives

Objective	Skill	Page(s)
Ac2002-1	**Creating and Using Databases**	
Ac2002-1-1	Create Access databases	26
Ac2002-1-2	Open database objects in multiple views	6, 37
Ac2002-1-3	Move among records	30
Ac2002-1-4	Format datasheets	44
Ac2002-2	**Creating and Modifying Tables**	
Ac2002-2-1	Create and modify tables	34
Ac2002-2-2	Add a predefined input mask to a field	140
Ac2002-2-3	Create Lookup fields	148
AC2002-2-4	Modify field properties	37, 140
Ac2002-3	**Creating and Modifying Queries**	
Ac2002-3-1	Create and modify select queries	126
Ac2002-3-2	Add calculated fields to select queries	118

(continued)

Objective	Skill	Page(s)
Ac2002-4	**Creating and Modifying Forms**	
Ac2002-4-1	Create and display forms	74, 94
Ac2002-4-2	Modify form properties	76, 85
Ac2002-5	**Viewing and Organizing Information**	
Ac2002-5-1	Enter, edit, and delete records	30, 134, 157
Ac2002-5-2	Create queries	118
Ac2002-5-3	Sort records	6, 108, 115
Ac2002-5-4	Filter records	6, 110, 113, 115
Ac2002-6	**Defining Relationships**	
Ac2002-6-1	Create one-to-many relationships	96
Ac2002-6-2	Enforce referential integrity	145
Ac2002-7	**Producing Reports**	
Ac2002-7-1	Create and format reports	162
Ac2002-7-2	Add calculated controls to reports	176
Ac2002-7-3	Preview and print reports	19, 182
Ac2002-8	**Integrating with Other Applications**	
Ac2002-8-1	Import data into Access	50, 52, 54, 57, 59, 60
Ac2002-8-2	Export data from Access	64
Ac2002-8-3	Create a simple data access page	261, 269

Expert MOS Objectives

Objective	Skill	Page(s)
Ac2002e-1	**Creating and Modifying Tables**	
Ac2002e-1-1	Use data validation	134, 138, 145
Ac2002e-1-2	Link tables	67
Ac2002e-1-3	Create Lookup fields and modify Lookup field properties	148
Ac2002e-1-4	Create and modify input masks	140

Objective	Skill	Page(s)
Ac2002e-2	**Creating and Modifying Forms**	
Ac2002e-2-1	Create a form in Design view	82, 193
Ac2002e-2-2	Create a switchboard and set startup options	188, 198
Ac2002e-2-3	Add subform controls to Access forms	96
Ac2002e-3	**Refining Queries**	
Ac2002e-3-1	Specify multiple query criteria	154
Ac2002e-3-2	Create and apply advanced filters	115
Ac2002e-3-3	Create and run parameter queries	126
Ac2002e-3-4	Create and run action queries	157
Ac2002e-3-5	Use aggregate functions in queries	128
Ac2002e-4	**Producing Reports**	
Ac2002e-4-1	Create and modify reports	162, 166, 171
Ac2002e-4-2	Add subreport controls to Access reports	176
Ac2002e-4-3	Sort and group data in reports	162
Ac2002e-5	**Defining Relationships**	
Ac2002e-5-1	Establish one-to-many relationships	96
Ac2002e-5-2	Establish many-to-many relationships	96
Ac2002e-6	**Operating Access on the Web**	
Ac2002e-6-1	Create and modify a data access page	261, 269
Ac2002e-6-2	Save PivotTable and PivotChart views to data access pages	273
Ac2002e-7	**Using Access tools**	
Ac2002e-7-1	Import XML documents into Access	63
Ac2002e-7-2	Export Access data to XML documents	64
Ac2002e-7-3	Encrypt and decrypt databases	212
Ac2002e-7-4	Compact and repair databases	204
Ac2002e-7-5	Assign database security	214, 225, 232
Ac2002e-7-6	Replicate a database	218
Ac2002e-8	**Creating Database Applications**	
Ac2002e-8-1	Create Access modules	90, 247, 252
Ac2002e-8-2	Use the Database Splitter	223
Ac2002e-8-3	Create an MDE file	237, 239

Taking a MOS Exam

As desktop computing technology advances, more employers rely on the objectivity and consistency of technology certification when screening, hiring, and training employees to ensure the competence of these professionals. As an employee, you can use technology certification to prove that you meet the standards set by your current or potential employer. The Microsoft Office Specialist (MOS) program is the only Microsoft-approved certification program designed to assist employees in validating their competence using Microsoft Office applications.

About the MOS Program

A Microsoft Office Specialist is an individual who has certified his or her skills in one or more of the Microsoft Office desktop applications of Microsoft Word, Microsoft Excel, Microsoft PowerPoint, Microsoft Outlook, Microsoft Access, Microsoft FrontPage, or Microsoft Project. The Microsoft Office Specialist Program typically offers certification exams at the "core" and "expert" skill levels. (The availability of Microsoft Office Specialist certification exams varies by application, application version, and language. Visit *http://www.microsoft.com/officespecialist* for exam availability.) The Microsoft Office Specialist Program is the only Microsoft-approved program in the world for certifying proficiency in Microsoft Office desktop applications and Microsoft Project. This certification can be a valuable asset in any job search or career advancement.

What Does This Logo Mean?

Approved Courseware

It means this courseware has been approved by the Microsoft Office Specialist Program to be among the finest available for learning Access 2002. It also means that upon completion of this courseware, you may be prepared to become a Microsoft Office Specialist.

Selecting a MOS Certification Level

In selecting the MOS certification(s) level that you would like to pursue, you should assess the following:

- The Office application and version(s) of the application with which you are familiar
- The length of time you have used the application
- Whether you have had formal or informal training

Candidates for the core-level MOS certification exams are expected to successfully complete a wide range of standard business tasks, such as formatting a document. Successful candidates generally have six or more months of experience with the application, including either formal instructor-led training with a MOS Authorized Instructor or self-study using MOS-approved books, guides, or interactive computer-based materials.

Candidates for expert-level certification, by comparison, are expected to complete more complex business-oriented assignments utilizing the application's advanced functionality, such as importing data and recording macros. Successful candidates generally have two or more years of experience with the application, again including formal instructor-led training with a MOS Authorized Instructor or self-study using MOS-approved materials.

MOS Exam Objectives

Every MOS certification exam is developed from a list of exam objectives, which are derived from studies of how the Office application is actually used in the workplace. Because these objectives dictate the scope of each exam, they provide you with critical information on how to prepare for MOS certification.

Tip

See the previous section, "MOS Objectives," for a complete list of objectives for Access.

MOS Approved Courseware, including Microsoft Press's Step by Step series, is reviewed and approved on the basis of its coverage of the MOS exam objectives.

The Exam Experience

The MOS certification exams are unique in that they are performance-based examinations that allow you to interact with a "live" version of the Office application as you complete a series of assigned tasks. All the standard menus, toolbars, and keyboard shortcuts are available—even the Help menu. MOS exams for Office XP applications consist of 25 to 35 questions, each of which requires you to complete one or more tasks using the Office application for which you are seeking certification. For example:

Prepare the document for publication as a Web page by completing the following three tasks:

1 Convert the memo to a Web page.

2 Title the page **Revised Company Policy**.

3 Name the memo **Policy Memo.htm**.

The duration of MOS exams ranges from 45 to 60 minutes, depending on the application. Passing percentages range from 70 to 80 percent correct.

The Exam Interface and Controls

After you fill out a series of information screens, the testing software starts the exam and the respective Office application. You will see the exam interface and controls, including the test question, in the dialog box in the lower right corner of the screen.

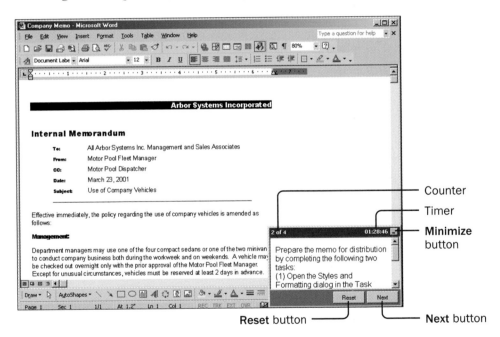

- If the exam dialog box gets in the way of your work, you can hide it by clicking the **Minimize** button in the upper right corner, or you can drag it to another position on the screen.

- The timer starts when the first question appears on your screen and displays the remaining exam time. If the timer and the counter are distracting, click the timer to remove the display.

Important

> The timer will not count the time required for the exam to be loaded between questions. It keeps track only of the time you spend answering questions.

- The counter tracks how many questions you have completed and how many remain.
- The **Reset** button allows you to restart work on a question if you think you have made an error. The **Reset** button will *not* restart the entire exam or extend the exam time limit.
- When you complete a question, click the **Next** button to move to the next question.

Important

> It is not possible to move back to a previous question on the exam.

Test-Taking Tips

- Follow all instructions provided in each question completely and accurately.
- Enter requested information as it appears in the instructions but without duplicating the formatting. For example, all text and values that you will be asked to enter will appear in the instructions as **bold** and **underlined**; however, you should enter the information without applying this formatting unless you are specifically instructed to do otherwise.
- Close all dialog boxes before proceeding to the next exam question unless you are specifically instructed otherwise.
- There is no need to save your work before moving on to the next question unless you are specifically instructed to do so.
- Do not cut and paste information from the exam interface into the application.
- For questions that ask you to print a document, spreadsheet, chart, report, slide, and so forth, nothing will actually be printed.
- Responses are scored based on the result of your work, not the method you use to achieve that result (unless a specific method is explicitly required), and not the time you take to complete the question. Extra keystrokes or mouse clicks do not count against your score.

■ If your computer becomes unstable during the exam (for example, if the application's toolbars or the mouse no longer functions) or if a power outage occurs, contact a testing center administrator immediately. The administrator will then restart the computer, and the exam will return to the point before the interruption occurred.

Certification

At the conclusion of the exam, you will receive a score report, which you can print with the assistance of the testing center administrator. If your score meets or exceeds the minimum required score, you will also be mailed a printed certificate within approximately 14 days.

For More Information

To learn more about becoming a Microsoft Office Specialist, visit *http://www.microsoft.com/officespecialist*.

To purchase a Microsoft Office Specialist certification exam, visit *http://www.microsoft.com/mspress/certification/officespecialist/*.

To learn about other Microsoft Office Specialist approved courseware from Microsoft Press, visit *http://microsoft.com/mspress/certification/officespecialist*.

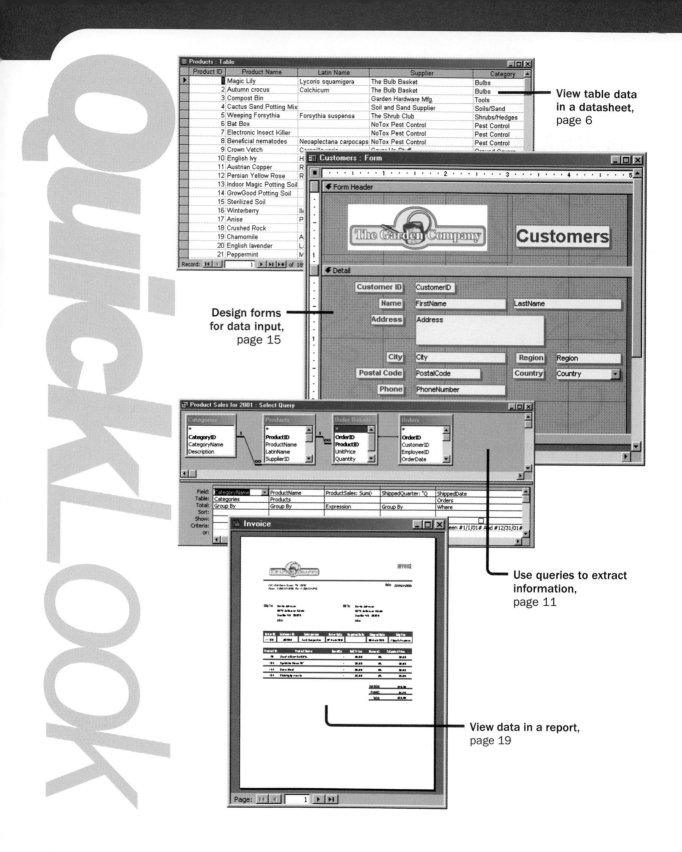

View table data
in a datasheet,
page 6

Design forms
for data input,
page 15

Use queries to extract
information,
page 11

View data in a report,
page 19

Chapter 1
Getting to Know Microsoft Access 2002

After completing this chapter, you will be able to:

✔ **Open an existing database.**

✔ **Open tables in different views.**

✔ **Open and run queries.**

✔ **Open a form in different views.**

✔ **Open a report in different views.**

This book gives you straightforward instructions for using Microsoft Access 2002 to create databases. It takes you from knowing little or nothing about Access—or, for that matter, about databases—to a level of expertise that will enable you to develop database applications for use by one person or by many.

This chapter introduces the concept of a database, explains a little about Access, and then takes you on a tour. The database you will use for the tour belongs to The Garden Company, a fictional garden supply and plant store. (You will be working with this database throughout this book.) Although looking at someone else's work might not be as exciting as jumping in and creating your own database, this tour will give you a firm foundation from which to begin working with Access to create your own databases.

In this chapter, you will open the GardenCo database, explore its structure, and look at some of the objects used to store and manipulate the data it contains. You will be working with the GardenCo database files that are stored in the following subfolders of the *SBS\Access\KnowAccess* folder: *Open*, *Tables*, *Queries*, *Forms*, and *Reports*.

Tip

To follow along with the exercises in this book, you need to install the practice files from the companion CD. (You cannot just copy the files.) You will find instructions for installing the files in the "Using the Book's CD-ROM" section at the beginning of the book.

What Is a Database?

In its most basic form, a database is the computer equivalent of an organized list of information. Typically, this information has a common subject or purpose, such as the list of employees shown here:

ID	Last Name	First Name	Title	Hire Date
1	Dale	Martha	Sales Rep	May 1, 1992
2	Fuller	Joanna	V.P., Sales	Aug 14, 1992
3	Lee	Mark	Sales Rep	Apr 1, 1992
4	Penn	Daniel	Sales Rep	May 3, 1993

This list is arranged in a **table** of columns and rows, called **fields** and **records** in database terms. Each column (field) stores a particular type of information about an employee: first name, last name, date of hire, and so on. Each row (record) contains information about a different employee.

If a database did nothing more than store information in a table, it would be as useful as a paper list. But because the database stores information in an electronic format, you can manipulate the information in powerful ways to extend its utility.

For example, a phone book for your city is probably sitting on a shelf within a few feet of you. If you want to locate a person or a business in your city, you can do so, because the information in the telephone book is organized in an understandable manner. If you want to get in touch with someone a little further away, you can go to the public library and use its collection of phone books, which probably includes one for each major city in the country. However, if you want to find the phone numbers of all the people in the country with your last name, or if you want the phone number of your grandmother's neighbor, these phone books won't do you much good because they aren't organized in a way that makes that information easy to find.

When the information published in a phone book is stored in a database, it takes up far less space, it costs less to reproduce and distribute, and, if the database is designed correctly, the information can be retrieved in many ways. The real power of a database isn't in its ability to store information; it is in your ability to quickly retrieve exactly the information you want from the database.

What's Special About Access?

Simple **database programs**, such as the Database component of Microsoft Works, can store information in only one table, which is often referred to as a flat file. These simple databases are often called **flat databases**. More complex database programs, such as Microsoft Access, can store information in multiple related tables, thereby creating what are often referred to as **relational databases**. If the information in a relational database is organized correctly, you can treat these multiple tables as a single storage area and pull information electronically from different tables in whatever order meets your needs.

A table is just one of the types of **objects** that you can work with in Access. The following graphic shows all the Access object types:

Of all these object types, only one—tables—is used to store information. The rest are used to manage, manipulate, analyze, retrieve, display, or publish the table information—in other words, to make the information as accessible and therefore as useful as possible.

Tip

For maximum compatibility with existing databases, the default format for new databases created with Access 2002 is Access 2000.

Over the years, Microsoft has put a lot of effort into making Access not only one of the most powerful consumer database programs available, but also one of the easiest to learn and use. Because Access is part of the Microsoft Office suite of programs, you can use many of the techniques you know from using other Office applications, such as Microsoft Word and Microsoft Excel, when using Access. For example, you can use familiar commands, buttons, and keyboard shortcuts to open and edit the information in Access tables. And because Access is integrated with other members of the suite, you can easily share information between Access and Word, Excel, or other programs.

Opening an Existing Database

The database for The Garden Company, which is called *GardenCo*, contains information about its employees, products, suppliers, and customers that is stored in a series of tables. As you complete the exercises in this book, you will work with these tables and develop an assortment of queries, forms, reports, data access pages, macros, and modules that can be used to enter, edit, and manipulate the information in the tables in many ways.

GardenCo

In this exercise, you will open the GardenCo database, explore some of its objects, and then close the database. You won't find a lot of detailed explanation here, because this is just an overview. The working folder for this exercise is *SBS\Access\KnowAccess\Open*. Follow these steps:

1 At the left end of the taskbar at the bottom of your screen, click the **Start** button, point to **Programs**, and then click **Microsoft Access**.

When Access first opens, your screen looks like this:

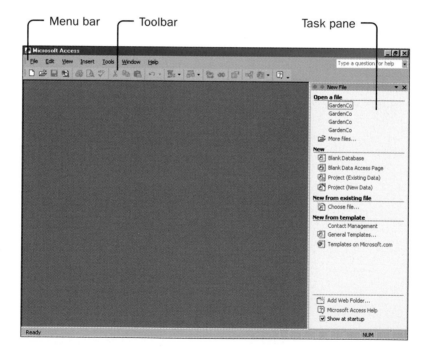

Important

What you see on your screen might not match the graphics in this book exactly. The screens in this book were captured on a monitor set to 800 x 600 resolution with 24-bit color and the Windows Standard color scheme. The book starts with the Access default settings, and the screens reflect any changes to those settings that are called for by the steps in the exercises.

Task pane
new for
OfficeXP

As with other Microsoft Office applications, Access has a menu bar and one or more toolbars across the top of the window. New to programs in Microsoft Office XP is the **task pane** shown at the right side of this window. In Access, a different version of the task pane appears when you click either **New** or **Search** on the **File** menu, or click **Office Clipboard** on the **Edit** menu.

Open

2   Click the **Open** button on the toolbar, and then browse to the *SBS\Access\KnowAccess\Open* folder, and double-click **GardenCo**.

The Garden Company introductory screen, called a **splash screen**, appears.

Tip

You will normally open a database by double-clicking its file name in Windows Explorer. (Access databases have a file name extension *.mdb*.) Or you can start Access and click **New** on the **File** menu to display the **New File** task pane, which offers a variety of options for opening new or existing databases.

3   Select the **Don't show this screen again** check box, and then click **OK**.

You see this **switchboard**, which is used to easily access the database objects needed to perform common tasks:

4 Click **Close Switchboard** to close the switchboard.

Restore

5 The database window is minimized as a small title bar in the lower left corner of your screen. Click the **Restore** button in this title bar to expand the database window.

The GardenCo **database window** looks like this:

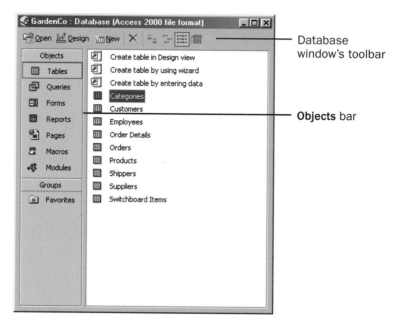

Across the top of the window is a toolbar and along the left edge is the **Objects** bar, which lists the Access database objects. Because **Tables** is selected, the right pane of the window lists the tables contained in the database.

6 Close the **GardenCo** database by clicking **Close** on the **File** menu.

Exploring Tables

Ac2002-1-2
Ac2002-5-3
Ac2002-5-4

Approved Courseware

Tables are the core database objects. Their purpose is to store information. The purpose of every other database object is to interact in some manner with one or more tables. An Access database can contain thousands of tables, and the number of records each table can contain is limited more by the space available on your hard disk than anything else.

Tip

For detailed information about Access specifications, such as the maximum size of a database or the maximum number of records in a table, click the Ask A Question box at the right end of the menu bar, type **Access specifications**, and press [Enter].

Every Access object has two or more **views**. For tables, the two most common views are **Datasheet view**, where you can see and modify the table's data, and **Design view**, where you can see and modify the table's structure. Clicking the **View** button toggles the view of the open table between Datasheet and Design views. You can also click the down arrow to the right of the **View** button and select a view from the drop-down list.

When you view a table in Datasheet view, you see the table's data in columns (fields) and rows (records), as shown here:

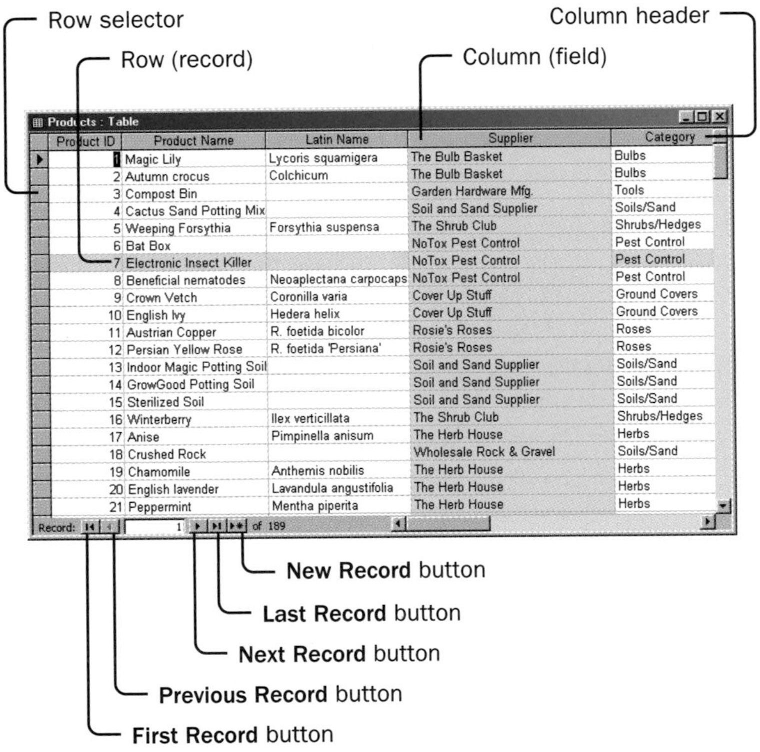

If two tables have one or more fields in common, you can embed the datasheet for one table in another. The embedded datasheet, which is called a **subdatasheet**, allows you to see the information in more than one table at the same time. For example, you might want to embed an Orders datasheet in a Customers table so that you can see the orders each customer has placed.

GardenCo

In this exercise, you will open existing tables in the GardenCo database and explore their structure in different views. The working folder for this exercise is *SBS\Access\KnowAccess\Tables*. Follow these steps:

1   Open the **GardenCo** database located in the working folder.

2   Click **Tables** on the **Objects** bar.

Details

Because the **Details** button is active on the toolbar at the top of the database window, a description of each of the objects listed in the window is displayed to the right of its name.

Tip

You can resize the columns in the database window by dragging the vertical bar that separates columns in the header. You can set the width of a column to the width of its widest entry by double-clicking the vertical bar.

Maximize

3   Click the **Maximize** button in the upper right corner of the database window.

The database window expands to fill the Access window, and you can now read the table descriptions. Note that the first three items in the **Name** column are not tables; they are shortcuts to three commands you can use to create a new table.

Tip

If you don't want these shortcuts at the top of each list of objects, click **Options** on the **Tools** menu, click the **View** tab in the **Options** dialog box, clear the **New object shortcuts** check box, and click **OK**.

Restore

4   Click the **Restore** button to shrink the database window again.

5   Click the **Categories** table, and then click the **Open** button at the top of the database window.

The table opens in Datasheet view, as shown here:

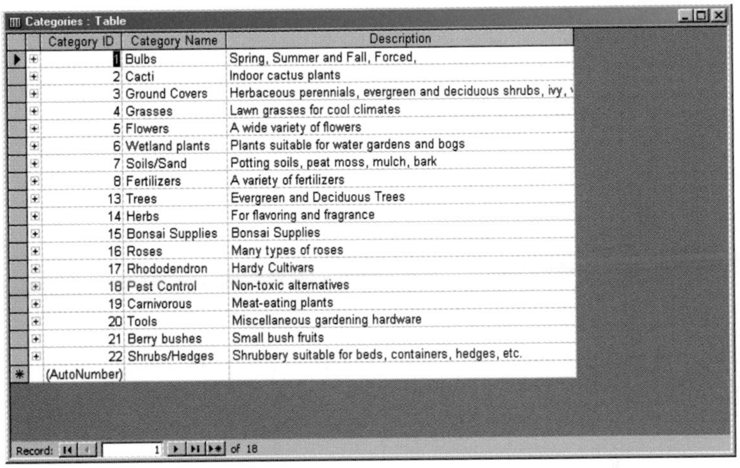

This datasheet contains a list of the categories of products sold by The Garden Company. As you can see, there are fields for Category ID, Category Name, and Description.

6 Click the plus sign to the left of the record for the Bulbs category.

Clicking the plus sign expands an embedded subdatasheet. You are now looking at category records from the Categories table and product records from the Products table simultaneously, as shown here:

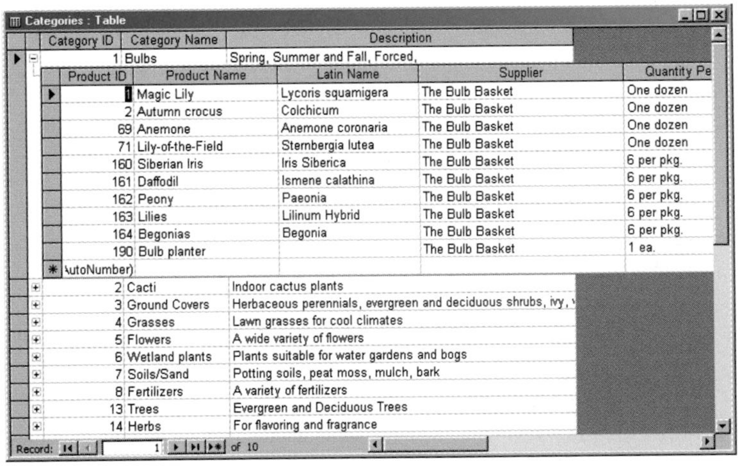

Notice that the plus sign has changed to a minus sign.

7 Click the minus sign to the left of the Bulbs record to collapse the sub-datasheet.

8 Close the **Categories** table by clicking **Close** on the **File** menu. If you are prompted to save changes to the table layout, click **Yes**.

Tip

You can also close a window by clicking the **Close** button in the window's upper right corner. When an object window is maximized, this button is called the **Close Window** button to avoid confusion with the **Close** button at the right end of the Access window's title bar. Be careful to click the correct button, or else you will quit Access.

9 On the **Objects** bar, double-click the **Orders** table to open it in Datasheet view, like this:

OrderID	CustomerID	EmployeeID	OrderDate	RequiredDate	ShippedDate	
11079	LANER	Carpenter, Lani	1/5/01		1/7/01	Big Things
11080	ACKPI	Carpenter, Lani	1/5/01		1/6/01	EZ Does It
11081	BROKE	Anderson, Amy	1/6/01		1/7/01	EZ Does It
11082	KHAKA	Anderson, Amy	1/6/01	1/12/01	1/8/01	Triple P De
11083	KOBMA	Carpenter, Lani	1/8/01	1/12/01	1/9/01	Triple P De
11084	COXAR	Anderson, Amy	1/12/01		1/14/01	Triple P De
11085	RANCY	Emanuel, Michael	1/12/01		1/13/01	EZ Does It
11086	OTALA	Emanuel, Michael	1/12/01		1/13/01	Triple P De
11087	THOJO	Carpenter, Lani	1/12/01		1/13/01	Big Things
11088	MILGE	Emanuel, Michael	1/13/01		1/14/01	Triple P De
11089	ESAPA	Anderson, Amy	1/14/01	1/19/01	1/16/01	EZ Does It
11090	HOHBO	Emanuel, Michael	1/14/01		1/16/01	Big Things
11091	HOLMI	Carpenter, Lani	1/15/01	1/20/01	1/19/01	EZ Does It
11092	ATKTE	Emanuel, Michael	1/16/01		1/19/01	Triple P De
11093	BENMA	Anderson, Amy	1/19/01		1/21/01	Big Things
11094	BALAM	Carpenter, Lani	1/22/01		1/23/01	Fast Fredd
11095	GANJO	Emanuel, Michael	1/22/01		1/24/01	Big Things
11096	CONST	Anderson, Amy	1/22/01		1/23/01	
11097	KAEJU	Anderson, Amy	1/22/01	1/27/01	1/23/01	EZ Does It
11098	HIGKI	Carpenter, Lani	1/22/01	1/27/01	1/23/01	
11099	KELRO	Carpenter, Lani	1/22/01	1/27/01	1/23/01	Big Things
11100	GAVER	Emanuel, Michael	1/23/01	1/28/01	1/24/01	Zippy's Exp

Record: 1 of 87

The navigation area at the bottom of the window indicates that this table contains 87 records and that the active record is number 1.

Next Record

10 Move the selection one record at a time by clicking the **Next Record** button several times.

The selection moves down the OrderID field, because that field contains the insertion point.

Tip

You can move the selection one record at a time by pressing the [↑] or [↓] key, one screen at a time by pressing the [Page Up] or [Page Down] key, and to the first or last field in the table by pressing [Ctrl]+[Home] or [Ctrl]+[End].

11 Move directly to record 40 by selecting the current record number, typing **40**, and pressing Enter .

12 Close the **Orders** table, clicking **No** if you are prompted to save changes to the table's layout.

13 Double-click **Products** in the list of tables to open it in Datasheet view.

Notice that this table contains 189 records.

View

14 Click the **View** button on the toolbar to switch the view of the Products table to Design view.

In Datasheet view, you see the data stored in the table, whereas in Design view, you see the underlying table structure.

Close

15 Close the **Products** table by clicking its **Close** button. If prompted to save changes to the table layout, click **No**.

16 Close the **GardenCo** database by clicking its **Close** button.

Exploring Queries

One way you can locate information in an Access database is to create **queries**. You use queries to locate information so that you can view, change, or analyze it in various ways. You can also use the results of queries as the basis for other Access objects.

A query is essentially a question. For example, you might ask, "Which records in the Customer table have the value 98052 in the Postal Code field?" When you **run a query** (the equivalent of asking a question), Access looks at all the records in the table or tables you have specified, finds those that match the criteria you have defined, and displays them in a datasheet.

In order for Access to be able to answer your questions, you have to structure queries in a very specific way. Each type of question has a corresponding type of query. The primary query types are select, crosstab, and parameter. Less common types are action, AutoLookup, and SQL (Structured Query Language). Access includes wizards that quickly guide you through the creation of the more common queries; the less common ones have to be created by hand in a **design grid** in Design view. Here's what a typical query looks like:

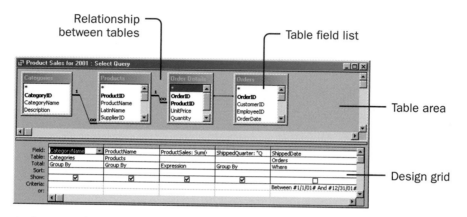

At the top of this query window are four small windows, listing the fields in the four tables that will be included in this query. The lines connecting the tables indicate that they are related by virtue of common fields. The first row of the grid contains the names of the fields to be included in the query, and the second row shows which table each field belongs to. The third row (labeled **Total**) enables you to perform calculations on the field values, and the fourth indicates whether the query results will be sorted on this field. A check mark in the check box in the fifth row (labeled **Show**) means that the field will be displayed in the results datasheet. (If the check box is not selected, the field can be used in determining the query results, but it will not be displayed.) The sixth row (labeled **Criteria**) contains criteria that determine which records will be displayed, and the seventh row (labeled **or**) sets up alternate criteria.

Don't worry if this all sounds a bit complicated at the moment. When you approach queries logically, they soon begin to make perfect sense. And don't worry if they sound like a lot of work. The **Query Wizard** is available to help you structure the query, and if you create a query that you are likely to run more than once, you can save it. It then becomes part of the database and is displayed in the database window when you click **Queries** on the **Objects** bar.

GardenCo

In this exercise, you will explore a few of the queries that have already been defined and saved in the GardenCo database. The working folder for this exercise is *SBS\Access\KnowAccess\Queries*. Follow these steps:

1 Open the **GardenCo** database located in the working folder.

2 Click **Queries** on the **Objects** bar.

The database window displays all the queries that have been saved as part of the GardenCo database.

3 Double-click the title bar of the database window to maximize the window.

Your screen looks like this:

Command icon

Update query icon

Delete query icon

Select query icon

The top two entries in this window are commands for creating queries. The remaining entries are queries that have already been created. The description of each query explains its purpose. The icon in the **Name** column is an indication of the query's type, as is the information in the **Type** column, which you can see by scrolling the window to the right.

Restore

4 Restore the database window to its original size by clicking the **Restore** button at the right end of the menu bar (not the title bar).

5 Open the **Products by Category** query in Datasheet view by selecting it and clicking the **Open** button at the top of the database window.

When you open the query, Access processes, or *runs*, it and produces a datasheet that displays the results shown on the next page.

The navigation bar tells you that 171 records are displayed. The Products table contains 189 records. To find out why 18 of the records are missing, you need to look at this query in Design view.

View

6   Click the **View** button on the toolbar to view the query in Design view, where it looks like this:

In the top part of the query window, two boxes list the fields of the tables this query is designed to work with. The bottom part is the design grid, where the query is formed. Each column of the grid can refer to one field from one of the tables above. Notice that <> Yes (*not equal to Yes*) has been entered in the **Criteria** row for the Discontinued field. This query therefore finds all the records that don't have a value of *Yes* in that field (in other words, that have not been discontinued).

Run

7   As an experiment, select **<>Yes** in the **Criteria** row for **Discontinued**, type **=Yes**, and then click the **Run** button on the toolbar.

Tip

You can also run a query by switching to Datasheet view.

You changed the query so that it finds all the records that have a value of Yes in the Discontinued field (in other words, that have been discontinued). Here are the results:

The 18 discontinued products account for the difference in the number of records in the Products table and the number of records displayed by the original query.

8 Close the query window, clicking **No** when prompted to save the design changes.

9 Close the **GardenCo** database.

Exploring Forms

Access tables are dense lists of raw information. If you create a database that only you will use, you will probably be very comfortable working directly with tables. But if you create a database that will be viewed and edited by people who don't know much about it—and don't necessarily want to know about it—working with your tables might be overwhelming. To solve this problem, you can design **forms** to guide users through your database, making it easier for them to enter, retrieve, display, and print information.

A form is essentially a window in which you can place **controls** that either give users information or enable them to enter information. Access provides a toolbox that includes many standard Windows controls, such as labels, text boxes, option buttons, and check boxes. With a little ingenuity, you can use these controls to create forms that look and work much like the dialog boxes in all Microsoft Windows applications.

You use forms to edit the records of the underlying tables or enter new records. As with tables and queries, you can display forms in several views. The three most common views are **Form view**, where you enter data; **Datasheet view**, which looks essentially like a table; and **Design view**, where you work with the elements of the form to refine the way it looks and works. The graphic on the next page shows what a form looks like in Design view.

This form consists of a **main form** that is linked to just one table. But a form can also include **subforms** that are linked to other tables. Arranged on the form are **label controls** containing text that appears on the form in Form view, and **text box controls** that will contain data from the table. Although you can create a form from scratch in Design view, you will probably use this view most often to refine the forms you create with a wizard.

GardenCo

In this exercise, you will take a look at a few of the forms in the GardenCo database that have been designed to make viewing tables, editing existing information, and adding new information easier and less error-prone. The working folder for this exercise is *SBS\Access\KnowAccess\Forms*. Follow these steps:

1 Open the **GardenCo** database located in the working folder.

2 Click **Forms** on the **Objects** bar, and then double-click **Switchboard** to open the main switchboard, which looks like this:

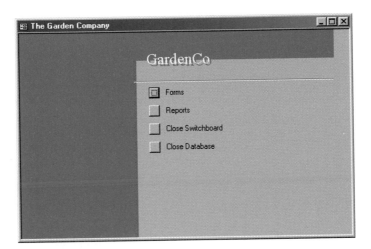

The Switchboard form has a customized title bar at the top, a title for the GardenCo database, and four command buttons. The first two buttons open switchboards—other forms—that have the same name as the button.

3   Click the **Forms** button on the switchboard to display the Forms switchboard.

4   Click **Edit/Enter Orders** to display this Orders form:

This form consists of a main form and a subform.

Next Record

5   Click the **Next Record** button on the navigation bar to display that record's information, and then click the **New Record** button (the asterisk) to display a blank form where you could enter a new order.

New Record

6   Close the **Orders** form, and click **Return** in the **Forms** switchboard to redisplay the main switchboard.

7   Click the **Close Switchboard** button.

8 In the database window, double-click **Products** in the **Forms** list to open this form:

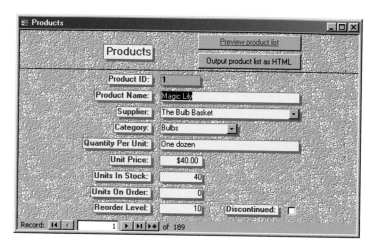

You use this form to edit the records of current products or enter new ones.

View

9 You are currently looking at the form in Form view. On the toolbar, click the **View** button's down arrow, and click **Datasheet View**.

Now the form looks essentially like the Products table in Datasheet view but without gridlines, as shown here:

Product ID:	Product Name:	Supplier:
1	Magic Lily	The Bulb Basket
2	Autumn crocus	The Bulb Basket
3	Compost Bin	Garden Hardware Mfg.
4	Cactus Sand Potting Mix	Soil and Sand Supplier
5	Weeping Forsythia	The Shrub Club
6	Bat Box	NoTox Pest Control
7	Electronic Insect Killer	NoTox Pest Control
8	Beneficial nematodes	NoTox Pest Control
9	Crown Vetch	Cover Up Stuff
10	English Ivy	Cover Up Stuff
11	Austrian Copper	Rosie's Roses
12	Persian Yellow Rose	Rosie's Roses
13	Indoor Magic Potting Soil	Soil and Sand Supplier
14	GrowGood Potting Soil	Soil and Sand Supplier
15	Sterilized Soil	Soil and Sand Supplier

Record: 1 of 189

10 Click the **View** button again to switch to Design view, and then maximize the form window.

Toolbox

11 If the toolbox is not displayed, click the **Toolbox** button on the toolbar.

Your screen now looks like this:

Tip

If the toolbox is in the way, drag it by its title bar to where it's not obscuring anything, as shown above.

12 Point to each of the icons in the toolbox until the name of the tool is displayed.

These are the tools you use to build custom forms for your database.

13 Close the **Products** form, and then close the database.

Exploring Reports

Ac2002-7-3

Approved Courseware

You use **reports** to display the information from your tables in nicely formatted, easily accessible ways, either on your computer screen or on paper. A report can include items of information selected from multiple tables and queries, values calculated from information in the database, and formatting elements such as headers, footers, titles, and headings.

You can look at reports in three views: Design view, where you can manipulate the design of a report in the same way that you manipulate a form; **Print Preview**, where you see your report exactly as it will look when printed; and **Layout Preview**, which shows you how all each element will look but without all the detail of Print Preview. A report in Design view looks as shown on the next page.

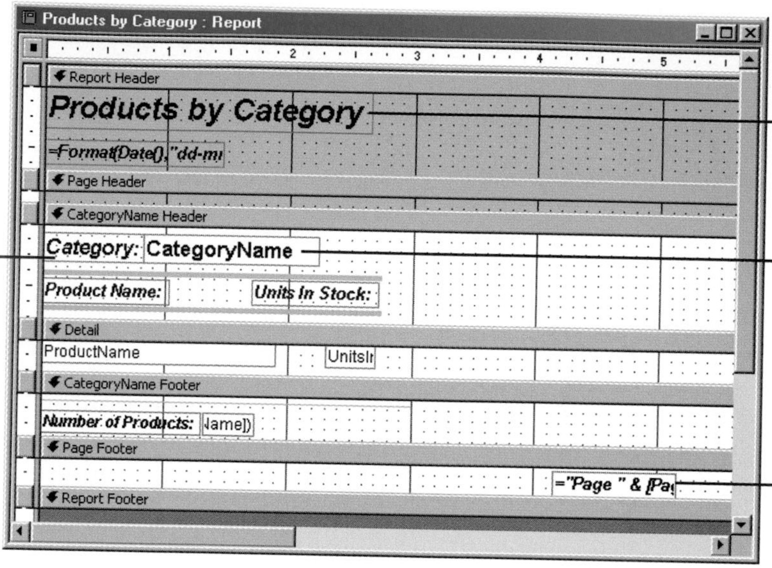

Report title
(appears on
first page)

Label
control

Text box
control

Page number
(appears on
every page)

GardenCo

In this exercise, you will take a look at a report that has been saved as part of the GardenCo database, just to get an idea of what is possible. The working folder for this exercise is *SBS\Access\KnowAccess\Reports*. Follow these steps:

1   Open the **GardenCo** database located in the working folder.

2   Click **Reports** on the **Objects** bar.

The top two entries in this window are commands you can use to create reports. The remaining entries are reports that have already been created.

3   Click **Customer Labels**, and then click the **Preview** button at the top of the database window to display the report.

This report prints customer names and addresses in a mailing label format. You are looking at it in a view that is much like Print Preview in other Microsoft Windows programs.

Tip

Access provides a wizard that can help you create a mailing label report. You can also use the Customer table in this database with Word's mail merge feature to create these labels.

4   Click in the form to change the zoom level.

Tip

If the report is too small to read in Print Preview, you can also select a zoom level in the **Zoom** box on the toolbar.

5   Close the **Customer Labels** report.

6   In the database window, click the **Invoice** report, and click the **Preview** button to see the invoice shown here:

7   Check out each page by clicking the navigation buttons at the bottom of the window.

View

8   Click the **View** button on the toolbar to display the report in Design view, and then maximize the report window so that your screen looks like the one shown on the following page.

In this view, the report looks similar to a form, and the techniques you use to create forms can also be used to create reports.

9 Close the **Invoice** report, and then close the **GardenCo** database.

10 If you are not continuing on to the next chapter, quit Access.

Exploring Other Access Objects

Tables, queries, forms, and reports are the objects you will use most frequently in Access. You can use them to create powerful and useful databases. However, if you need to create a sophisticated database, you can use data access pages, macros, and modules to substantially extend the capabilities of Access. To round out this introduction to Access databases, this section provides a brief overview of these objects.

Pages

To enable people to view and manipulate your database information via an intranet or the Internet, you can create **pages**, also known as **data access pages**. Working with a data access page on the Web is very much like working directly with a table or form in Access—users can work with the data in tables, run queries, and enter information in forms.

Although publishing database information on the Web seems like a fairly difficult task, Access provides a wizard that does most of the tedious work of creating data access pages for you. You can use a wizard-generated page as-is, or you can add your own personal touch in Design view.

Macros

You use **macros** to have Access respond to an event, such as the click of a button, the opening of a form, or the updating of a record. Macros can be particularly handy when you expect that other people who are less experienced with Access than you will work in your database. For example, you can make routine database actions, such as opening and closing forms or printing reports, available as command buttons on switchboards. And by grouping together an assortment of menu commands and having users carry them out via a macro with the click of a button, you can ensure that everyone does things the same way.

Modules

More powerful than macros, **modules** are Microsoft Visual Basic for Applications (VBA) programs. VBA is a high-level programming language developed by Microsoft for the purpose of creating Windows applications. A common set of VBA instructions can be used with all Microsoft Office programs, plus each program has its own set. Whereas macros can automate four to five dozen actions, VBA includes hundreds of commands and can be extended indefinitely with third-party add-ins. You could use VBA to carry out tasks that are too complex to be handled with macros, such as opening an Excel spreadsheet and retrieving specific information.

Tip

The Microsoft Office XP installation CD-ROM includes several sample databases that illustrate many of the principles of creating and using a database. One of these, the Northwind Traders database, is used as an example in many topics in Access online Help, so it is a particularly good database for you to explore. You'll find a link to this database on the Access **Help** menu, under **Sample Databases**.

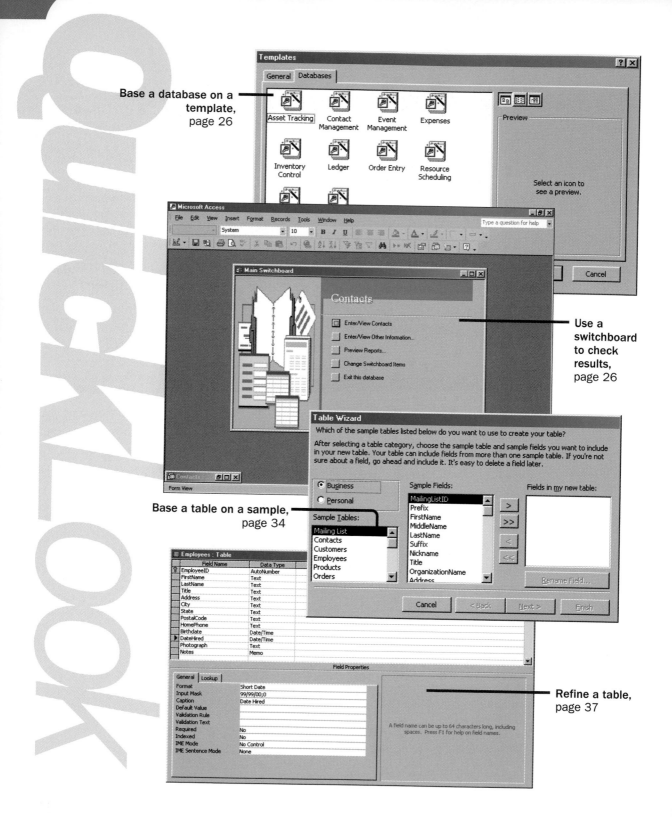

Base a database on a template, page 26

Use a switchboard to check results, page 26

Base a table on a sample, page 34

Refine a table, page 37

Chapter 2
Creating a New Database

After completing this chapter, you will be able to:

✔ Create a new database structure using a wizard.

✔ Check the work of the wizard.

✔ Create an empty database, and add tables using a wizard.

✔ Refine the way your data is displayed.

✔ Manipulate columns and rows in tables.

Creating the structure for a database is easy. But an empty database is no more useful than an empty Microsoft Word document or an empty Microsoft Excel worksheet. It is only when you fill, or **populate**, a database with data in tables that it starts to serve a purpose. As you add queries, forms, and reports, it becomes easier to use. If you customize it with a switchboard and your tools, it moves into the realm of being a **database application**.

Not every database has to be refined to the point that it can be classified as an application. Databases that only you or a few experienced database users will work with can remain fairly rough-hewn. But if you expect an administrative assistant to enter data or your company's executives to generate their own reports, then spending a little extra time in the beginning to create a solid database application will save a lot of work later. Otherwise, you'll find yourself continually repairing damaged files or walking people through seemingly easy tasks.

Microsoft Access takes a lot of the difficult and mundane work out of creating and customizing a database by providing **wizards** that you can use to create entire databases or individual tables, forms, queries, and other objects. It is generally easier to use a wizard to create something that is similar to what you need and then modify it than it is to create the same thing by hand.

In this chapter you will first use a wizard to rapidly create the structure for a sophisticated contact management database, complete with tables, queries, forms, and reports. After exploring this database and entering a few records to get an idea of what a wizard can provide in the way of a starting point, you will discard this database and start working on a simpler contacts database for The Garden Company. By the end of this chapter, you will have a GardenCo database containing three tables that will serve as the foundation for many of the exercises in this book.

In this chapter, you'll be creating a couple of databases from scratch in the working folder for this chapter, *SBS\Access\CreateDB\CreatingDB*. You will also use the Contacts and GardenCo database files that are stored in the following subfolders of the working folder: *CheckingDB*, *Refining*, and *Manipulating*.

Creating a Database Structure the Simple Way

Ac2002-1-1

Approved Courseware

In the distant past (a few years ago in computer time), creating a database structure from scratch involved first analyzing your needs and then laying out the database design on paper. You would decide what information you needed to track and how to store it in the database. Creating the database structure could be a lot of work, and after you had created it and entered data, making changes could be difficult. Wizards have changed this process. Committing yourself to a particular database structure is no longer the big decision it once was. Using the **Database Wizard**, you can create a dozen database applications in less time than it used to take to sketch the design of one on paper. Access wizards may not create exactly the database application you want, but they can quickly create something very close.

In this exercise, you will use the **Database Wizard** to create a new database structure. In this case, the new database will contain the structure for a contact management database. The working folder for this exercise is *SBS\Access\CreateDB\CreatingDB*. Follow these steps:

New

1   If the **New File** task pane is not displayed, open it by clicking the **New** button on the Access toolbar.

2   In the **New from template** section of the task pane, click **General Templates**, and then click the **Databases** tab to display these options:

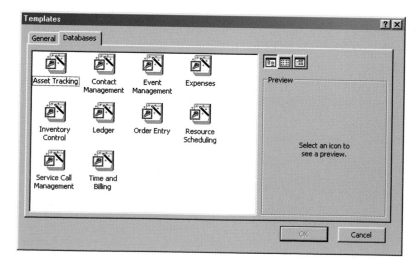

Tip

The **Database Wizard** uses predefined **templates** to create fairly sophisticated database applications. In addition to the templates provided with Access, if you are connected to the Internet, you will find additional templates and other resources by following the link to **Templates on Microsoft.com** that is in the **New from template** section of the **New File** task pane.

3 Double-click **Contact Management**.

The **File New Database** dialog box appears so that you can provide a name for your new database and specify where to store it:

Tip

The default folder for storing Access database files is *My Documents*. You can change this default to any other folder by clicking **Options** on the **Tools** menu when a database file is open, entering a new path in the **Default database folder** box on the **General** tab, and clicking **OK**.

4 Browse to *SBS\Access\CreateDB\CreatingDB* (the working folder for this exercise), replace *Contact Management* with **Contacts** in the **File Name** box, and click **Create**.

Tip

Naming conventions for an Access database file follow those for Microsoft Windows files. A file name can contain up to 215 characters including spaces, but creating a file name that long is not recommended. File names cannot contain the following characters: \ / : * ? " < > |. The extension for an Access database file is *.mdb*.

First the database window is displayed, and then you see the first page of the **Database Wizard**, which tells you the type of information that will be stored in this database.

5 This page requires no input from you, so click **Next** to move to the second page of the **Database Wizard**:

This page lists the three tables that will be included in the Contact Management database. The box on the right lists the fields you might want to include in the table selected in the box on the left. Required fields have a check mark in their check boxes. Optional fields are italic. You can select the check box of an optional field to include it in the selected table.

6 Click each table name, and browse through its list of fields, just to see what is available. Then indicate that you want to include all the selected fields in the three tables by clicking **Next** to move to the next page of the wizard.

On this page, you can select from a list of predefined styles that determine what the elements of the database will look like.

Tip

Whenever the wizard's **Back** button is active (not gray), you can click it to move back through previous pages and change your selections. If the **Finish** button is active, you can click it at any time to tell a wizard to do its job with no further input from you. Most of the options set by a wizard can be modified later, so clicking **Finish** does not mean that whatever the wizard creates is cast in stone.

7 Click each of the styles to see what they look like. Then click **Blends**, and click **Next**.

8 Click each of the report styles to see what they look like. Then click **Bold**, and click **Next**.

9 Change the proposed database name to **Contacts**, leave the **Yes, I'd like to include a picture** check box clear, and click **Next**.

The **Next** button is unavailable on this page, indicating that this is the wizard's last page. By default, the **Yes, start the database** check box is selected, and the **Display Help on using a database** check box is clear.

10 Leave the default settings as they are, and click **Finish**.

The process of creating a database can take from several seconds to a minute. While the wizard creates the database, an alert box tells you what is happening and how far along the process is. When the wizard finishes, it opens the newly created Contacts database with this switchboard displayed:

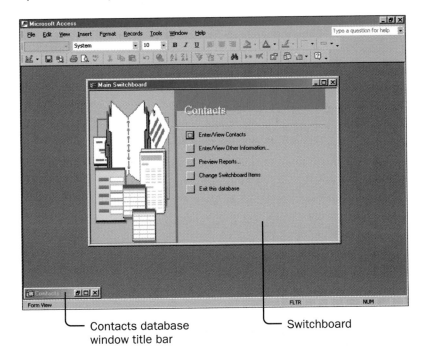

Contacts database window title bar

Switchboard

Close

11 Click the **Close** button at the right end of the Main Switchboard window's title bar.

12 When the switchboard opened, the Contacts database window was minimized. (You can see its title bar in the lower left corner of the Access window.) Click the **Close** button at the right end of this title bar to close the database.

Checking the Work of a Wizard

Ac2002-1-3
Ac2002-5-1

Approved Courseware

Using a wizard to create a database is quick and painless, but just what do you end up with? The **Database Wizard** creates a database application, complete with a switchboard, several tables, and some other objects. In many cases, all you have to do to have a working database application is add the data. If the wizard's work doesn't quite suit your needs, you can modify any of the database objects or use another type of wizard to add more objects.

For example, if you tell the **Database Wizard** to create a contact management database, it creates three tables. It doesn't create any queries for this type of database, but it does for some of the other types. It creates forms that you can use to enter or view data, and two reports that you can use to list contacts or summarize the calls made or received during the week. Finally, it creates a switchboard so that users can quickly access the parts of the database needed to perform specific tasks.

Contacts

In this exercise, you'll use the switchboard to take a quick tour of the Contacts database that the **Database Wizard** has created. You can't check out some of the objects unless the database contains data, so along the way, you will enter information in several of the tables. The working folder for this exercise is *SBS\Access\CreateDB\CheckingDB*. Follow these steps:

1 Open the **Contacts** database located in the working folder.

2 In the switchboard, click the **Enter/View Other Information** button to display the Forms Switchboard window.

This switchboard has two buttons: the first opens a form you can use to enter or view contact types, and the second returns you to the Main Switchboard window.

3 Click **Enter/View Contact Types** to display this Contact Types form:

Contact Types	▢▢✕
▶	
Contact Type ID	(AutoNumber)
Contact Type	
Record: ◀◀ ◀ 1 ▶ ▶▶ ▶✳ of 1	

If the underlying Contact Types table contained any records, you could use this form to view them. The only action you can take now is to add a new record.

4 Type **Supplier** in the **Contact Type** box, and press [Enter].

As you typed, Access supplied the entry for the **Contact Type ID** field. Access keeps track of this number and enters the next available number in this field whenever you add a new record.

5 Repeat the previous step to enter records for **Customer** and **Shipper**.

6 Now that the underlying Contact Types table contains a few records, use the **navigation buttons** at the bottom of the form to scroll through them. Then click the **Close** button to close the Contact Types form.

Important

With most computer applications, **saving** your work often is important to avoid losing it if your computer crashes or the dog chews through the power cord. With Access, it is not only *not* important to save your data, it is *not possible* to manually save it. When you move the insertion point out of a record after entering or editing information, Access saves that record. This mixed blessing means that you don't have to worry about losing your changes, but you do have to remember that any data entry changes you make are permanent and can be undone only by editing the record again.

7 Click **Return to Main Switchboard**.

8 Click **Enter/View Contacts** to display this Contacts form:

You use this two-page form to enter records in the underlying Contacts table or to view records that are already there. The form has buttons at the bottom to switch between pages and to open other forms from which you can place calls (**Dial**) or where you can record information about communications you've had with the contact (**Calls**).

9 Enter some information on this form—your own first and last name will do—and notice that when you enter your name, Access provides a contact ID.

10 Click the **2** button at the bottom of the form to move to page 2, and then expand the list of contact types.

The list contains the three types you just entered in the Contact Types table through the Contact Types form.

11 Select one of the contact types.

12 Return to the first page, click in the **Work Phone** box to place the insertion point there, type **555-0100**, and press [Enter].

13 Click in the **Work Phone** box again, and click the **Dial** button.

The **AutoDialer** dialog box appears, with the contents of the box that is currently selected on the form displayed as a potential number to dial.

Tip

This dialog box is not part of Access; it is a Windows utility. When you click the **Dial** button, VBA code attached to the button calls the utility. If you were to click **Setup**, the **Windows Phone And Modem Options** dialog box would be displayed. (If you don't have a modem installed, the **Install New Modem** dialog box appears instead.)

14 Click **Cancel** to close the **AutoDialer** dialog box, and then click the **Calls** button to display this Calls form:

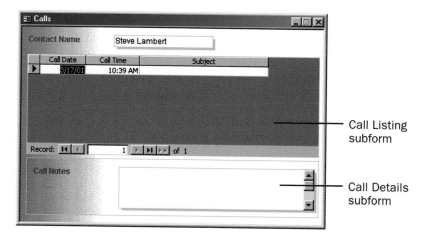

Call Listing subform

Call Details subform

This form includes the Call Listing subform, which lists any previous calls you have recorded, and the Call Details subform, which displays details of the selected call. You can record information about communications (phone calls, e-mail exchanges, and so on) that you've had with this contact.

15 Click in the **Subject** cell of the new record, and enter **Order information** as the subject.

Access adds a **New Record** line, where the **Call Date** and **Call Time** fields default to the current date and time, as shown here:

New
Record
line

16 Click in the **Call Notes** box, and type a short note.

17 Click the **Close** button to close the Calls form, and then click **Close** again to close the Contacts form.

18 Click **Preview Reports** to display the Reports Switchboard window.

19 Preview the two short reports by clicking the button for each one, reading it, and then closing it.

When you preview the Weekly Call Summary report, the Report Date Range form is displayed to allow you to enter a range of dates for the report. If you accept the default range of the current week, the summary of the call you just added is included in the report.

20 Click **Return to Main Switchboard**, and then click the **Close** button to close the Main Switchboard window without closing the database.

21 Double-click the database window's title bar to restore the window, which looks like this:

22 Explore all the tables, forms, and reports in the database by clicking each object type on the **Objects** bar and then opening the individual objects.

You won't be able to open the Report Date Range form directly, because it is designed to be opened by VBA code that supplies the information that the form needs.

23 Close the **Contacts** database.

Creating Tables the Simple Way

When you use the **Database Wizard** to create a contact management database, the database has all the **components** needed to store basic information about people. But suppose The Garden Company needs to store different types of information for different types of contacts. For example, it might want to maintain different types of information about employees, customers, and suppliers. In addition to the standard information—such as names, addresses, and phone numbers—the company might want to track these other kinds of information:

■ Employee Social Security number, date of hire, marital status, deductions, and pay rate

■ Customer order and account status

■ Supplier contact, current order status, and discounts

The company could add a lot of extra fields to the Contacts table and then fill in just the ones it needs for each contact type, but cramming all this information into one table would soon get pretty messy. Instead, it should create a database with one table for each contact type: employee, customer, and supplier.

The **Database Wizard** doesn't offer exactly this combination of tables, so in this exercise, you will create a GardenCo database with an empty structure. You will then add several tables to the database using the **Table Wizard**. The working folder for this exercise is *SBS\Access\CreateDB\CreatingDB*. Follow these steps:

New

1 Click the **New** button on the toolbar to display the **New File** task pane.

2 In the **New** section of the task pane, click **Blank Database**.

3 Browse to the working folder for this exercise, type **GardenCo** as the name of the new database, and click **Create**.

Access displays a database window that contains no tables, queries, forms, or other database objects. (You can confirm that the database is empty by clicking each of the object types on the **Objects** bar.)

4 Click the **New** button on the database window's toolbar to display the **New Table** dialog box.

Tip

Instead of clicking the **New** button, you can click the **New Object** button's down arrow, and then click **Table**; or you can click **Tables** on the **Objects** bar, and then double-click **Create table by using wizard**; or you can click **Table** on the **Insert** menu.

5 Double-click **Table Wizard** to display the wizard's first page, shown here:

![Table Wizard dialog box]

You can display a list of either business tables or personal tables. Although these categories are generally oriented toward business or personal use, depending on the nature of your business or preferences, you might find the sample table you want in either list.

6 Take a few minutes to browse through the business list, and then check the **Personal** button to see those sample tables.

Each category contains a list of sample tables. When you click an item in the **Sample Tables** list, the **Sample Fields** list to the right displays all the fields available for that table. (You can add more fields after creating the table if you need them.) Selecting an item in the **Sample Fields** list and then clicking the **>** button moves the selected field to the **Fields in my new table** list. Clicking the **>>** button moves *all* sample fields to the **Fields in my new table** list. The **<** and **<<** buttons remove one or all fields from your new table list.

7 With the **Business** category selected, select **Customers** in the **Sample Tables** list.

8 Click the **>>** button to copy all the fields to the **Fields in my new table** list, and then click **Next** to move to the next page of the wizard.

On this page you can provide a name for your new table and specify whether the wizard should set a **primary key** for the table. A primary key consists of one or more fields that differentiate one record from another.

9 Leave **Customers** as the table name, click **No, I'll set the primary key**, and then click **Next**.

The wizard suggests **CustomerID** as the field that will uniquely identify records, and asks what type of data the field will contain.

10 Click **Numbers and/or letters I enter when I add new records**, and then click **Next** to move to the last page of the wizard.

You can select one of the three option buttons on this page to determine whether the table should open in Design view or in Datasheet view, or whether a wizard-generated form should open so that you can enter data.

11 Accept the default selection, **Enter data directly into the table**, and click **Finish** to create and open the Customers table.

12 Scroll horizontally through the table to view all the fields created by the wizard based on your selections on its first page. Then close the table.

The Customers table now appears in the database window.

13 Start the **Table Wizard** again, this time by double-clicking **Create table by using wizard** in the database window.

14 Select **Employees** in the **Sample Tables** list, and move only the following fields to the **Fields in my new table** list, by selecting each field in the **Sample Fields** list and clicking the **>** button:

EmployeeID
FirstName
LastName
Title
Address
City
StateOrProvince
PostalCode
HomePhone
Birthdate
DateHired
Photograph
Notes

15 In the **Fields in my new table** list, select **StateOrProvince**, click **Rename Field**, change the name of the field to **State**, and click **OK**.

16 Click the **Next** button twice to move two pages forward, naming the table **Employees** and allowing Access to create a primary key.

Because one table already exists in the database, the wizard attempts to establish a relationship between the tables and displays a new page.

17 You will be able to establish relationships later, so skip over this page by clicking **Next**.

18 Click **Finish**, and then close the **Employees** table.

19 Repeat steps 13 through 18 to create a **Suppliers** table that includes all the fields provided. Click **Finish** to accept all the suggestions and defaults.

20 Close the **Suppliers** table.

Three tables are now listed in the **Tables** pane of the database window.

21 Close the database.

Refining How Data Is Displayed

Ac2002-1-2
Ac2002-2-4

Approved Courseware

When you use the **Table Wizard** to create tables and populate them with the fields you specify, it sets a variety of **properties** for each field. These properties determine what data be entered in a field and how the data will look on the screen.

The field properties set by Access are a good starting place, and most of them are probably fine as they are. However, suppose some of the properties don't meet your needs. You can change some of them without affecting the data stored in the table; others might affect the data, so it pays to be cautious about making drastic changes until you have some experience working with Access.

GardenCo

In this exercise, you will review and edit a few of the property settings for one of the tables in the GardenCo database located in the working folder for this exercise, *SBS\Access\CreateDB\Refining*. Follow these steps:

1 Open the **GardenCo** database located in the working folder.

2 In the database window, double-click **Employees** in the **Tables** pane to open the table in Datasheet view, as shown on the next page.

Your table window might be a different size than this one. Notice that any field name that is composed of two words has a space between the words, whereas the name you specified in the wizard had no space. Remember this when you are looking at the table in Design view later.

Tip

As with other Microsoft Office XP applications, you can change the size of the window by moving the pointer to a corner and, when the pointer becomes a double-headed arrow, dragging to expand or reduce the size of the window.

View

3   Click the **View** button on the toolbar to display the table in Design view, like this:

Primary key

In Design view, the top portion of the window contains a list of the table's fields. The **Field Name** column contains the names you specified when you created the table. Notice that there are no spaces in the names. The **Data Type** column specifies the type of data that the field can contain. The **Description** column can contain a description of the field.

Notice the **Primary Key** icon to the left of the EmployeeID field. The value in the primary key field is used to uniquely identify each record; that is, no two records can have the same value in this field. You can take responsibility for entering this value, or you can let Access help you with this chore. When the data type of a field is set to **AutoNumber**, Access fills this field in every new record with the next available number.

Tip

If you no longer want the table to have a primary key, select the field designated as the primary key in the top portion of the window, and click **Primary Key** on the **Edit** menu. If you want to assign a different field as the primary key, select that field, and click **Primary Key** on the **Edit** menu.

4   Click in the **Data Type** cell for the **EmployeeID** field—the one with **AutoNumber** in it—and then click the down arrow that appears.

The cell expands to show a list of all possible **data types**. Each data type cell contains this list, allowing you to set the appropriate data type for each field. The data type setting restricts data entry to that specific type. If you try to enter data that is incompatible with that type, Access rejects it.

Tip

For a description of all the data types, search for the *data type* topic in Access online Help.

5   Press the [Esc] key to close the list without changing the data type.

6   Click in each box in the **Field Properties** section at the bottom of the table window.

The number of properties in the **Field Properties** section varies with each data type. For example, the **AutoNumber** data type has five properties, four of which have drop down lists from which you can select settings. As you click each property, a description of that property appears in the area on the right, as shown on the next page.

Click this down arrow to see property options.

Property description

The **Field Size** property determines the size and type of value that can be entered in the field. For example, if this property is set to **Long Integer**, the field will accept entries from –2,147,483,648 to 2,147,483,647. If the data type is **AutoNumber**, entries in this field will start with 1, so you could conceivably have over two billion employees before you outgrew this table.

The **Increment** setting for the **New Values** property specifies that Access should use the next available sequential number. The alternative (which you can see by expanding the list for this cell) is **Random**.

The **Format** property determines how data from the field is displayed on the screen and in print; it does not control how it is stored. Some data types have predefined formats, and you can also create custom formats.

Remember that when you displayed the table in Datasheet view, some of the field names had spaces in them? The way the field names are displayed in Datasheet view is controlled by the **Caption** property. If there is an entry for this property, it is used in place of the actual field name.

The **Yes (No Duplicates)** setting for the **Indexed** property indicates that the information in this field will be indexed for faster searching, and that duplicate values are not allowed. For the primary key field, this property is automatically set to **Yes (No Duplicates)**, but a field can also be indexed without being a primary key.

Tip

For more information about a particular property, click in its box, and press [F1] to see the pertinent Access online Help topic.

7 With the **EmployeeID** field still selected (as indicated by the arrow in the **row selector**), click in the **Format** box, and enter three zeros (**000**).

The ID number generated by Access will now be displayed as three digits. If the number isn't three digits long, it will be padded on the left with zeros.

8 Click the **Photograph** field, and change its data type from **OLE Object** to **Text**.

The **Table Wizard** included the **Photograph** field in this table and set this field's data type to **OLE Object** so that you can store a graphic in the field. But you will be storing the file name of a graphic, not the graphic itself, so **Text** is a more appropriate data type.

9 Click in the **HomePhone** field to display these properties:

The data type for **HomePhone** is **Text**, even though the data will be a string of numbers. Because this type of entry can also contain parentheses, dashes, and spaces and is not the type of number that you would use in a calculation, **Text** is the appropriate data type.

Looking at the **Field Properties** section for this field, you can see that fields with this data type have more properties than fields with the **AutoNumber** data type.

The **Field Size** property for a field with the **Text** data type determines the number of characters that can be entered in the field. If you attempt to enter too many characters, Access displays a warning message, and you won't be able to leave the field until you reduce the number of characters to this many or fewer.

The **Caption** property is set to **Home Phone**. This name will be used at the top of the field's column in Datasheet view. The wizard supplies these descriptive names, but you can change them.

10 Click in the **DateHired** field to display the properties shown here:

The **Format** property for this field is set to **Short Date**, which looks like this: 4/21/01. If a valid date is entered in just about any standard format, such as 21 April 01, this property displays the date as 4/21/01.

Important

Exercises in this book that use the short date format assume that the year display is set to two digits (M/d/yy) in the **Regional Settings Properties** dialog box in Microsoft Windows 98, or the **Regional Options** dialog box in Microsoft Windows 2000. You can check this on your computer by opening Control Panel (click **Start**, move the pointer over **Settings**, and click **Control Panel**) and then double-clicking **Regional Settings** or **Regional Options**, as appropriate. In either case, the setting is found on the **Date** tab.

This field also has its **Input Mask** property set to **99/99/00;0**. An **input mask** controls how data looks when you enter it and the format in which it is stored. Each 9 represents an optional numeral, and each 0 represents a required one. When you move to this field to enter a date in Datasheet view, you will see a mask that looks like this: __/__/__. The mask indicates that the date must be entered in the 4/21/01 format, but as soon as you press [Enter] to move to the next field, the date will change to whatever format is specified by the **Format** property.

Another interesting property is **Validation Rule**. None of the wizard-generated tables use **validation rules**, because the rules are too specific to the data being entered to anticipate, but let's take a quick look at how they work.

11 Click in the **Validation Rule** box, and enter **<Now()**. Then click in the **Validation Text** box, and enter **"Date entered must be today or earlier."**

This rule states that the date entered must be before (less than) the current instant in time, as determined by the system clock of the computer where the database is stored. If you enter a date in the future, Access will not accept it and will display the validation text in an alert box.

Important

The **Format**, **Input Mask**, and **Validation Rule** properties seem like great ways to be sure that only valid information is entered in your tables. But if you aren't careful, you can make data entry difficult and frustrating. Test your properties carefully before releasing your database for others to use.

View

12 Click the **View** button to return to Datasheet view, clicking **Yes** when prompted to save the table.

Tip

When you try to switch from Design view to Datasheet view after making changes (and sometimes even if you haven't made any changes), you are presented with an alert box stating that you must save the table. If you click **No**, you remain in Design view. If you click **Yes**, Access saves your changes and switches to Datasheet view. If you want to switch views without saving changes that you have made inadvertently, click **No**, and then click the table's **Close** button. When Access displays another alert box, click **No** to close the table without saving any changes.

13 Enter a future date in both the **Birthdate** and **DateHired** fields.

The **Birthdate** field, which has no validation rule, accepts any date, but the **DateHired** field won't accept a date beyond the one set on your computer.

14 Click **OK** to close the alert box, change the **DateHired** value to a date in the past, and click the **Close** button to close the Employees table.

15 In the database window, select **Suppliers**, and click the **Design** button to open the table in Design view.

16 Double-click the **StateOrProvince** field name to select it, and change it to **State**. Then click the **Caption** property in the **Field Properties** section, and change it to **State**, too.

17 Delete the **Country/Region**, **PaymentTerms**, **EmailAddress**, and **Notes** fields by clicking in the row selector and pressing the ⌦ key.

Tip

Access alerts you that deleting the **EmailAddress** field requires deleting the field and all its indexes. Click **Yes**. (You will see this alert again in step 19; click **Yes** each time to delete the fields.)

18 Click the **Close** button to close the Suppliers table, clicking **Yes** to save your changes.

19 Open the **Customers** table in Design view, and delete the following fields: **CompanyName**, **CompanyOrDepartment**, **ContactTitle**, **Extension**, **FaxNumber**, **EmailAddress**, and **Notes**.

20 Click in the **CustomerID** field, and change the **Field Size** property to **5**.

21 Change these fields and their captions: *ContactFirstName* to **FirstName** and **First Name**, *ContactLastName* to **LastName** and **Last Name**, *BillingAddress* to **Address**, *StateOrProvince* to **Region**, and *Country/Region* to **Country**.

22 Click the **Close** button to close the Customers table, clicking **Yes** to save it.

23 Close the **GardenCo** database.

Manipulating Table Columns and Rows

Ac2002-1-4

Approved Courseware

When you refine a table's structure by adding fields and changing field properties in Design view, you are affecting the data that is stored in the table. But sometimes you will want to adjust the table itself to get a better view of the data. If you want to look up a phone number, for example, but the names and phone numbers are several columns apart, you will have to scroll the table window to get the information you need. You might want to rearrange columns or hide a few columns to be able to see the fields you are interested in at the same time.

You can manipulate the columns and rows of an Access table without in any way affecting the underlying data. You can size both rows and columns, and you can also hide, move, and freeze columns. You can save your table formatting so that the table will look the same the next time you open it, or you can discard your table adjustments without saving them.

GardenCo

In this exercise, you will open a table and manipulate its columns and rows. To make the value of table formatting more apparent, you will work with a version of the GardenCo database that has several tables containing many records. The working folder for this exercise is *SBS\Access\CreateDB\Manipulate*. Follow these steps:

1   Open the **GardenCo** database located in the working folder.

2   Click **Tables** on the **Objects** bar.

3   Double-click the **Customers** table to open it in Datasheet view.

4   Drag the vertical bar at the right edge of the **Address** column header to the left until the column is about a half inch wide.

Customer ID	First Name	Last Name	Address	City	Region	Postal Code	Country
CHANE	Neil	Charney	1842 10	Sidney	BC	V3X 2Y5	Canada
CLAJA	Jane	Clayton	785 Bea	Sidney	BC	V3U 2Y5	Canada
LINEL	Jose	Lugo	23 Tsaw	Tsawassen	BC	T2G 8M4	Canada
MUNST	Stuart	Munson	7320 Ec	Vancouver	BC	V3L 2K1	Canada
TANYO	Susan M.	Tjamberg	1900 Oa	Vancouver	BC	V3F 2T1	Canada
MORJO	Jon	Morris	490 Full	Vancouver	BC	V3H 2K1	Canada
WAICO	Connie	Waite	3319 Hi	Vancouver	BC	V3F 2Y1	Canada
ALBST	Steve	Alboucq	130 17tl	Vancouver	BC	V3Y 2K1	Canada
AKEKI	Kim	Akers	1932 52	Vancouver	BC	V3G 2T1	Canada
TIAMI	Mike	Tiano	5540 Rc	Victoria	BC	Y3B 2X4	Canada
FLEBR	Brian	Fleming	537 Orc	Victoria	BC	Y3C 2W4	Canada
DREKA	Kate	Dresen	1630 Hi	Carmel Valley	CA	68492	USA
MINPA	Patti	Mintz	47 Euca	Escondido	CA	26371	USA
FLOKA	Kathie	Flood	8887 W	Glendale	CA	32891	USA
MILER	Eric	Miller	23 High	Granada Hills	CA	33216	USA
MATJO	Joseph	Matthews	96 Jeffe	Loma Linda	CA	12893	USA
CAMMI	Michael L.	Campbell	89 W. H	Palo Alto	CA	43201	USA
CAMDA	David	Campbell	22 Mark	San Francisco	CA	41102	USA
SEIPE	Peter	Seidenspinner	9308 Da	San Francisco	CA	42877	USA
SAXJE	Jenny	Sax	98 N. H	San Francisco	CA	41950	USA
POLCA	Carole	Poland	10 Pepf	San Jose	CA	98766	USA
SIMDA	David	Simpson	45 Park	San Jose	CA	51589	USA

Record: 1 of 110

The column is now too narrow to display the entire address.

5   Point to the vertical bar between the **Address** and **City** column headers, and double-click.

The column to the left of the vertical bar is now the minimum width that will display all the text in that field in all records. This technique is particularly useful in a large table where you can't easily determine the length of a field's longest entry.

6   On the left side of the datasheet, drag the horizontal bar between any two record selectors downward.

As you can see here, the height of all rows in the table increases:

Customers : Table						
Customer ID	First Name	Last Name	Address	City	Region	Postal Code
CHANE	Neil	Charney	1842 10th Avenue	Sidney	BC	V3X 2Y5
CLAJA	Jane	Clayton	785 Beale St.	Sidney	BC	V3U 2Y5
LINEL	Jose	Lugo	23 Tsawassen Blvd.	Tsawassen	BC	T2G 8M4
MUNST	Stuart	Munson	7320 Edwards Ave.	Vancouver	BC	V3L 2K1
TANYO	Susan M.	Tjamberg	1900 Oak St.	Vancouver	BC	V3F 2T1
MORJO	Jon	Morris	490 Fulton Dr.	Vancouver	BC	V3H 2K1
WAICO	Connie	Waite	3319 Hillside Dr.	Vancouver	BC	V3F 2Y1

Record: 1 of 110

7 On the **Format** menu, click **Row Height** to display the **Row Height** dialog box.

8 Select the **Standard Height** check box, and then click **OK**.

The height of all rows is returned to the default setting. (You can also set the rows to any other height in this dialog box.)

9 Click in the **First Name** column, and then click **Hide Columns** on the **Format** menu.

The First Name column disappears, and the columns to its right shift to the left. If you select several columns before clicking **Hide Columns**, they all disappear.

Tip

You can select adjacent columns by clicking in the header of one, holding down the [Shift] key, and then clicking in the header of another. The two columns and any columns in between are selected.

10 To restore the hidden field, click **Unhide Columns** on the **Format** menu to display this dialog box:

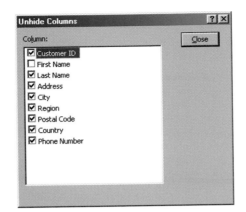

11 Select the **First Name** check box, and then click **Close**.

Access redisplays the First Name column.

12 Drag the right side of the database window to the left to reduce its size so that you cannot see all fields in the table.

13 Point to the **Customer ID** column header, hold down the mouse button, and drag through the **First Name** and **Last Name** column headers. Then with the three columns selected, click **Freeze Columns** on the **Format** menu.

Now as you scroll the window horizontally to view columns that are off the screen to the right, the first three columns will remain in view.

14 On the **Format** menu, click **Unfreeze All Columns** to restore the columns to their normal condition.

15 Close the table without saving your changes, and then close the **GardenCo** database.

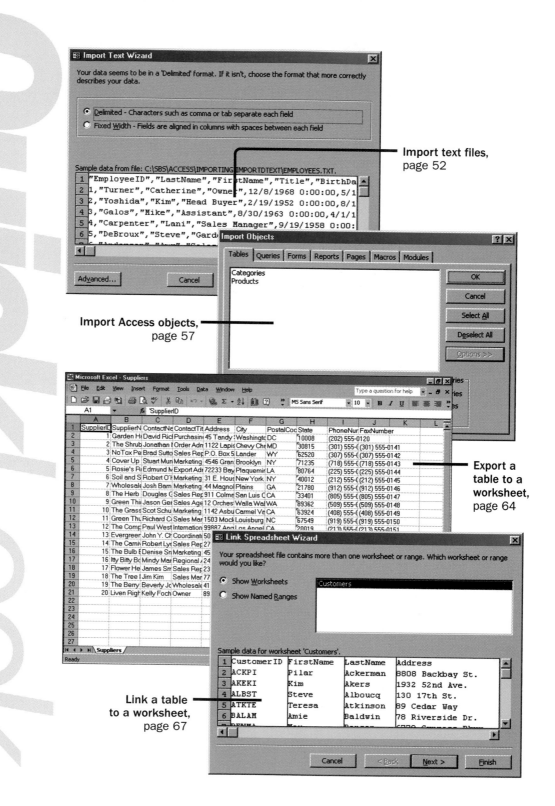

Import text files,
page 52

Import Access objects,
page 57

Export a table to a worksheet,
page 64

Link a table to a worksheet,
page 67

Chapter 3
Getting Information Into and Out of a Database

After completing this chapter, you will be able to:

✔ Import information from various programs.

✔ Import information from other Access databases.

✔ Export information to other programs.

✔ Link database content to other databases.

Not many people enjoy typing information in a database, so one of your goals when designing a **relational database** is to structure the tables in such a way that the same information never has to be entered more than once. If, for example, you are designing a database to track customer orders, you don't want sales clerks to have to type the name of the customer in each order. Unless you are running a mortuary, you will probably have repeat customers. So you need a customer table to hold all the pertinent information about each customer, and you can then simply reference a customer ID in each order. If information about a customer changes, you have to update it in only one place in the database: the customer table. In this way, the only item of customer information in the order records (the ID) remains accurate. An added benefit of this system is that you reduce the confusion that can result from typos and from having the same information appear in different formats throughout the database.

Good database design saves keystrokes while entering new information and maintaining the database, but even more time and effort can be saved in another way. As a Microsoft Office XP application, Microsoft Access can easily share information with the other applications in the Office suite. But it also makes it easy to populate a database by **importing** information in numerous other formats. If the information that you intend to store in an Access database has already been entered into almost any other electronic document, it is quite likely that you can move it into Access without retyping it.

If your information is still being actively maintained in another application and you want to bring it into Access to analyze it, create reports, or easily export it to another format, you should consider **linking** your Access database to the existing information in its original application rather than importing the information. When you link to data in another application, you can view and edit it in both applications, and what you see in Access is always up to date.

Many companies that store accounting, manufacturing, marketing, sales, and other information on their computers have discovered the advantages of sharing this information within the company through an **intranet**, or with the rest of the world through the Internet. With Access, you can speed up this process by **exporting** the information stored in a database as Hypertext Markup Language (HTML) and Extensible Markup Language (XML) pages.

In this chapter, you'll import information stored in various formats into the GardenCo database. You'll also export some of their data to several standard formats. After all this importing and exporting, you will experiment with viewing and updating information in another application by linking to it. You will be working with GardenCo database files and several other sample files that are stored in the following subfolders of the *SBS\Access\Importing* folder: *ImportExcel, ImportDText, ImportFText, ImportAccess, ImportDbase, ImportHTML, ImportXML, Export, Link,* and *OfficeLink*.

Importing Information from Excel

Ac2002-8-1

Approved Courseware

Access works well with Microsoft Excel. You can import entire **worksheets** or a **named range** from a worksheet into either a new table (one that is created during the import) or an existing table. You can also import specific fields from a worksheet or range.

Excel is a good intermediate format to use when importing information that isn't set up quite right. For example, if you want to add or remove fields, combine or split fields, or use complex math functions to manipulate data before importing it into Access, Excel is a great place to do it.

GardenCo
Customers

In this exercise, you will import information about The Garden Company's customers, which is stored in an Excel worksheet, into the Customers table in the GardenCo database. The working folder for this exercise is *SBS\Access\Importing\ImportExcel*. Follow these steps:

1 Open the **GardenCo** database located in the working folder.

2 On the **File** menu, point to **Get External Data**, and then click **Import**.

3 In the **Files of type** list, click **Microsoft Excel**.

4 Browse to the *SBS\Access\Importing\ImportExcel* folder, click **Customers**, and then click **Import.**

Access displays the first page of the **Import Spreadsheet Wizard**, which is shown here:

On this page, you can browse the contents of any worksheets or named ranges in the spreadsheet you just selected. You can scroll horizontally and vertically to view the worksheet's columns and rows, which are displayed in the lower pane.

5   With **Customers** selected in the list of worksheets, click **Next** to display this page of the wizard:

6   Select the **First Row Contains Column Headings** check box, and click **Next**.

The background for the top row changes to gray, and when you scroll up and down, the top row no longer scrolls.

7 Click **In an Existing Table**, select the **Customers** table from the adjacent drop-down list, and click **Next**.

Important

When importing into an existing table, all the field names and data types must match exactly; otherwise, Access can't import the file and displays an error. If the structure matches but data in a field is too large or has some other minor problem, Access might import the record containing the field into an ImportError table, rather than into the desired one. You can fix the problem there and then copy and paste the record into the correct table.

8 Click **Finish** to import the file.

Access informs you that the file was imported.

9 Click **OK** to close the message box, and then open the **Customers** table to confirm that Access imported the customer list.

10 Close the **Customers** table, and then close the database.

Importing Information from a Delimited Text File

Ac2002-8-1

Approved Courseware

Text files are the common denominator of documents. Almost every application that works with words and numbers can generate some kind of a text file, in addition to files in its **native format**. Access can import tabular data (tables and lists) from text files if the data has been stored in a recognizable format. The most common formats are delimited and fixed width.

In a **delimited text file**, each record ends in a carriage return, and each field is separated from the next by a comma or some other special character, called a **delimiter**. If a field contains one of these special characters, you must enclose the entire field in quotation marks. (Some people enclose all fields in quotation marks to avoid having to locate and enclose the special cases.)

GardenCo
Employees

In this exercise, you will import information about The Garden Company's employees, which is stored in a **comma-delimited text file**, into the Employees table in the GardenCo database. The working folder for this exercise is *SBS\Access\Importing\ImportDText*. Follow these steps:

1 Open the **GardenCo** database located in the working folder.

2 On the **File** menu, point to **Get External Data**, and then click **Import**.

3 In the **Files of type** list, click **Text Files**.

Tip

Text files typically have an extension of *.txt*. However, some programs save delimited text files with a *.csv* or *.tab* extension. You will also occasionally see text files with an extension of *.asc* (for **ASCII**). Fixed-width files are sometimes stored with an extension of *.prn* (for *printer*), but Access doesn't recognize this extension, so you will have to rename it to one it does recognize. All of the acceptable extensions are treated the same way by Access.

4 Browse to the *SBS\Access\Importing\ImportDText* folder, click **Employees**, and then click **Import**.

Access displays the first page of the **Import Text Wizard**, shown here:

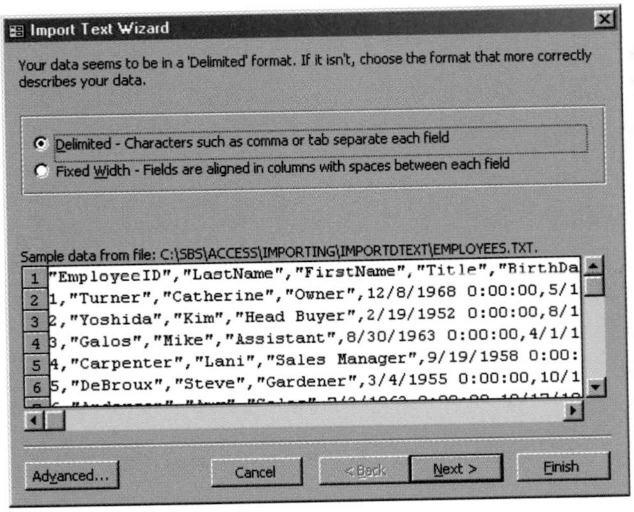

You can see that each field is enclosed in quotation marks, and there is a comma between them. Access recognized that the selected file is delimited and has selected that option.

5 Click the **Advanced** button to display the default import specifications for this file.

You don't need to change anything in the **Employees Import Specification** dialog box, but you can see that you could fine-tune the import process here.

Tip

If you want to import several files that deviate in some way from the default settings, you can specify the new settings and save them. Then as you open each of the other files, you can display this dialog box and click the **Specs** button to select and load the saved specifications.

6 Click **Cancel** to close the **Employees Import Specification** dialog box, and then click **Next** to display this page of the wizard:

The wizard breaks the file into fields, based on its assumption that items are separated by commas. From the neat columns you see here, this assumption is obviously a good one. But if the columns are jumbled, you can choose a different delimiter from the options at the top of this page.

7 Select the **First Row Contains Field Names** check box, and then click **Next**.

The background of the first row becomes gray to indicate that these entries are field names.

8 Click **In an Existing Table**, select **Employees** from the drop-down list, and click **Next**.

9 Click **Finish** to import the text file into the Employees table.

A message informs you that the file was imported.

10 Click **OK** to close the message box, and then open the **Employees** table to confirm that Access imported nine records from the employees list.

11 Close the **Employees** table, and then close the database.

Importing Information from a Fixed-Width Text File

Ac2002-8-1

Approved Courseware

The only way to get the data of many older applications into Access is to export the data to a **fixed-width text file** and then import that file into Access. In a fixed-width text file, the same field in every record contains exactly the same number of characters. If the actual data doesn't fill a field, the field is padded with spaces so that the starting point of the data in the next field is the same number of characters from the beginning of every record. For example, if the first field contains 12 characters, the second field always starts 13 characters from the beginning of the record, even if the actual data in the first field is only 4 characters.

Fixed-width text files used to be difficult to import into databases, because you had to carefully count the number of characters in each field and then specify the field sizes in the database layout or the import program. If the text in any field were even one character off, all records from that point on would be jumbled. That is no longer a problem with Access, because the **Import Text Wizard** makes importing a fixed-width text file simple.

GardenCo
Suppliers

In this exercise, you will import a fixed-width text file into the Suppliers table in the GardenCo database. The working folder for this exercise is *SBS\Access\Importing \ImportFText*. Follow these steps:

1   Open the **GardenCo** database located in the working folder.

2   On the **File** menu, point to **Get External Data**, and then click **Import**.

3   In the **Files of type** list, click **Text Files**.

4   In the working folder for this exercise, click **Suppliers**, and then click **Import** to display the first page of the **Import Text Wizard**, shown here:

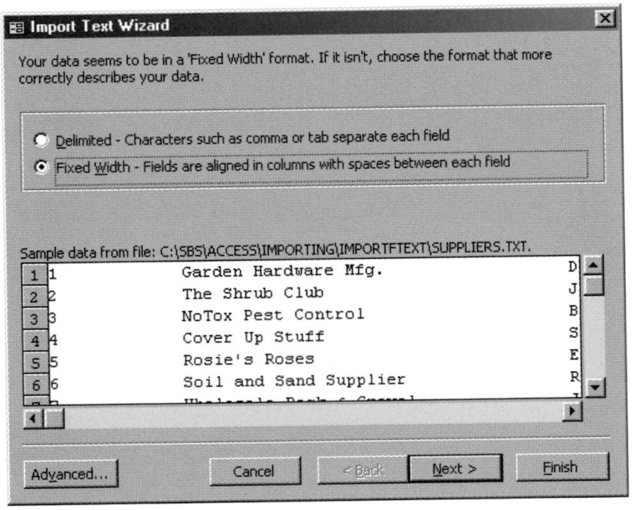

The wizard found that chunks of text seemed to line up, so it selected **Fixed Width** as the format.

5   Click **Next** to display the second page of the wizard, shown on the following page.

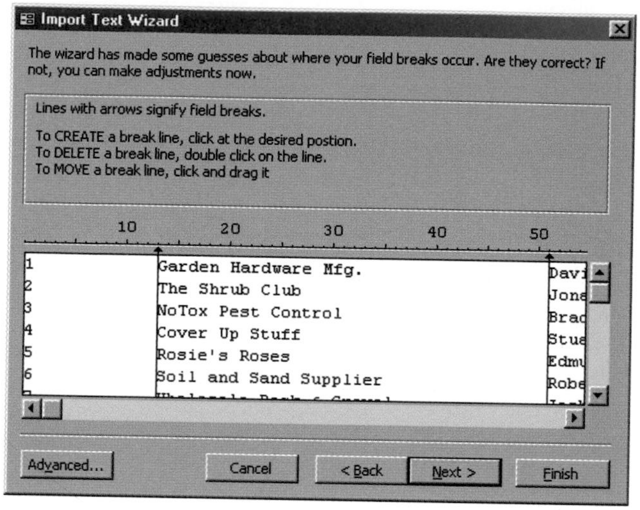

The wizard breaks the file into fields based on its assumption that a column of one or more spaces extending through all records marks the end of a field. If you take a casual glance at the fields, the wizard seems to have done its job well, but take a closer look.

6 Use the horizontal scroll bar to scroll through the fields until you get to the two fields that contain phone numbers, which are shown here:

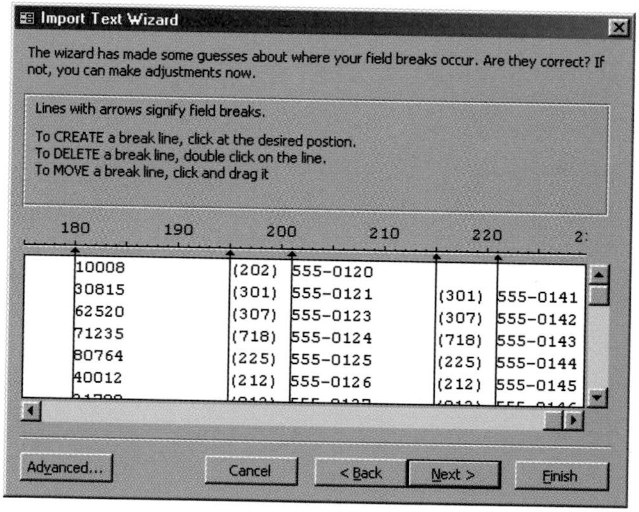

As you can see, the wizard broke each phone number into two fields because a column of spaces separates the area code from the number. Breaking the numbers this way would be fine if you wanted to store the area codes in separate fields, but you don't want to do that in this database.

7 Double-click the dividing line at column 201 to remove it. Then repeat this step for the dividing line at column 221, and click **Next**.

Tip

If necessary, you can also add or move lines in the table. Simply follow the wizard's directions.

8 Click **In an Existing Table**, select **Suppliers** from the drop-down list, and then click **Next**.

9 Click **Finish** to import the text file into the Suppliers table.

Access informs you that the file was imported.

10 Click **OK** to close the message box, and then open the **Suppliers** table to confirm that Access imported 20 records from the suppliers list.

11 Close the **Suppliers** table, and then close the database.

Importing Information from an Access Database

Ac2002-8-1

Approved Courseware

Suppose you already have an Access database that includes tables of information about products and orders and another that includes contact information. Now you wish you had just one database so that all the information you use on a regular basis is in one place. You had to create the existing databases by hand and then type in all the data, and you don't relish the thought of having to retype anything. You can take advantage of this earlier work by importing the product and orders information into the contacts database, rather than recreating it all.

You can easily import one or more of the standard Access objects: tables, queries, forms, reports, pages, macros, and modules. When importing a table, you have the option of importing just the table definition (the structure that you see in Design view), or both the definition and the data. When importing a query, you can import it as a query or you can import the results of the query as a table.

When you import an Access object, the entire object is imported as an object of the same name in the active database. You don't have the option of importing selected fields or records. If the active database already has an object of the same name, Access imports the object with a number added to the end of its name.

Tip

If you need only some of the fields or records from a table in another database, you can create a query in the other database to select just the information you need, and then import the results of the query as a table. Alternatively, you can import the table and then either edit it in Design view or use queries to clean it up.

GardenCo
Products

In this exercise, you will import a couple of tables from a Products database into the GardenCo database. The working folder for this exercise is *SBS\Access\Importing \ImportAccess*. Follow these steps:

1 Open the **GardenCo** database located in the working folder.

2 On the **File** menu, point to **Get External Data**, and then click **Import**.

3 In the **Files of type** list, make sure **Microsoft Access** is selected.

4 Browse to the *SBS\Access\Importing\ImportAccess* folder, click **Products**, and then click **Import** to open the **Import Objects** dialog box.

As you might guess from looking at the tabs across the top of this dialog box, you can import any type of Access object from this database.

5 Click the **Options** button to expand the dialog box to display these import options:

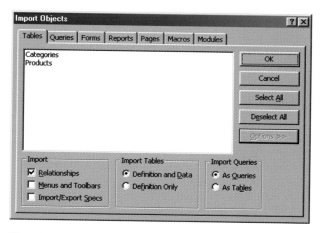

The default options are fine for the current task, but if it were necessary, you could use these options to refine the import process.

6 Click **Select All** to select the two tables listed.

You can also click individual tables one at a time to select them.

7 Click **OK** to import the tables.

8 Open the new **Categories** and **Products** tables to confirm that records were imported. Then close them.

9 Close the database.

Importing Information from Other Databases

Ac2002-8-1

Approved Courseware

Importing information from databases other than Access is usually an all-or-nothing situation, and quite often, what you get isn't in the exact format you need. You might find, for example, that **transaction records** include redundant information, such as the name of the product or purchaser, in every record. Or information about people might include the full name and address in one field, when you would like separate fields for the first name, last name, street address, and so on. You can choose to import information as it is and manipulate it in Access, or you can move it into some other program, such as Excel or Word, and manipluate it there before importing it into Access.

Access can import data from the following versions of dBASE, Lotus 1-2-3, and Paradox:

Program	Versions
dBASE	III, IV, and 5
Lotus 1-2-3	WK1, WK3, WJ2
Paradox	3, 4, 5, 7-8

GardenCo
Shippers

In this exercise, you will import information from a dBASE file into the Shippers table in the GardenCo database. The working folder for this exercise is *SBS\Access\Importing\ImportDbase*. Follow these steps:

1   Open the **GardenCo** database located in the working folder.

2   On the **File** menu, point to **Get External Data**, and then click **Import** to open the **Import** dialog box.

3   In the **Files of type** list, click **dBASE 5**.

4   In the *SBS\Access\Importing\ImportDbase* folder, click **Shippers.dbf**, and then click **Import**.

   After a few seconds of processing, Access lets you know that the file was imported. There are no options to select; whatever was in the file was imported.

5   Click **OK** to close the message box, close the **Import** dialog box, and then open the **Shippers** table to confirm that five records were imported properly.

6   Close the table and the database.

Importing Information from an HTML File

Ac2002-8-1

Approved Courseware

You might be familiar with the **Hypertext Markup Language (HTML)**, which is used to create Web pages. HTML uses **tags** to control the appearance and alignment of text when it is displayed in a Web browser. To display a table on a Web page, the table's elements—rows and cells—are enclosed in appropriate **HTML tags**. For example, a simple HTML table might look like this:

```
       .
       .
       .
<table>
<tr>
    <td>LastName</td><td>FirstName</td>
</tr>
    <td>Anderson</td><td>Amy</td>
</table>
       .
       .
       .
```

Of course, a lot of other tags and text would appear above and below this little table, and few tables are this simple. But you can get the general idea. With an HTML document, it is the <table>, <tr> (table row), and <td> (table data) tags that make the data look like a table when viewed in a Web browser.

All Office XP programs can save a document in HTML format, and to a limited extent, they can read or import a document saved in HTML format by another program. If you attempt to import an HTML document into Access, it will **parse** the document and identify anything that looks like structured data. You can then look at what Access has found and decide whether or not to import it.

Important

If you want to import data into an existing table but the structure of the data isn't the same as the table structure, it is often easier to import the data into Excel, massage it there, and then import it into Access.

GardenCo
NewCust

In this exercise, you will import new customer information that is stored in an HTML document into the Customers table in the GardenCo database. The working folder for this exercise is *SBS\Access\Importing\ImportHTML*. Follow these steps:

1   Open the **GardenCo** database located in the working folder.

2   Open the **Customers** table, and notice that it contains 107 records. Close the table.

3   On the **File** menu, point to **Get External Data**, and then click **Import**.

4   In the **Files of type** list, click **HTML Documents**.

5   Browse to the *SBS\Access\Importing\ImportHTML* folder, click **NewCust**, and then click **Import** to display the first page of the **Import HTML Wizard**, shown here:

Import HTML Wizard				
Microsoft Access can use your column headings as field names for your table. Does the first row specified contain column headings?				
☐ First Row Contains Column Headings				
1 CustomerID	LastName	FirstName	Address	City
2 YOURO	Young	Rob	231 N. Ukiah Rd.	Aloh
3 ZIMKA	Zimprich	Karin	472 Lexington Ave.	Carn
4 ZUVLE	Zuvela	Leonard	76 Kings Way	Fall

Advanced...   Cancel   < Back   Next >   Finish

The wizard has found the table in the NewCust file and displays its contents, divided into rows and columns. If the file contains multiple tables or lists, the wizard lists them here, and you can select the one you want to import.

6   Select the **First Row Contains Column Headings** check box.

The background of the first row becomes gray to indicate that the entries in this row are field names.

7 Click the **Advanced** button to display the **Import Specification** dialog box, shown here:

In the **Field Information** section, the data type of the **PostalCode** field is set to **Long Integer** because, in the file being imported, this field contains what appear to be large numbers. You don't need to manipulate these numbers mathematically, and you might want to change them to the ZIP+4 Code format or to a foreign code. Additionally, you are importing this information to the Customers table, which already considers postal codes to be text, so you need to change this setting.

8 Click in the **Data Type** cell for **PostalCode**, and then click **Text** in the drop-down list.

9 Click **OK**, and then click **Next** to display the next page of the wizard.

10 Click **In an Existing Table**, select **Customers** from the drop-down list, and then click **Next**.

11 Click **Finish** to import the new customers into the Customers table.

12 In the message box that appears, click **OK** to close it, and then open the **Customers** table.

The table now contains 110 records.

13 Close the **Customers** table and the database.

Importing XML Data

Ac2002e-7-1

Extensible Markup Language (XML) files are often used for exchanging information between applications, both on and off the Web. XML files are similar to HTML files in two ways: both are plain text files that use tags to format their content, and both use start and end tags. However, HTML tags describe how elements should look, whereas XML tags specify the structure of the elements in a document. Also, as its name implies, the XML tag set is extensible—there are ways to add your own tags. Here is an example of a simple XML file:

```
<?xml version="1.0"?>
<ORDER>
                <CUSTOMER>Nancy Davolio</CUSTOMER>
                <PRODUCT>
                 <ITEM>Sterilized Soil</ITEM>
                 <PRICE>$8.65</PRICE>
                 <QUANTITY>1 bag</QUANTITY>
                </PRODUCT>
</ORDER>
```

This file describes an order that Nancy Davolio (the customer) placed for one bag (the quantity) of Sterilized Soil (the item) at a cost of $8.65 (the price). As you can see, when the data's *structure* is tagged, rather than just its *appearance*, you can easily import the data into a table of a database.

GardenCo
Orders
OrderDetails
Order-
Details.xsd

In this exercise, you will import the Orders and Order Details XML documents into the GardenCo database. The working folder for this exercise is *SBS\Access \Importing\ImportXML*. Follow these steps:

1 Open the **GardenCo** database located in the working folder.

2 On the **File** menu, point to **Get External Data**, and then click **Import**.

3 In the **Files of type** list, click **XML Documents**.

4 Browse to the *SBS\Access\Importing\ImportXML* folder.

Notice that there is one file named *Orders* and two files named *Order Details* in this folder. Of the two Order Detail files, one has the extension *.xml* (which you won't see unless your computer is set to display file extensions), and the other has the extension *.xsd*. XML consists of data and a **schema**, which describes the structure of the data. Applications that export to XML might combine the data and schema in one .xsd file, as with Orders, or might create an .xml file to hold the data and an .xsd file to hold the schema, as with Order Details. If the application exports two separate files, you will have to have both files to import both the data and the structure into Access.

5 Click **Orders**, click **Import** to open the **Import XML** dialog box, and then click the **Options** button to display the import options shown at the bottom of this dialog box:

> **Import XML**   ? X
>
> Orders
>
> OK
> Cancel
> Help
> Options >>
>
> Import Options
> ○ Structure Only
> ● Structure and Data
> ○ Append Data to Existing Table(s)

6 Click **OK** to accept the default to import structure and data.

The Orders file contains both the XML data and the schema. Access imports it and creates the Orders table.

7 Click **OK** to close the message that the import process is complete.

8 Repeat step 2 to open the **Import** dialog box.

9 Click **Order Details** (the .xml file), and then click **Import**.

10 Click **OK** in the **Import XML** dialog box to accept the default to import both structure and data.

Access imports both the Order Details.xml and Order Details.xsd files and creates the Order Details table.

11 Click **OK** when the import is complete, and then open and view both the Orders and Order Details tables to confirm that the data and structure were imported.

12 Close the database.

Exporting Information to Other Applications

Ac2002-8-2
Ac2002e-7-2

Approved Courseware

You can export Access database objects in a variety of formats. The specific formats available depend on the object you are trying to export. Tables, for example, can be exported in pretty much the same formats in which they can be imported. Macros, on the other hand, can be exported only to another Access database.

The following table lists the export formats available for each object:

Object	Export Formats
Table	Access, dBASE, Excel, FoxPro, HTML, Lotus 1-2-3, Paradox, Text, Active Server Pages (ASP), Microsoft Internet Information Server (IIS), Rich Text Format (RTF), Word Merge, XML, Open Database Connectivity (ODBC)
Query	Access, dBASE, Excel, HTML, Lotus 1-2-3, Paradox, Text, ASP, IIS, RTF, Word Merge, XML, ODBC
Form	Access, Excel, HTML, Text, ASP, IIS, RTF, XML
Report	Access, Excel, HTML, Text, RTF, Snapshot, XML
Page	Access, Data Access Page (DAP)
Macro	Access
Module	Access, Text

Tables and queries can be exported to most versions of the listed formats. Forms and reports are more limited, but even so, exporting to the formats you are most likely to use is pretty straightforward. The ones that get a little tricky are Active Server Pages (ASP), Microsoft Internet Information Server (IIS), and Open Database Connectivity (ODBC).

GardenCo

In this exercise, you will export the Suppliers table from the GardenCo database in a format that can be used by Excel. Then you'll export the Customers table to an XML document. The working folder for this exercise is *SBS\Access\Importing\Export*.

Tip

To complete this exercise, you will need to have Excel 97 or later installed on your computer.

Follow these steps:

1 Open the **GardenCo** database located in the working folder.

2 In the database window, click the **Suppliers** table.

3 On the **File** menu, click **Export** to display the **Export Table 'Suppliers' To** dialog box.

4 With the working folder for this exercise active, check that **Suppliers** is the name in the **File name** box.

5 Select **Microsoft Excel 97-2002** in the **Save as type** list.

6 Click **Export**.

Access exports the table and closes the dialog box.

7 Start Microsoft Windows Explorer, browse to the *SBS\Access\Importing \Export* folder, and double-click **Suppliers** to open it in Excel.

The new worksheet looks like this:

8 Quit Excel, and minimize Windows Explorer.

9 Click the title bar of the database window to activate it, and with the Suppliers table still selected, click **Export** on the **File** menu.

10 In the *SBS\Access\Importing\Export* folder, select **XML Documents** in the **Save as type** box, accept **Suppliers** as the file name, and click the **Export** button to open the **Export XML** dialog box.

11 Make sure both **Data (XML)** and **Schema of the data** are selected, and then click **OK**.

12 Switch to Windows Explorer, and notice that Access exported the Suppliers table as both an *.xml* and an *.xsd* file.

Tip

You can combine the data and schema in one file by clicking the **Advanced** button, clicking the **Schema** tab, and then selecting the appropriate option.

13 Repeat steps 9 and 10 and try exporting the Suppliers table in various other formats by changing the options in the **Save As Type** box. Then view the exported files to see the results.

Tip

If you export to an HTML file, you can view the table in a browser such as Microsoft Internet Explorer. To see the tags that define the structure of the table, either view the source in the browser or open the file in a text editor.

14 Close the database, and close Windows Explorer.

Linking a Database to Information in Another Database

Ac2002e-1-2

Approved Courseware

Instead of importing data into an Access database from another application, you can leave the data in the other application and link to it. Although working with data that is stored in your own database is faster, safer, and more flexible, sometimes linking is preferable.

The most common reason for linking to data in another Access database or a different application is because you don't own the data. Perhaps another department in your organization maintains the data in a **SQL database**, and they are willing to give you permission to read the tables and queries but not to change them. Other reasons are security and ease of distribution of data.

Important

If you link to a file on a **local area network (LAN)**, be sure to use a **universal naming convention (UNC) path**, rather than a **mapped network drive**. A UNC path includes the computer name as well as the drive letter and folder names, so it is less likely to change.

GardenCo
LinkDatabase

In this exercise, you will first link a table in the GardenCo database to a table in another Access database and then link to a named range in an Excel worksheet. The working folder for this exercise is *SBS\Access\Importing\Link*. Follow these steps:

1 Open the **GardenCo** database located in the working folder.

2 On the **File** menu, point to **Get External Data**, and then click **Link Tables**.

3 When the **Link** dialog box appears, leave **Files of type** as **Microsoft Access**, browse to the *SBS\Access\Importing\Link* folder, and click the **LinkDatabase** file. Then click **Link** to display the **Link Tables** dialog box.

4 Click **Shippers** as the name of the table in LinkDatabase that you want to link to, and click **OK**.

The dialog box closes, and a table named *Shippers1* is added to the database window. (Access adds *1* to the table name because the GardenCo database already contains a table named *Shippers*.) Notice that the table's icon has an arrow to its left, indicating that its data is linked, rather than stored in the database.

5 Open the table to confirm that it contains a list of shipping companies, and then close it.

6 Repeat step 2 to open the **Link** dialog box again.

7 In the **Files of type** list, select **Microsoft Excel**.

8 With the *SBS\Access\Importing\Link* folder still be active, select the **Link-Worksheet** file, and then click **Link** to display the first page of the **Link Spreadsheet Wizard**, shown here:

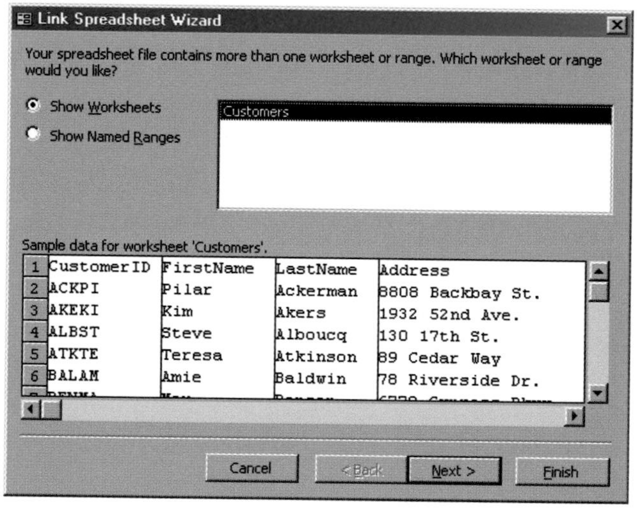

You can browse through all the worksheets and named ranges in the selected spreadsheet.

9 Click **Show Named Ranges**, click **SpecialCustomers** in the list of ranges, and then click **Next**.

10 Leave the **First Row Contains Column Headings** check box cleared, because this particular named range doesn't have column headings, and then click **Next**.

11 Click **Finish**, and then click **OK** when the message box appears.

Access has added a new table, named *SpecialCustomers*, to the database window. The table's icon has an arrow to its left to indicate that it is a linked table, but the icon itself has an Excel logo instead of an Access logo.

Delete

12 You don't really need these two linked tables in the GardenCo database, so delete them by selecting each one, clicking the **Delete** button, and then clicking **Yes** to confirm the deletion.

13 Close the database.

Other Ways to Share Access Data

All the methods of importing and exporting data described in this chapter work well, but they aren't the only ways to share information with other applications.

Sometimes the quickest and easiest way to get information into or out of a database is to just copy it and paste it where you want it. This technique works particularly well for getting data *out of* an Access table and into Word or Excel. If you paste into Word, the data becomes a Word table, complete with a header row containing the field captions as column headings. If you paste into Excel, the data is displayed in the normal row-and-column format on the worksheet.

Getting data *into* an Access table using this technique is a little more complicated. The data you are pasting must meet all the criteria for entering it by hand (input mask, validation rules, field size, and so on), and you have to have the correct cells selected when you use the **Paste** command. If Access encounters a problem when you attempt to paste a group of records, it displays an error message and pastes the problem records into a Paste Errors table. You can then troubleshoot the problem in that table, fix whatever is wrong, and try copying and pasting again.

Tip

You can also copy an entire table from one Access database into another. Simply open both databases, copy the table from the source database to the Clipboard, and then paste it in the destination database. Access prompts you to give the new table a name, and asks if you want to paste the table structure only, paste the structure and data, or append the data to an existing table.

OfficeLinks

GardenCo

Another quick way to share the information in an Access database with Word or Excel is through the **OfficeLinks** button on the toolbar. Clicking this button's down arrow displays a menu of three commands you can use to merge the data in the table with a Word mail merge document, to publish the table in a Word document, or to instantly export the table to an Excel worksheet.

In this exercise, you will experiment with copying records. This technique requires a little more effort than using the **OfficeLinks** button, but gives you the option of moving just part of a table to Excel or Word. The working folder for this exercise is *SBS\Access\Importing\OfficeLink*.

Tip

To complete this exercise, you will need to have Excel and Word installed on your computer.

Follow these steps:

1 Open the **GardenCo** database located in the working folder, and then open the **Customers** table.

Copy

2 Select about six records by pointing to the row selector of the first record you want to select (the pointer changes to a right arrow), holding down the mouse button and dragging to the last record you want to select. Then click the **Copy** button on the toolbar.

Paste

3 Start Excel, and with cell A1 of a new blank worksheet selected, click the **Paste** button on Excel's toolbar.

Toolbar Options

If the Paste button is not visible, click the **Toolbar Options** button to display a palette of additional buttons, and then click the **Paste** button on the palette.

Excel pastes the records you copied in Access, complete with the same column headings. (You will have to widen the columns to see all the data.)

4 Press [Alt]+[Tab] to switch back to Access.

5 Select a block of cells in the middle of the table by moving the pointer over the left edge of the first one you want to select, and when the pointer changes to a fat cross, dragging until you have selected all the desired cells.

6   Click the **Copy** button (the **Clipboard** task pane and the Office Assistant might appear), press `Alt`+`Tab` to move back to Excel, click a cell below the records you pasted previously, and then click the **Paste** button.

Excel pastes in the new selection, again with column headings.

7   The data you copied is still in the Clipboard, so start Word, and click the **Paste** button on Word's toolbar.

Word pastes the selection into a nicely formatted table with the title *Customers*, reflecting the name of the table from which this data came.

8   Quit Word and Excel without saving your changes.

9   Close the **Clipboard** task pane, the **Customers** table, and the database.

10   If you are not continuing on to the next chapter, quit Access.

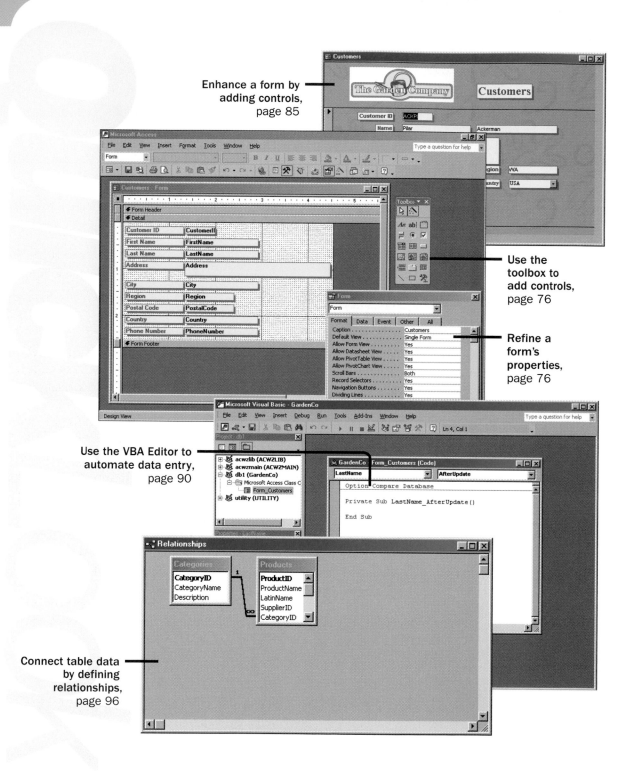

Enhance a form by
adding controls,
page 85

Use the
toolbox to
add controls,
page 76

Refine a
form's
properties,
page 76

Use the VBA Editor to
automate data entry,
page 90

Connect table data
by defining
relationships,
page 96

Chapter 4
Simplifying Data Entry with Forms

After completing this chapter, you will be able to:

✔ **Create a form using a wizard.**
✔ **Refine the properties and layout of a form.**
✔ **Add controls and VBA code that help enter data.**
✔ **Create a form using AutoForm.**
✔ **Create a form based on more than one table.**

A database that contains the day-to-day records of an active company is useful only if it can be kept up to date and if particular items of information can be found quickly. Although Microsoft Access is fairly easy to use, entering, editing, and retrieving information in Datasheet view is not a task you would want to assign to someone who's not familiar with Access. Not only would these tasks be tedious and inefficient, but working in Datasheet view leaves far too much room for error, especially if details of complex transactions have to be entered into several related tables. The solution to this problem, and the first step in the conversion of this database to a database application, is to create and use forms.

A form is an organized and formatted view of some or all of the fields from one or more tables or queries. Forms work interactively with the tables in a database. You use **controls** on the form to enter new information, to edit or remove existing information, or to locate information. Like printed forms, Access forms can include **label controls** that tell users what type of information they are expected to enter, as well as **text box controls** in which they can enter the information. Unlike printed forms, Access forms can also include a variety of other controls, such as **option buttons** and **command buttons**, that transform Access forms into something very much like a Microsoft Windows dialog box or one page of a wizard.

Tip

Some forms are used to navigate among the features and functions of a database application and have little or no connection with its actual data. A **switchboard** is an example of this type of form.

As with other Access objects, you can create forms by hand or with the help of a wizard. Navigational and housekeeping forms, such as switchboards, are best created by hand in Design view. Forms that are based on tables, on the other hand, should always be created with a wizard and then refined by hand—not because it is difficult to drag the necessary text box controls onto a form, but because there is simply no point in doing it by hand.

For this chapter, you will create some forms to hide the complexity of the GardenCo database from the people who will be entering and working with its information. First you will discover how easy it is to let the **Form Wizard** create forms that you can then modify to suit your needs. You'll learn about the controls you can place on a form, and the properties that control its function and appearance. After you have created a form containing controls, you will learn how to tell Access what to do when a user performs some action in a control, such as clicking or entering text. You will also take a quick look at subforms (forms within a form). You will be working with the GardenCo database files and other sample files that are stored in the following subfolders of the *SBS\Access\Forms* folder: *FormByWiz, Properties, Layout, Controls, Events, AutoForm,* and *Subform.*

Creating a Form Using a Wizard

Ac2002-4-1

Approved Courseware

Before you begin creating a form, you need to know what table it will be based on and have an idea of how the form will be used. Having made these decisions, you can use the **Form Wizard** to help create the basic form. Remember though, that like almost any other object in Access, after the form is created you can always go into Design view to customize the form if it does not quite meet your needs.

GardenCo

In this exercise, you'll create a form that will be used to add new customer records to the Customers table of The Garden Company's database. The working folder for this exercise is *SBS\Access\Forms\FormByWiz*. Follow these steps:

1 Open the **GardenCo** database located in the working folder.

2 On the **Objects** bar, click **Forms**.

3   Double-click **Create form by using wizard** to start the **Form Wizard**, whose first page looks like this:

4   In the **Tables/Queries** drop-down list, click **Table: Customers** to display the fields from that table in the **Available Fields** list.

5   Click the **>>** button to move all the fields from the Customers table to the **Selected Fields** list, and then click **Next**.

You use the second page of the **Form Wizard** to select the layout of the fields on the new form. When you click an option on the right side of the page, the preview area on the left side shows what the form layout will look like with that option applied.

6   Select **Columnar**, and then click **Next**.

In this page, you can click a style option to see how the selected style will look when applied to the form.

7   Select the **Sumi Painting** style from the list, and click **Next**.

8   Because this form is based on the Customers table, Access suggests *Customers* as the form's title. Accept this suggestion, leave the **Open the form to view or enter information** option selected, and click **Finish**.

The new Customers form opens, displaying the first customer record in the Customers table, like this:

Customers	
Customer ID	ACKPI
First Name	Pilar
Last Name	Ackerman
Address	8808 Backbay St.
City	Bellevue
Region	WA
Postal Code	88337
Country	USA
Phone Number	(206) 555-0194

Record: I◄ ◄ 1 ► ►I ►* of 110

9 Use the navigation controls at the bottom of the form to scroll through a few of the records.

10 Close the form and the database.

Refining Form Properties

Ac2002-4-2

Approved Courseware

As with tables, you can work with forms in multiple views. The two most common views are Form view, which you use to view or enter data, and Design view, which you use to add controls to the form or change the form's properties or layout.

When you use the **Form Wizard** to create a form in a column format, every field you select from the underlying table is represented by a text box control and its associated label control. A form like this one, which is used to enter or view the information stored in a specific table, is linked, or **bound**, to that table. Each text box—the box where data is entered or viewed—is bound to a specific field in the table. The table is the **record source**, and the field is the **control source**. Each control has a number of properties, such as font, font size, alignment, fill color, and border. The wizard assigns default values for these properties, but you can change them to improve the form's appearance.

GardenCo
tgc_bkgrnd

In this exercise, you will edit the properties of the Customers form so that it suits the needs of the people who will be using it on a daily basis. The working folder for this exercise is *SBS\Access\Forms\Properties*. Follow these steps:

1 Open the **GardenCo** database located in the working folder.

2 With **Forms** selected on the **Objects** bar, select **Customers** in the list of forms, and click the **Design** button.

This form opens in Design view, like this:

Text box control — Toolbox

Label control —

When a form is created, some of its properties are inherited from the table on which it is based. In this case, the names assigned to the text boxes (*FirstName*, *LastName*, and so on) are the field names from the Customers table, and the labels to the left of each text box reflect the **Caption** property of each field. The size of each text box is determined by the **Field Size** property.

Tip

After a form has been created, its properties are not bound to their source. Changing the table's field properties has no impact on the corresponding form property, and vice versa.

3 Change the font of the **Customer ID** label by clicking the label and clicking **Microsoft Sans Serif** in the **Font** list on the Formatting toolbar. (If you don't see **Microsoft Sans Serif**, click **MS Sans Serif**.)

4 With the label still selected, click **8** in the **Font Size** list to make the font slightly smaller.

5 Right-click the **CustomerID** text box (not its label), and click **Properties** on the shortcut menu to display this **Properties** dialog box for the **CustomerID** text box:

Text Box: CustomerID	☒

CustomerID ▼

| Format | Data | Event | Other | All |

Name	CustomerID	▲
Control Source	CustomerID	
Format		
Decimal Places	Auto	
Input Mask		
Default Value		
IME Hold	No	
IME Mode	No Control	
IME Sentence Mode	None	
Validation Rule		
Validation Text		▼

All the settings available on the toolbar are also available (with other settings) in a **Properties** dialog box that is associated with each control. You can use this dialog box to display the properties of any object on the form, including the form itself: simply select the object from the drop-down list at the top of the dialog box.

You can display related types of properties by clicking the appropriate tab: **Format**, **Data**, **Event**, or **Other**. Or you can display all the properties by clicking the **All** tab.

6 Click the **Format** tab, scroll to the **Font Name** property, and change it to **Microsoft Sans Serif** (or **MS Sans Serif**). Then set **Font Size** to **8**, and set **Font Weight** to **Bold**.

On the form behind the dialog box, you can see how these changes affect the *CustomerID* text in the text box.

Tip

When you are working in Design view with the **Properties** dialog box open, you can drag the dialog box by its title bar to the side of the screen so that you can see the changes you're making to the form.

7 Click **FirstName_Label** in the drop-down list at the top of the **Properties** dialog box to select the label to the left of the **FirstName** text box.

8 Repeat step 6 to change the font settings for this control.

These different ways of selecting a control and changing its properties provide some flexibility and convenience, but you can see that it would be a bit tedious to apply any of them to a few dozen controls on a form. The next two steps provide a faster method.

9   Press ⌃+Ⓐ to select all the controls in the **Detail** section of the form.

Tip

Small black handles appear around all the controls to indicate that they are selected. The title bar of the **Properties** dialog box now displays *Multiple selection*, and the **Objects** list is blank. Only the **Format** settings that have the same settings for all the selected controls are displayed. Because the changes you made in the previous steps are not shared by all the selected controls, the **Font Name**, **Font Size**, and **Font Weight** settings are now blank.

10   To apply the settings to all the selected controls, set the **Font Name**, **Font Size**, and **Font Weight** as you did in step 6.

11   With all controls still selected, click **Back Style** on the **Format** tab, and set it to **Normal.**

The background of the labels will no longer be transparent.

12   Click **Back Color**, and then click the **...** button at the right end of the box to display this **Color** dialog box:

13   Click pale yellow, and click **OK**.

The background of all the controls changes to pale yellow.

Tip

14 Set **Special Effect** to **Shadowed**, and set **Border Color** to a shade of green.

You can either click the **...** button and make a selection, or type a color value such as **32768** in the **BorderColor** box.

15 Click the **Detail** section to deselect all the controls. Your form should now look something like this:

16 Click the label to the left of **FirstName**, and in the **Properties** dialog box, change the caption to **Name**.

17 Repeat step 16 to change *Phone Number* to **Phone**.

Tip

You can edit the **Caption** property of a label or the **Control Source** property of a text box by selecting it, clicking its text, and then editing the text as you would in any other Windows application. However, take care when editing the **Control Source** property, which defines where the content of the text box comes from.

18 Remove the label to the left of **LastName** by clicking it and then pressing the ⌸ key.

19 Select all the labels, but not their corresponding text boxes, by holding down the ⇧ key as you click each of them. Then in the **Properties** dialog box, set the **Text Align** property to **Right**.

20 On the **Format** menu, point to **Size**, and then click **To Fit** to size the labels to fit their contents, as shown here:

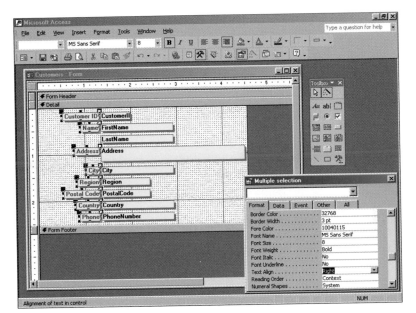

Tip

The order in which you make formatting changes, such as the ones above, can have an impact on the results. If you don't see the expected results, click the **Undo** button or press [Ctrl]+[Z] to step back through your changes, and then try again.

21 Now select all the text boxes but not their corresponding labels, and in the **Properties** dialog box, change the **Left** setting to **1.5"** to insert a little space between the labels and the text boxes.

22 Change **Font Weight** to **Normal**, and then click anywhere outside the controls to deselect them.

23 To change the background to one that better represents The Garden Company, select **Form** from the drop-down list of objects at the top of the **Properties** dialog box, click the **Picture** property—which shows *(bitmap)*—and then click the **...** button to open the **Insert Picture** dialog box.

24 Browse to the *SBS\Access\Forms\Properties* folder, change the **Files of type** setting to **Graphics Interchange Format**, and double-click **tgc_bkgrnd**.

The form's background changes, and the path to the graphic used for the new background is displayed in the **Picture** property, as shown on the next page.

25 Click the **Save** button to save the design of your Customers form.

26 Close the form and the database.

Refining Form Layout

Ac2002e-2-1

Approved Courseware

The forms created by a wizard are functional, not fancy. However, it's fairly easy to customize the layout to suit your needs. You can add and delete labels, move both labels and text controls around of the form, add logos and other graphics, and otherwise improve the layout of the form to make it attractive and easy to use.

As you work with a form's layout, it is important to pay attention to the shape of the pointer, which changes shape to indicate the manner in which you can change the selected item. Because a text box and its label sometimes act as a unit, you have to be careful to notice the pointer's shape before making any change. This table explains what action each shape indicates:

Shape		Action
🖐	Hand	Drag to move both controls together, as one.
👆	Pointing finger	Drag to move just the control.
↕	Vertical arrows	Drag the top or bottom border to change the height.
↔	Horizontal arrows	Drag the right or left border to change the width.
↘	Diagonal arrows	Drag the corner to change both the height and width.

GardenCo

In this exercise, you will rearrange the label and text box controls on the Customers form to make them more closely fit the way people will work with them. The working folder for this exercise is *SBS\Access\Forms\Layout*. Follow these steps:

1 Open the **GardenCo** database located in the working folder.

2 Open the **Customers** form in Design view.

3 If necessary, drag the lower right corner of the Form window down and to the right until you can see the **Form Footer** at the bottom of the form and have an inch or so of blank area to the right of the background, like this:

The form is divided into three sections: **Form Header**, **Detail**, and **Form Footer**. Only the **Detail** section currently has anything in it.

4 Point to the right edge of the **Detail** background, and when the pointer changes to a two-way arrow, drag the edge of the background to the right until you can see about five full grid sections.

5 Click the **LastName** text box, and then slowly move the pointer around its border, from black handle to black handle, noticing how it changes shape.

6 Move the pointer over the **LastName** text box and when it changes to a hand, drag it up and to the right of the **FirstName** text box.

7 One by one, select each control, resize it, and move it to the location shown in this graphic:

Tip

To fine-tune the size or position of a control, click it, move the pointer over the control until it becomes the shape for the change you want, and then press the appropriate arrow key—←, ↓, ↑, or →—to move the control, in small increments, in a specific direction.

8 Now you'll create and save a style based on this form so that you can apply it to any new form you create in the future, instead of having to make all of these manual adjustments each time. On the **Format** menu, click **AutoFormat** to display the **AutoFormat** dialog box:

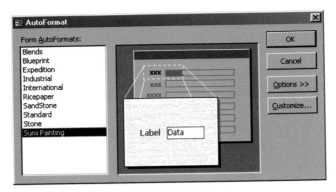

9 Click the **Customize** button to display the **Customize AutoFormat** dialog box.

10 Click **Create a new AutoFormat based on the Form 'Customers'**, and then click **OK**.

11 In the **New Style Name** dialog box, type **The Garden Company** as the name of the new style, and then click **OK**.

Back in the **AutoFormat** database, the new style appears in the **Form Auto-Formats** list. From now on, this style will be available in any database you open on this computer.

12 Click **OK** to close the **AutoFormat** dialog box.

Save

13 Click the **Save** button.

14 Close the form and the database.

Adding Controls to a Form

Ac2002-4-2

Approved Courseware

Every form has three basic sections: **Form Header**, **Detail**, and **Form Footer**. When you use a wizard to create a form, the wizard adds a set of controls for each field that you select from the underlying table to the **Detail** section and leaves the **Form Header** and **Form Footer** sections blank. Because these sections are empty, Access collapses them, but you can size all the sections by dragging their **selectors**. Although labels and text box controls are perhaps the most common controls found on forms, you can also enhance your forms with many other types of controls. For example, you can add groups of option buttons, check boxes, and list boxes to present people with choices instead of making them type entries in text boxes.

More Controls

The most popular controls are stored in the toolbox. Clicking the **More Controls** button displays a list of all the other controls that Access has discovered on your computer. The controls displayed when you click the **More Controls** button are not necessarily associated with Access or even with another Microsoft Office application. The list includes every control that any application has installed and registered on your computer.

Important

> Some controls, such as the Calendar Control, can be very useful. Others might do nothing when you add them to a form, or might do something unexpected and not entirely pleasant. If you feel like experimenting, don't do so in a database that is important to you.

GardenCo
tgc_logo2

In this exercise, you will use the Customers form from the GardenCo database to add a graphic and a caption to the **Form Header** section. You will also replace the Country text box control in the **Detail** section with a combo box control. The working folder for this exercise is *SBS\Access\Forms\Controls*. Follow these steps:

1 Open the **GardenCo** database located in the working folder.

2 Open the **Customers** form in Design view.

3 Point to the horizontal line between the **Form Header** section selector and the **Detail** section selector and, when the pointer changes to a double arrow, drag the **Detail** section selector down about 1 inch.

The form now looks like this:

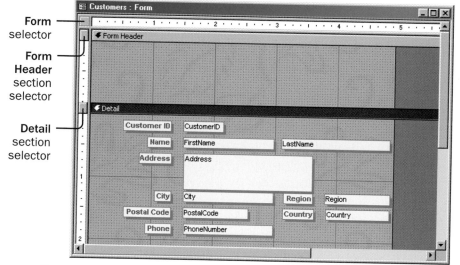

Toolbox

4 If the toolbox isn't displayed, click the **Toolbox** button on the toolbar.

You can also check the **Toolbox** command on the **View** menu. To keep the toolbox open but out of the way, you can dock it along one edge of the screen.

5 To get an idea of what controls are available, move the pointer over the buttons in the toolbox, pausing just long enough to display each button's ScreenTip.

Image

6 Click the **Image** control in the toolbox, and then drag a rectangle about 1 inch high and 3 inches wide at the left end of the **Form Header** section.

When you release the mouse button, Access displays the **Insert Picture** dialog box, where you can select an image to insert in the control.

7 Make sure that the *SBS\Access\Forms\Controls* folder is selected and that **Graphics Interchange Format** is the **Files of type** setting. Then double-click **tgc_logo2**.

The Garden Company logo appears inside the image control, like this:

Tip

If the control isn't large enough, the image is cropped. You can enlarge the control to display the entire image. (You might also have to enlarge the **Form Header** section.)

Label

8 To add a caption to the header, click the **Label** control in the toolbox, and then drag another rectangle in the header section.

Access inserts a label control containing the insertion point, ready for you to enter a caption.

9 Type the caption **Customers**, and press Enter.

The Customers label takes on the formatting of the other labels.

10 With the **Customers** label selected, press the ▢ key to display the **Properties** dialog box.

11 Change **Font Size** to **18**, and change **Text Align** to **Center**. Then close the **Properties** dialog box.

12 On the **Format** menu, point to **Size**, and then click **To Fit**.

13 Adjust the size and position of the two controls you added until they look something like this:

Control
Wizards

14 If the **Control Wizards** button is active in the toolbox (has a border around it), click it to deselect it.

Deselecting this button enables you to create a control with all the default settings without having to work through the wizard's pages.

Combo Box

15 Insert a combo box in the **Details** section by clicking the **Combo Box** control in the toolbox and then dragging a rectangle just below the current **Country** text box.

When you release the mouse, Access displays a combo box control, which is **unbound** (not attached to a field in the Customers table).

Format Painter

16 Copy the formatting of the **Country** text box to the new combo box control by clicking the **Country** text box, clicking the **Format Painter** button on the toolbar, and then clicking the combo box control.

Both the combo box control and its label take on the new formatting.

17 Select the combo box again, and then display the **Properties** dialog box.

18 Click the **Data** tab, set **Control Source** to **Country**, and then type the following in the **Row Source** box:

```
SELECT DISTINCT Customers.Country FROM Customers;
```

(Note that there is no space between *Customers* and *Country*; there is only a period.)

This line is a query that extracts one example of every country in the Country field of the Customers table and displays the results as a list when you click the box's arrow.

The **Properties** dialog box now looks like this (you'll have to widen it to display the whole query):

```
┌─────────────────────────────────────────────────────────────┐
│ 📋 Combo Box: Combo20                                    [X] │
│ ┌─────────────────────────────────┬─┐                        │
│ │ Combo20                         │▼│                        │
│ └─────────────────────────────────┴─┘                        │
│ ┌──────┬──────┬───────┬───────┬─────┐                        │
│ │Format│ Data │ Event │ Other │ All │                        │
│ Control Source . . . . . . . . . │Country│            ▼ ... ▲│
│ Input Mask . . . . . . . . . . .                             │
│ Row Source Type . . . . . . . . Table/Query                  │
│ Row Source . . . . . . . . . . . SELECT DISTINCT Customers.Country FROM Customers │
│ Bound Column . . . . . . . . . . 1                           │
│ Limit To List . . . . . . . . . . No                         │
│ Auto Expand . . . . . . . . . . . Yes                        │
│ Default Value . . . . . . . . .                              │
│ Validation Rule . . . . . . . . .                            │
│ Validation Text . . . . . . . . .                            │
│ Enabled . . . . . . . . . . . . . Yes                     ▼  │
└─────────────────────────────────────────────────────────────┘
```

Tip

If you need to add a new customer from a country that is not on the list, you can type the new country in the combo box. After the record is added to the database, that country shows up when the combo box list is displayed.

19 If necessary, set the **Row Source Type** to **Table/Query**.

20 Click the label to the left of the combo box, click the dialog box's **Format** tab, change the caption to **Country**, and close the dialog box.

21 Delete the original **Country** text box and its label, and move the new combo box and label into their place, resizing them as needed.

22 Click the **View** button to see your form, which looks similar to this:

23 Scroll through a couple of records, and display the combo box's list to see how you can select a country.

24 You don't need the **record selector**—the gray bar along the left edge of the form—so return to Design view, and display the **Properties** dialog box for the entire form by checking the **Form** selector and pressing ⌑. Then on the **Format** tab, change **Record Selectors** to **No**. While you're at it, change **Scroll Bars** to **Neither**. Then close the **Properties** dialog box.

25 Save the form's new design, and switch to Form view for a final look.

26 Close the form and the database.

Using VBA to Enter Data in a Form

Ac2002e-8-1

As you may have suspected by now, almost everything in Access, including the Access program itself, is an object. One of the characteristics of objects is that they can recognize and respond to **events**, which are essentially actions. Different objects recognize different events. The basic events, recognized by almost all objects, are Click, Double Click, Mouse Down, Mouse Move, and Mouse Up. Most objects recognize quite a few other events. A text control, for example, recognizes about 17 different events; a form recognizes more than 50.

Tip

You can see the list of events recognized by an object by looking at the **Event** tab on the object's **Properties** dialog box.

While you use a form, objects are signaling events, or **firing events**, almost constantly. However, unless you attach a **macro** or **Microsoft Visual Basic for Applications (VBA) procedure** to an event, the object is really just firing blanks. By default, Access doesn't do anything obvious when it recognizes most events. So without interfering with the program's normal behavior, you can use an event to specify what action should happen. You can even use an event to trigger the running of a macro or a Visual Basic for Applications (VBA) procedure that performs a set of actions.

Sound complicated? Well, it's true that events are not things most casual Access users tend to worry about. But because knowing how to handle events can greatly increase the efficiency of objects like forms, you should take a glimpse of what they're all about while you have a form open.

For example, while looking at customer records in the GardenCo database, you might have noticed that the CustomerID is composed of the first three letters of the customer's last name and the first two letters of his or her first name, all in capital letters. This technique will usually generate a unique ID for a new customer. If you try to enter an ID that is already in use, Access won't accept the new entry, and you'll have to add a number or change the ID in some other way to make it unique. Performing trivial tasks, such as combining parts of two words and then converting the results to capital letters, is something a computer excels at. So rather than typing the ID for each new customer record that is added to The Garden Company's database, you can let VBA do it instead.

GardenCo
AftUpdate

In this exercise, you will write a few lines of VBA code and attach the code to the After Update event in the LastName text box on the Customers form. When you change the content of the text box and attempt to move somewhere else on the form, the Before Update event is fired. In response to that event, Access updates the record in the source table, and then the After Update event is fired. This is the event you are going to work with. This is by no means an in-depth treatment of VBA, but this exercise will give you a taste of VBA's power. The working folder for this exercise is *SBS\Access\Forms\Events*. Follow these steps:

1 Open the **GardenCo** database located in the working folder.

2 With **Forms** selected on the **Objects** bar, click **Customers** in the list of forms, and click the **Design** button.

3 Click the **LastName** text box to select it, and if necessary, press F4 to open the **Properties** dialog box.

91

4   Click the **Event** tab to see these options:

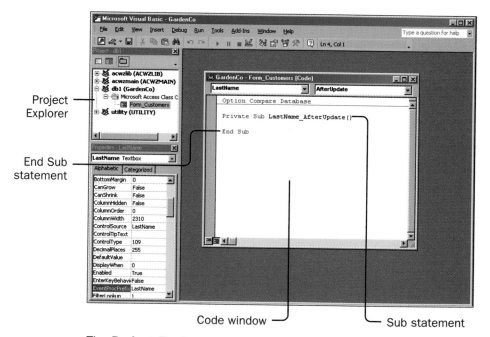

This tab lists the events that the **LastName** text box control can respond to.

5   You want to attach VBA code to the After Update event, so click **After Update** in the list, and then click the **...** button.

The **Choose Builder** dialog box appears, offering you the options of building an expression, a macro, or VBA code.

6   Click **Code Builder**, and then click **OK** to open the VBA Editor, shown here:

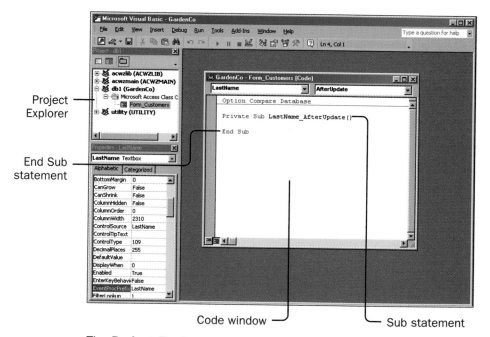

The **Project Explorer** pane lists any objects you have created to which you can attach code; in this case, only the Customers form (**Form_Customers**) is listed. As you create more forms and reports, they will appear here.

The Code window displays a placeholder for the procedure that Access will use to handle the After Update event for the LastName text control. This procedure is named *Private Sub LastName_AfterUpdate()*, and at the moment it contains only the Sub and End Sub statements that mark the beginning and end of any procedure.

7 Type the following lines between the Sub and End Sub statements, or open the file named *AftUpdate* in the *SBS\Access\Forms\Events* folder, and copy and paste the lines:

```
'Create variables to hold first and last names
' and customer ID
Dim fName As String
Dim lName As String
Dim cID As String

'Assign the text in the LastName text box to
' the lName variable.
lName = Forms!customers!LastName.Text

'You must set the focus to a text box before
' you can read its contents.
Forms!customers!FirstName.SetFocus
fName = Forms!customers!FirstName.Text

'Combine portions of the last and first names
' to create the customer ID.
cID = UCase(Left(lName, 3) & Left(fName, 2))

'Don't store the ID unless it is 5 characters long
' (which indicates both names filled in).
If Len(cID) = 5 Then
    Forms!customers!CustomerID.SetFocus

    'Don't change the ID if it has already been
    ' entered; perhaps it was changed manually.
    If Forms!customers!CustomerID.Text = "" Then
        Forms!customers!CustomerID = cID
    End If
End If

'Set the focus where it would have gone naturally.
Forms!customers!Address.SetFocus
```

Important

When a line of text is preceded by an apostrophe, the text is a comment that explains the purpose of the next line of code. In the VBA Editor, comments are displayed in green.

View Microsoft
Access

8 Save the file, click the **View Microsoft Access** button to return to the Access window, and then close the **Properties** dialog box.

9 In Form view, size the window as necessary. Then on the **Navigation** bar, click the **New Record** button to create a new record.

New Record

10 Press the ⊞ key to move the insertion point to the text box for the First-Name field, type **John**, press ⊞ to move to the text box for the LastName field, type **Coake**, and then press ⊞ again.

If you entered the VBA code correctly, *COAJO* appears in the **CustomerID** text box.

11 Change the first and last name to something else and notice that the **CustomerID** text box doesn't change even if the names from which it was derived do change.

12 Press the ⎋ key to remove your entry, and then try entering the last name first, followed by the first name.

Access does not create a Customer ID. The code does what it was written to do but not necessarily what you want it to do, which is to create an ID regardless of the order in which the names are entered. There are several ways to fix this problem. You could write a similar procedure to handle the After Update event in the **FirstName** text box, or you could write one procedure to handle both events and then jump to it when either event occurs. You won't do either in these exercises, but if you are interested, you can look at the code in the database file for the next exercise to see the second solution.

13 Press ⎋ to clear your entries, and then close the **Customers** form and the database.

14 Press ⎇+⊞ to switch to the VBA Editor, which is still open, and close the editor.

Creating a Form Using an AutoForm

Ac2002-4-1

Approved Courseware

Although a form doesn't have to include all the fields from a table, when it is used as the primary method of creating new records, it usually does include all of them. The quickest way to create a form that includes all the fields from one table is to use an **AutoForm**. And as with the forms created by a wizard, you can easily customize these forms.

GardenCo

In this exercise, you will create an AutoForm that displays information about each of the products carried by The Garden Company. The working folder for this exercise is *SBS\Access\Forms\AutoForm*. Follow these steps:

1 Open the **GardenCo** database located in the working folder.

2 On the **Objects** bar, click **Forms**.

3 On the database window's toolbar, click the **New** button to display this **New Form** dialog box, which lists all the ways you can create a form:

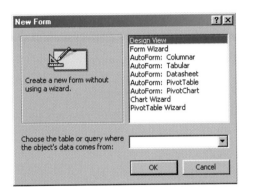

4 Click **AutoForm: Columnar** in the list of choices, select the **Categories** table from the drop-down list at the bottom of the dialog box, and then click **OK**.

The dialog box closes, and after a moment a new Categories form is displayed in Form view.

Save

5 Click the **Save** button, accept the default name of *Categories* in the **Save As** dialog box, and click **OK** to view your form, which looks like this:

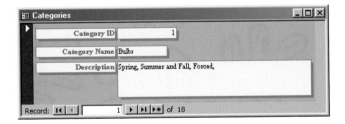

Tip

When AutoForm creates a form, Access applies the background style you selected the last time you used the **Form Wizard** (or the default style, if you haven't used the wizard). If your form doesn't look like this one, switch to Design view, and on the **Format** menu, click **AutoFormat**. You can then select **The Garden Company** style from the list displayed.

6 This form looks pretty good as it is, but switch to Design view so that you can make a few minor changes.

7 Delete the word *Category* from the **Category Name** label.

8 The **CategoryID** value is provided by Access and should never be changed, so you need to disable that text box control. Click and, if necessary, press [F4] to display the control's **Properties** dialog box.

9 On the **Data** tab, change **Enabled** to **No**, and close the dialog box.

10 Switch to Form view, and scroll through a few categories. Try to edit entries in the **Category ID** field to confirm that you can't.

11 You don't need the record selector for the form, so return to Design view, and display the form's **Properties** dialog box by clicking the **Form** selector and pressing [F4]. Then on the **Format** tab, change **Scroll Bars** to **Neither** and **Record Selectors** to **No**.

12 Save and close the **Categories** form.

13 Close the database.

Adding a Subform to a Form

Ac2002-6-1
Ac2002e-2-3
Ac2002e-5-1
Ac2002e-5-2

Approved Courseware

A form can display information (fields) from one or more tables or queries. If you want to display fields from several tables or queries on one form, you have to give some thought to the **relationships** that must exist between those objects.

In Access, a relationship is an association between common fields in two tables, and it allows you to relate the information in one table to the information in another table. For example, in the GardenCo database a relationship can be established between the Categories table and the Products table because both tables have a CategoryID field.

Each product is in only one category, but each category can contain many products, so this type of relationship—the most common—is known as a **one-to-many relationship**.

As you create forms and queries, Access might recognize some relationships between the fields in the underlying tables. However, it probably won't recognize all of them without a little help from you.

GardenCo

In this exercise, you will first define the relationship between the Categories and Products tables in the GardenCo database. You will then add a **subform** to a form. For each category displayed on the main form, this subform will display all the products in that category. The working folder for this exercise is *SBS\Access\Forms \Subform*. Follow these steps:

1 Open the **GardenCo** database located in the working folder.

Relationships

2 On the Access toolbar, click the **Relationships** button to open the Relationships window.

Show Table

3 If the **Show Table** dialog box isn't displayed, click the **Show Table** button on the toolbar. Then double-click **Categories** and **Products** in the list displayed. Close the **Show Table** dialog box to view the Relationships window, which looks like this:

4 Point to **CategoryID** in one table, and drag it on top of **CategoryID** in the other table.

Access displays the **Edit Relationships** dialog box, which lists the fields you have chosen to relate and offers several options, as shown here:

```
┌─────────────────────────────────────────────────────┐
│ Edit Relationships                          ? X      │
│                                                      │
│ Table/Query:       Related Table/Query:   ┌────────┐ │
│ Categories    ▼    Products          ▼    │ Create │ │
│ ┌──────────────┬───────────────────┐ ▲    └────────┘ │
│ │ CategoryID ▼ │ CategoryID        │      ┌────────┐ │
│ ├──────────────┼───────────────────┤      │ Cancel │ │
│ │              │                   │ ▼    └────────┘ │
│ └──────────────┴───────────────────┘      ┌──────────┐
│ ☐ Enforce Referential Integrity          │ Join Type..│
│   ☐ Cascade Update Related Fields         └──────────┘
│   ☐ Cascade Delete Related Records        ┌──────────┐
│                                           │Create New..│
│ Relationship Type:   One-To-Many          └──────────┘
└─────────────────────────────────────────────────────┘
```

Other Types of Relationships

In addition to one-to-many relationships, you can create **one-to-one relationships** and **many-to-many relationships**, but they are not as common.

In a one-to-one relationship, each record in one table can have one and only one related record in the other table. This type of relationship isn't commonly used because it is easier to put all the fields in one table. However, you might use two related tables instead of one to break up a table with many fields, or to track information that applies to only some of the records in the first table.

A many-to-many relationship is really two one-to-many relationships tied together through a third table. For example, the GardenCo database contains Products, Orders, and Order Details tables. The Products table has one record for each product sold by The Garden Company, and each product has a unique ProductID. The Orders table has one record for each order placed with The Garden Company, and each record in it has a unique OrderID. However, the Orders table doesn't specify which products were included in each order; that information is in the Order Details table, which is the table in the middle that ties the other two tables together. Products and Orders each have a one-to-many relationship with Order Details. Products and Orders therefore have a many-to-many relationship with each other. In plain language, this means that every product can appear in many orders, and every order can include many products.

5 Select the **Enforce Referential Integrity** check box, select the other two check boxes, and then click **Create**.

Tip

Access uses a system of rules called **referential integrity** to ensure that relationships between records in related tables are valid, and that you don't accidentally delete or change related data. When the **Cascade Update Related Fields** check box is selected, changing a primary key value in the primary table automatically updates the matching value in all related records. When the **Cascade Delete Related Records** check box is selected, deleting a record in the primary table deletes any related records in the related table.

Access draws a line representing the one-to-many relationship between the **CategoryID** fields in each of the tables, as shown here:

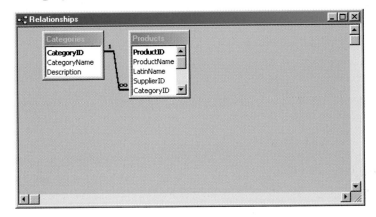

Tip

You can edit or delete a relationship by right-clicking the line and clicking the appropriate command on the shortcut menu.

6 Close the Relationships window, clicking **Yes** when prompted to save the window's layout.

7 Open the **Categories** form in Design view.

Toolbox

8 Enlarge the Form window, and drag the **Form Footer** section selector down about 1 inch to give yourself some room to work.

9 If the toolbox isn't displayed, click the **Toolbox** button.

Control Wizards

10 Make sure the **Control Wizards** button in the toolbox is active (has a border around it).

11 Click the **Subform/Subreport** button, and drag a rectangle in the lower portion of the **Details** section.

A white object appears on the form, and the first page of the **Subform Wizard** opens.

Subform/ Subreport

12 Leave **Use existing Tables and Queries** selected, and click **Next**.

13 In the **Tables/Queries** list, click **Table: Products**.

14 Add the **ProductName**, **CategoryID**, **QuantityPerUnit**, **UnitPrice**, and **UnitsInStock** fields to the **Selected Fields** list by clicking each one and then clicking the **>** button. Then click **Next** to display the third page of the wizard:

SubForm Wizard
Would you like to define which fields link your main form to this subform yourself, or choose from the list below?
⊙ Choose from a list.   ○ Define my own.
Show Products for each record in Categories using CategoryID
None
Cancel   < Back   Next >   Finish

Because the Category ID field in the subform is related to the Category ID field in the main form, the wizard selects **Show Products for each record in Categories using CategoryID** as the **Choose from a list** option.

Tip

If the wizard can't figure out which fields are related, it selects the **Define my own** option and displays list boxes in which you can specify the fields to be related.

15 Click **Next** to accept the default selection, and then click **Finish** to accept the default name for the subform and complete the process.

Access displays the Categories form in Design view, with an embedded Products subform. The size and location of the subform is determined by the original rectangle you dragged on the form.

16 Adjust the size and location of the objects on your form so that it resembles this one:

17 Notice the layout of the subform, and then click **View** to switch to Form view, where the form looks like the one shown on the next page.

The format of the subform has totally changed. In Design view, it looks like a simple form, but in Form view, it looks like a datasheet.

18   Switch back to Design view, make any necessary size adjustments, and if necessary, open the **Properties** dialog box.

19   Click the **Form** selector in the upper left corner of the subform twice.

The first click selects the Products subform control, and the second click selects the form. A small black square appears on the selector.

20   On the **Format** tab of the **Properties** dialog box, change both **Record Selectors** and **Navigation Buttons** to **No**.

While on this tab, notice the **Default View** property, which is set to **Datasheet**. You might want to return to this property and try the other options after finishing this exercise.

21   Switch back to Form view, and drag the dividers between column headers until you can see all the fields. Here are the results:

Category ID			1
Name	Bulbs		
Description	Spring, Summer and Fall, Forced,		

Products subform

	Product Name	Category	Quantity Per	Unit Price	Units In Stock
▶	Magic Lily	Bulbs	One dozen	$40.00	40
	Autumn crocus	Bulbs	One dozen	$18.75	37
	Anemone	Bulbs	One dozen	$28.00	26
	Lily-of-the-Field	Bulbs	One dozen	$38.00	34
	Siberian Iris	Bulbs	6 per pkg.	$12.95	30
	Daffodil	Bulbs	6 per pkg.	$12.95	24
	Peony	Bulbs	6 per pkg.	$19.95	20
	Lilies	Bulbs	6 per pkg.	$10.50	18
	Begonias	Bulbs	6 per pkg.	$18.95	12
	Bulb planter	Bulbs	1 ea.	$6.95	6

Record: I◀ ◀ | 1 | ▶ ▶I ▶* of 18

Tip

You can quickly adjust the width of columns to fit their data by double-clicking the double arrow between column headings.

First Record

22 Click the navigation buttons to scroll through several categories. When you are through, click the **First Record** button to return to the first category (Bulbs).

As each category is displayed at the top of the form, the products in that category are listed in the datasheet in the subform.

23 Click the category name to the right of the first product.

The arrow at the right end of the box indicates that this is a combo box.

24 Click the arrow to display the list of categories, and change the category to **Cacti**.

Next Record

25 Click the **Next Record** navigation button to move to the next category (Cacti).

You can see that the first product is now included in this category.

26 Display the list of categories, and then restore the first product to the **Bulbs** category.

27 You don't want people to be able to change a product's category, so return to Design view. Then, in the subform, click the **CategoryID** text box control, and press ⌈Del⌉.

Important

You included the **CategoryID** field when the wizard created this subform because it is the field that relates the Categories and Products tables. The underlying Products table uses a combo box to display the name of the category instead of its ID number, so that combo box also appears on the subform.

28 Save the form, switch back to Form view, and then adjust the width of the subform columns and the size of the Form window until your form looks like this one:

29 Close the **Categories** form, saving your changes to both the form and the subform.

30 Close the database.

31 If you are not continuing on to the next chapter, quit Access.

Creating a Form and Subform with a Wizard

If you know, when you create a form, that you are going to add a subform, you can do the whole job with the **Form Wizard**, like this:

1   On the **Objects** bar, click **Forms**, and then click the **New** button on the database window's toolbar.

2   Click **Form Wizard**, select the form's base table from the list at the bottom of the page, and then click **OK**.

3   Verify that the table you selected is shown in the **Table/Queries** list, and then click the **>>** button to include all the fields in the new form.

4   Drop down the **Tables/Queries** list, and select the subform's base table.

5   Double-click the desired fields to add them to the list of selected fields, and then click **Next**.

6   Accept the default options, and click **Next**.

7   Accept the default **Datasheet** option, and click **Next**.

8   Click **Finish** to create the form and subform.

You can then clean up the form to suit your needs, just as you did in the previous exercise.

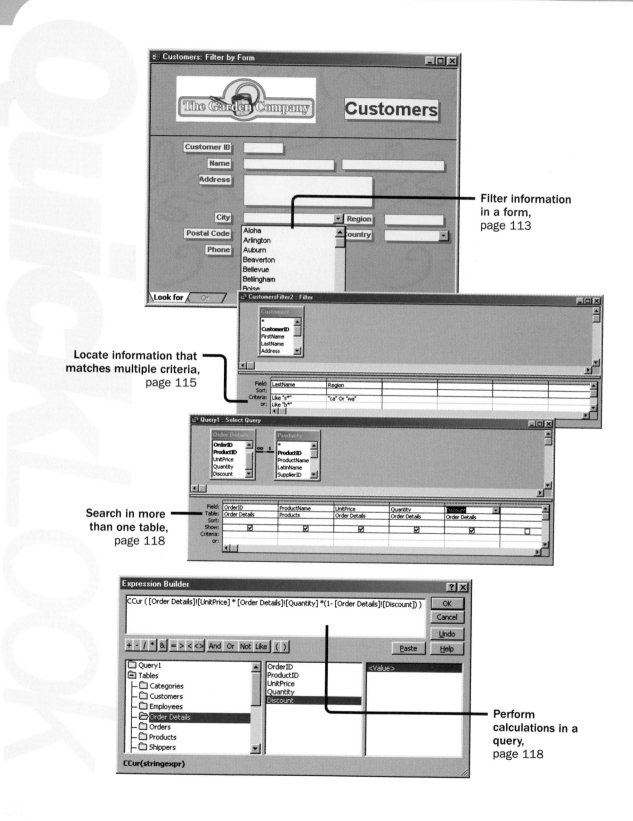

Filter information in a form, page 113

Locate information that matches multiple criteria, page 115

Search in more than one table, page 118

Perform calculations in a query, page 118

Chapter 5
Locating Specific Information

After completing this chapter, you will be able to:

✔ Sort information on one or more fields.

✔ Filter information in various ways.

✔ Create queries that find information in one or more tables.

✔ Create a query to perform calculations.

A database is a repository for information. It may hold a few records in one table or thousands of records in many related tables. No matter how much information is stored in a database, it is useful only if you can locate the information you need when you need it. In a small database you can find information simply by scrolling through a table until you spot what you are looking for. But as a database grows in size and complexity, locating specific information becomes more difficult.

Microsoft Access provides a variety of tools you can use to organize the display of information in a database and to locate specific items of information. Using these tools, you can focus on just part of the information by quickly sorting a table based on any field (or combination of fields), or you can filter the table so that information containing some combination of characters is displayed (or excluded from the display). With a little more effort, you can create queries to display specific fields from specific records from one or more tables. You can even save these queries so that you can use them over and over again.

A query can do more than simply return a list of records from a table. You can use functions in a query that perform calculations on the information in the table to produce the sum, average, count, and other mathematical values.

In this chapter, you will learn how to pinpoint precisely the information you need in a database using sorting and filtering tools, and queries. You will be working with the GardenCo database files that are stored in the following subfolders of the *SBS\Access\Queries* folder: *Sort, FilterDS, FilterForm, AdvFilter, QueryDS, QueryWiz,* and *Aggregate*.

Sorting Information

Ac2002-5-3

Approved Courseware

Information stored in a table can be sorted in either ascending or descending order, based on the values in one or more fields in the table. You could, for example, sort a customer table alphabetically based first on the last name of each customer and then on the first name. Such a sort would result in this type of list, which resembles those found in telephone books:

Last	First
Smith	Denise
Smith	James
Smith	Jeff
Thompson	Ann
Thompson	Steve

Occasionally you might need to sort a table to group all entries of one type together. For example, to qualify for a discount on postage, The Garden Company might want to sort customer records on the postal code field to group the codes before printing mailing labels.

GardenCo

In this exercise, you will learn several ways to sort the information in a datasheet or a form. The working folder for this exercise is *SBS\Access\Queries\Sort*. Follow these steps:

1 Open the **GardenCo** database located in the working folder.

2 Open the **Customers** table in Datasheet view.

Sort Ascending

3 To sort by Region, click anywhere in the **Region** column, and then click the **Sort Ascending** button.

Tip

You can also use the **Sort Ascending** or **Sort Descending** commands on the **Records** menu; or you can right-click the column in the datasheet and click either command on the shortcut menu.

The records are rearranged in order of region.

Sort Descending

4 To reverse the sort order, while still in the **Region** column, click the **Sort Descending** button.

The records for Washington State (WA) are now at the top of your list. In both sorts, the region was sorted alphabetically, but the City field was left in a seemingly random order, when what you really want to see is the records arranged by city within each region.

How Access Sorts

The concept of sorting seems pretty intuitive, but sometimes your computer's approach to such a concept is not so intuitive. Sorting numbers is a case in point. In Access, numbers can be treated as text or as numerals. Because of the spaces, hyphens, and punctuation typically used in street addresses, postal codes, and telephone numbers, the numbers in these fields are usually treated as text, and sorting them follows the logic applied to sorting all text. Numbers in a price or quantity field, on the other hand, are typically treated as numerals. When Access sorts text, it sorts first on the first character in the selected field in every record, then on the next character, then on the next, and so on—until it runs out of characters. When Access sorts numbers, it treats the contents of each field as a single value, and sorts the records based on that value. This tactic can result in seemingly strange sort orders. For example, sorting the list in the first column of the following table as text produces the list in the second column. Sorting the same list as numerals produces the list in the third column.

Original	Sort as Text	Sort as Number
1	1	1
1234	11	2
23	12	3
3	1234	4
11	2	5
22	22	11
12	23	12
4	3	22
2	4	23
5	5	1234

If a field with the Text data type contains numbers, you can sort the field numerically by padding the numbers with leading zeros so that all entries are the same length. For example, 001, 011, and 101 are sorted correctly even if the numbers are defined as text.

Tip

Access can sort on more than one field, but it sorts consecutively from left to right. So the fields you want to sort must be adjacent, and they must be arranged in the order in which you want to sort them.

5   To move the **Region** field to the left of the **City** field, click its header to select the column, and then drag the column to the left until a dark line appears between **Address** and **City**.

6   Because **Region** is already selected, hold down the ⌈shift⌋ key and click the **City** header to extend the selection so that both the **Region** and **City** columns are selected.

7   Click the **Sort Ascending** button to arrange the records with the regions in ascending order and the city names also in ascending order within each region (or in this case, each state).

Tip

You can sort records while viewing them in a form. Simply click the box of the field on which you want to base the sort, and then click one of the **Sort** buttons. However, you can't sort on multiple fields in Form view.

8   The order of the columns in the Customers table doesn't really matter, but go ahead and move the **Region** column back to where it was.

9   Save and close the **Customers** table.

10 Close the database.

Filtering Information in a Table

Ac2002-5-4

Approved Courseware

Sorting the information in a table organizes it in a logical manner, but you still have the entire table to deal with. If your goal is to locate all records containing information in one or more fields that match a particular pattern, one of the available **Filter** commands will satisfy your needs. For example, you could quickly create a filter to locate every customer of The Garden Company who lives in Seattle. Or you could find everyone who placed an order on January 13. Or you could locate all customers who live outside of the United States.

You can apply simple filters while viewing information in a table or a form. These filters are applied to the contents of a selected field, but you can apply another filter to the results of the first one to further refine your search.

Tip

The **Filter** commands you will use in this exercise are available by pointing to **Filter** on the **Records** menu; by clicking buttons on the toolbar; and on the shortcut menu. However, not all **Filter** commands are available in each of these places.

GardenCo

In this exercise, you will practice several methods of filtering information in a table. The working folder for this exercise is *SBS\Access\Queries\FilterDS*. Follow these steps:

1 Open the **GardenCo** database located in the working folder.

2 Open the **Customers** table in Datasheet view.

Filter By
Selection

3 Click any instance of **Sidney** in the **City** field, and then click the **Filter By Selection** button.

   The number of customers displayed in the table changes from 110 to 2 because only two customers live in Sidney.

Important

When you filter a table, the records that don't match the filter aren't removed from the table; they are simply not displayed.

Remove Filter

4 Click the **Remove Filter** button to redisplay the rest of the customers.

5 What if you want a list of all customers who live anywhere that has a postal code starting with *V3F*? Find an example of this type of postal code in the table, select the characters **V3F**, and then click the **Filter By Selection** button again.

   Only the two records with postal codes starting with *V3F* are now visible.

6 Click **Remove Filter**.

7 What if this table is enormous and you aren't sure if it contains even one *V3F*? Right-click any postal code, click **Filter For** on the shortcut menu, type **V3F*** in the cell, and press Enter to see the same results.

   The asterisk (*) is a wildcard that tells Access to search for any entry in the postal code field that starts with *V3F*.

8 To find out how many customers live outside the United States, remove the current filter, right-click the **Country** field in any USA record, and click **Filter Excluding Selection** on the shortcut menu.

   You see all customers from other countries (in this case, only Canada).

Wildcards

When you don't know or aren't sure of a character or set of characters, you can use **wildcard characters** as placeholders for those unknown characters in your search criteria. The most common wildcards are:

Character	Description	Example
*	Match any number of characters.	*Lname = Co** returns Colman and Conroy
?	Match any single alphabetic character.	*Fname = eri?* returns Eric and Erik
#	Match any single numeric character.	*ID = 1##* returns any ID from 100 through 199

9 To experiment with one more filtering technique, remove the filter, save and close the **Customers** table, and open the **Orders** table in Datasheet view.

10 To find all orders taken by Michael Emanuel on January 23, right-click **Emanuel, Michael** in the **Employee** field, and click **Filter By Selection** on the shortcut menu.

11 Right-click **1/23/01** (or the equivalent date) in the **OrderDate** field, and again click **Filter By Selection** on the shortcut menu.

You now have a list of Michael's orders on the 23rd. You could continue to refine this list by filtering on another field, or you could sort the results by clicking in a field and then clicking one of the **Sort** buttons.

Tip

After you have located just the information you want and have organized it appropriately, you can display the results in a form or report. Simply click the **New Object** button on the toolbar, and follow the directions.

12 Remove the filters by clicking the **Remove Filter** button.

13 Save and close the **Orders** table.

14 Close the database.

Tip

You can use the **Filter** commands to filter the information in a table when you are viewing it in a form. The **Filter For** command is often useful with forms because you don't have to be able to see the desired selection.

Filtering By Form

Ac2002-5-4

Approved Courseware

The **Filter By Form** command provides a quick and easy way to filter a table based on the information in several fields. If you open a table and then click the **Filter By Form** button, what you see looks like a simple datasheet. However, each of the blank cells is a combo box with a scrollable drop-down list of all the entries in that field, like this:

You can make a selection from the list and click the **ApplyFilter** button to display only the records containing your selection.

Using **Filter By Form** on a table that has only a few fields, such as this one, is easy. But using it on a table that has a few dozen fields gets a bit cumbersome. Then it's easier to use **Filter By Form** in the form version of the table. If you open a form and then click **Filter By Form**, you see an empty form. Clicking in any box and then clicking its down arrow displays a list of all the entries in the field, as shown here:

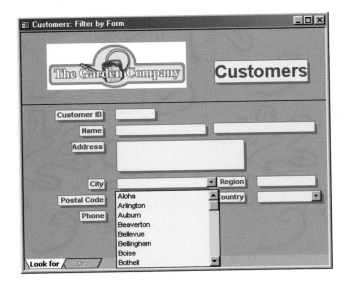

If you make a selection and click the **ApplyFilter** button, clicking the **Next Record** navigation button displays the first record that meets your selection criteria, then the next, and so on.

Tip

Filter By Form offers the same features and techniques whether you are using it in a form or a table. Because defining the filter is sometimes easier in a form and viewing the results is sometimes easier in a table, you might consider using **AutoForm** to quickly create a form for a table. You can then use the form with **Filter By Form** rather than the table, and then switch to Datasheet view to look at the results.

GardenCo

In this exercise, you will try to track down a customer whose last name you have forgotten. You're pretty sure the name starts with *S* and the customer is from California or Washington, so you're going to use **Filter By Form** to try and locate the customer's record. The working folder for this exercise is *SBS\Access\Queries\FilterForm*. Follow these steps:

1 Open the **GardenCo** database located in the working folder.

2 Click **Forms** on the **Objects** bar, and double-click **Customers** to open the Customers form in Form view.

Filter By Form

3 Click the **Filter By Form** button on the toolbar.

The Customers form, which displays the information from one record, is replaced by its Filter By Form version, which has a blank box for each field and the **Look for** and **Or** tabs at the bottom.

4 Click the second **Name** box, type **s***, and press ⏎ to tell Access to display all last names starting with S.

Access converts your entry to the proper format, or **syntax**, for this type of expression: *Like "s*"*.

5 Click the **Region** box, and select **CA** from the drop-down list.

Apply Filter

6 Click the **Apply Filter** button to see only the customers living in California whose last names begin with S.

Access replaces the filter window with the regular Customers form, and the navigation bar at the bottom of the form indicates that three filtered records are available.

7 Click the **Filter By Form** button to switch back to the filter.

Your filter criteria are still displayed. When you enter filter criteria using any method, they are saved as a form property and are available until replaced by other criteria.

8   To add the customers from another state, click the **Or** tab.

This tab has the same blank cells as the **Look for** tab. You can switch back and forth between the two tabs to confirm that your criteria haven't been cleared.

Tip

When you display the **Or** tab, a second **Or** tab appears so that you can include a third state if you want.

9   Type **s*** in the **LastName** box, type or select **WA** in the **Region** box, and then click the **Apply Filter** button.

You can scroll through the filtered Customers form to view the six matched records.

10   Close the **Customers** form, and then close the database.

Locating Information That Matches Multiple Criteria

Ac2002-5-3
Ac2002-5-4
Ac2002e-3-2

Approved Courseware

Filter By Selection, **Filter For <input>**, and **Filter By Form** are quick and easy ways to hone in on the information you need, as long as your filter criteria are fairly simple. But suppose The Garden Company needs to locate all the orders shipped to midwest states between specific dates by either of two shippers. When you need to search a single table for records that meet multiple criteria or that require complex expressions as criteria, you can use the **Advanced Filter/Sort** command.

You work with the **Advanced Filter/Sort** command in the design grid shown here:

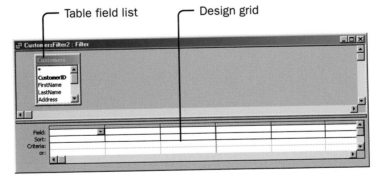

You can use this **design grid** to work with only one table.

Tip

If you create a simple query in the filter window that you think you might like to use again, you can save it as a query. Either click **Save As Query** on the **File** menu; click the **Save As Query** button on the toolbar; or right-click in the filter window, and then click **Save As Query** on the shortcut menu.

GardenCo

In this exercise, you will create a filter to locate customers in two states by using the **Advanced Filter/Sort** command. After locating the customers, you will experiment a bit with the design grid to get a better understanding of its filtering capabilities. The working folder for this exercise is *SBS\Access\Queries\AdvFilter*. Follow these steps:

1 Open the **GardenCo** database located in the working folder.

2 Click **Tables** on the **Objects** bar, and double-click **Customers** to open the Customers table in Datasheet view.

3 On the **Records** menu, point to **Filter**, and then click **Advanced Filter/Sort**.

Access opens the filter window with the **Customers** field list in the top area.

4 If the design grid is not blank, click **Clear Grid** on the **Edit** menu.

5 Double-click **LastName** to copy it to the **Field** cell in the first column of the design grid.

6 Click in the **Criteria** cell under **LastName**, type **s***, and press [Enter].

Access changes the criterion to "*Like "s*"*".

7 Scroll to the bottom of the **Customers** field list, and double-click **Region** to copy it to the next available column of the design grid.

8 Click in the **Criteria** cell under **Region**, type **ca or wa**, and press [Enter].

The design grid looks like this:

CustomersFilter2 : Filter	
Customers	
City	
Region	
PostalCode	
Country	
PhoneNumber	
Field:	LastName	Region
Sort:		
Criteria:	Like "s*"	"ca" Or "wa"
or:		

Your entry has changed to "*ca" Or "wa*". The filter will now match customers with a last name beginning with s who live in California or Washington.

9 On the **Filter** menu, click **Apply Filter/Sort** to view these records that match the criteria:

Tip

You can keep an eye on both the filter window and the table window if you reduce both in size.

10 On the **Records** menu, click **Filter** and then **Advanced Filter/Sort** to return to the filter window.

11 Click in the **or** cell in the **LastName** column, type **b***, and press [Enter]. The design grid now looks like this:

12 On the **Filter** menu, click **Apply Filter/Sort**.

The result includes records for all customers with a last name that begins with *s* or *b*, but some of the *b* names live in Montana and Oregon. If you look again at the design grid, you can see that the filter is formed by combining the fields in the **Criteria** row with the *And* operator, combining the fields in the **or** row with the *And* operator, and then using the *Or* operator to combine the two rows. So the filter is searching for customers with names beginning with *s* who live in California or Washington, or customers with names beginning with *b*, regardless of where they live.

13 Return to the filter window, type **ca or wa** in the **or** cell under **Region**, and press [Enter].

14 Apply the filter again to see only customers from California and Washington.

15 Close the **Customers** table, without saving your changes, and then close the database.

Expressions

The word **expressions**, as used in Access, is synonymous with *formulas*. An expression is a combination of **operators**, **constants**, **functions**, and **control properties** that evaluates to a single value. Access builds formulas using the format *a=b+c*, where *a* is the result and *=b+c* is the expression. An expression can be used to assign properties to tables or forms, to determine values in fields or reports, as part of queries, and in many other places in Access.

The expressions you use in Access combine multiple **criteria** to define a set of conditions that a record must meet before Access will select it as the result of a filter or query. Multiple criteria are combined using logical, comparison, and arithmetic operators. Different types of expressions use different operators.

The most common **logical operators** are *And*, *Or*, and *Not*. When criteria are combined with the *And* operator, a record is selected only if it meets them all. When criteria are combined with the *Or* operator, a record is selected if it meets any one of them. The *Not* operator selects all records that don't match its criterion.

Common **comparison operators** include < (less than), > (greater than), and = (equal). These basic operators can be combined to form <= (less than or equal to), >= (greater than or equal to), and <> (not equal to). The *Like* operator is sometimes grouped with the comparison operators and is used to test whether or not text matches a pattern.

The common **arithmetic operators** are + (add), - (subtract), * (multiply), and / (divide), which are used with numerals. A related operator, & (a text form of +) is used to concatenate—or put together—two text strings.

Creating a Query in Design View

Ac2002-3-2
Ac2002-5-2

Approved Courseware

Sorting and filtering information is quick, easy, and useful. When you want to work with more than one table, however, you need to move beyond filters and into the realm of queries. The most common type of query selects records that meet specific conditions, but there are several other types, as follows:

- A **select query** retrieves data from one or more tables and displays the results in a datasheet. You can also use a select query to group records and calculate sums, counts, averages, and other types of totals. You can work with the results of a select query in Datasheet view to update records in one or more related tables at the same time.

- A **parameter query** prompts you for information to be used in the query—for example, a range of dates. This type of query is particularly useful if the query is the basis for a report that is run periodically.

- A **crosstab query** calculates and restructures data for easier analysis. It can calculate a sum, average, count, or other type of total for data that is grouped by two types of information—one down the left side of the datasheet and one across the top. The cell at the junction of each row and column displays the results of the query's calculation.

- An **action query** updates or makes changes to multiple records in one operation. It is essentially a select query that performs an action on the results of the selection process. Four types of actions are available: **delete queries**, which delete records from one or more tables; **update queries**, which make changes to records in one or more tables; **append queries**, which add records from one or more tables to the end of one or more other tables; and **make-table queries**, which create a new table from all or part of the data in one or more tables.

Tip

Access also includes SQL queries, but you won't be working with this type of query in this book.

Filters and Sorts vs. Queries

The major differences between using filtering or sorting and using a query are:

- The **Filter** and **Sort** commands are usually faster to implement than queries.

- The **Filter** and **Sort** commands are not saved, or are saved only temporarily. A query can be saved permanently and run again at any time.

- The **Filter** and **Sort** commands are applied only to the table or form that is currently open. A query can be based on multiple tables and other queries, which don't have to be open.

You can create a query by hand or by using a wizard. Regardless of how you create the query, what you create is a statement that describes the conditions that must be met for records to be matched in one or more tables. When you run the query, the matching records appear in a datasheet in Datasheet view.

GardenCo

In this exercise, you will create an order entry form that salespeople can fill in as they take orders over the phone. The form will be based on a select query that combines information from the Order Details table and the Products table. The query will create a datasheet listing all products ordered with the unit price, quantity ordered, discount, and extended price. Because the extended price isn't stored in the database, you will calculate this amount directly in the query. The working folder for this exercise is *SBS\Access\Queries\QueryDes*. Follow the steps on the next page.

119

1 Open the **GardenCo** database located in the working folder.

2 On the **Objects** bar, click **Queries**.

3 Double-click **Create query in Design view**.

Access opens the query window in Design view and then opens the **Show Table** dialog box, like this:

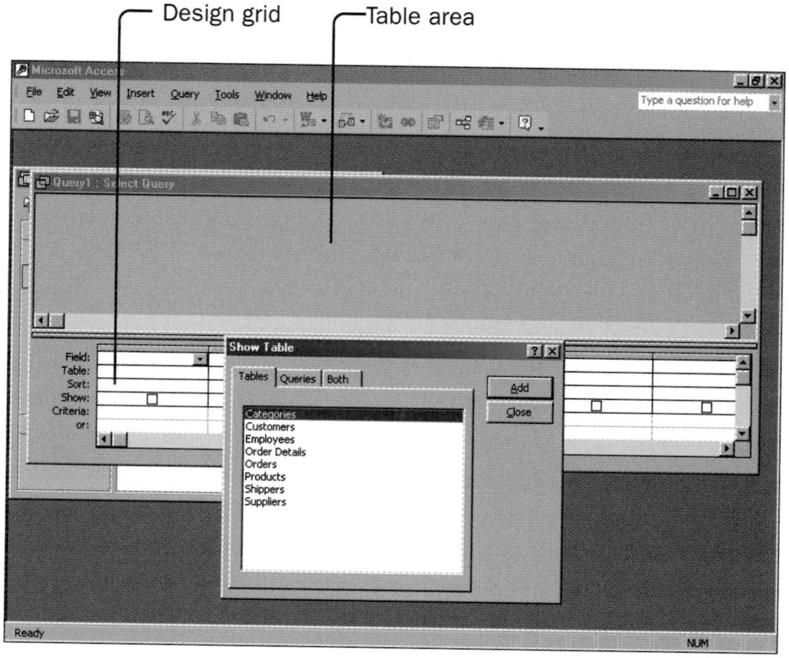

You use the **Show Table** dialog box to specify which tables and saved queries to include in the current query.

4 With the **Tables** tab active, double-click **Order Details** and **Products** to add both tables to the query window. Then close the dialog box.

Each table you added is represented in the top portion of the window by a small field list window with the name of the table—in this case, Order Details and Products—in its title bar, as shown here:

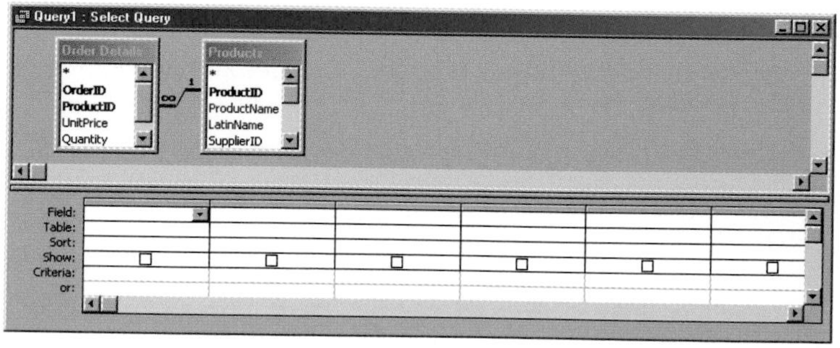

At the top of each list is an asterisk, which represents all the fields in the list. Primary key fields in each list are bold. The line from **ProductID** in the Order Details table to **ProductID** in the Products table indicates that these two fields are related.

Tip

To add more tables to a query, reopen the **Show Tables** dialog box by right-clicking the top portion of the query window and clicking **Show Table** on the shortcut menu; or by clicking the **Show Tables** button on the toolbar.

The lower area of the query window is taken up by a design grid where you will build the query's criteria.

5 To include fields in the query, you drag them from the lists at the top of the window to consecutive columns in the design grid. Drag the following fields from the two lists:

From Table	Field
Order Details	OrderID
Products	ProductName
Order Details	UnitPrice
Order Details	Quantity
Order Details	Discount

Tip

You can quickly copy a field to the next open column in the design grid by double-clicking the field. To copy all fields to the grid, double-click the title bar above the field list to select the entire list, and then drag the selection over the grid. When you release the mouse button, Access adds the fields to the columns in order. You can drag the asterisk to a column in the grid to include all the fields in the query, but you also have to drag individual fields to the grid if you want to sort on those fields or add conditions to them.

The query window now looks like the one shown on the next page.

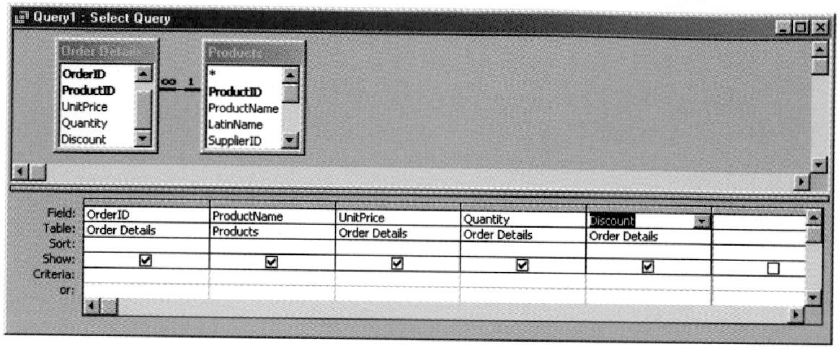

Run

6 Click the **Run** button to run the query and display the results in Datasheet view, like this:

OrderID	Product Name	UnitPrice	Quantity	Discount
11091	Autumn crocus	$18.75	4	0
11079	Compost Bin	$58.00	1	0
11083	Compost Bin	$58.00	1	0
11138	Compost Bin	$58.00	1	0
11152	Compost Bin	$58.00	1	0
11085	Cactus Sand Potting Mix	$4.50	2	0
11093	Cactus Sand Potting Mix	$4.50	2	0
11121	Cactus Sand Potting Mix	$4.50	1	0
11132	Cactus Sand Potting Mix	$4.50	1	0
11148	Cactus Sand Potting Mix	$4.50	1	0
11114	Weeping Forsythia	$18.00	3	0
11147	Weeping Forsythia	$18.00	1	0
11082	Bat Box	$14.75	3	0

Record: 1 of 215

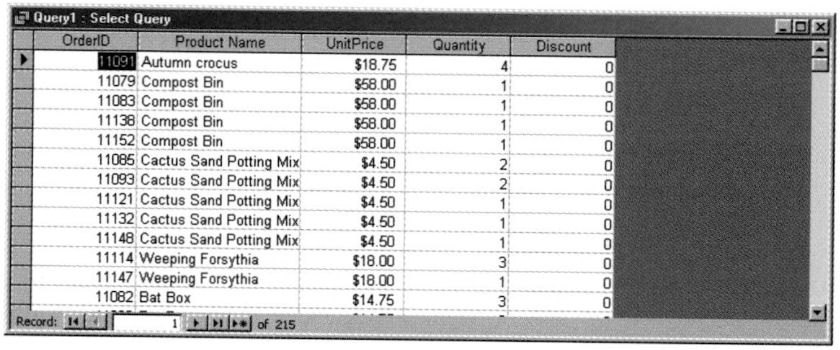

The results show that the query is working so far. There are two things left to do: sort the results on the **OrderID** field and add a field for calculating the extended price, which is the unit price times the quantity sold minus any discount.

View

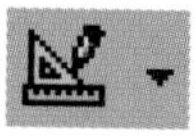

7 Click the **View** button to return to Design view.

The third row in the design grid is labeled *Sort*. If you click in the **Sort** cell in any column, you can specify whether to sort in ascending order, descending order, or not at all.

8 Click in the **Sort** cell in the **OrderID** column, click the down arrow, and click **Ascending**.

Neither of the tables includes an extended price field. There is no point in entering this information in a table, because you will use the Expression Builder to insert an expression in the design grid that computes this price from existing information.

9 Right-click the **Field** row of the first blank column in the design grid (the sixth column), and click **Build** on the shortcut menu.

The **Expression Builder** dialog box opens, as shown here:

Operator buttons ─────┐   ┌───── Expression box

Elements area

Here is the expression you will build:

`<CCur([Order Details].[UnitPrice]*[Quantity]*(1-[Discount])/100)*100>`

The only part of this expression that you probably can't figure out is the CCur function, which converts the results of the math inside its parentheses to currency format.

10 Double-click the **Functions** folder in the first column of the elements area, and then click **Built-In Functions**.

The categories of built-in functions are displayed in the second column.

11 Click **Conversion** in the second column to limit the functions in the third column to those in that category. Then double-click **Ccur** in the third column.

The Expression Builder now looks like the one shown on the next page.

Expression Builder

When an expression is a valid filter or query option, you can usually either type the expression or use the Expression Builder to create it. You open the Expression Builder by either clicking **Build** on a shortcut menu or clicking the **...** button (sometimes referred to as the **Build** button) at the right end of a box that can accept an expression.

The Expression Builder isn't a wizard; it doesn't lead you through the process of building an expression. But it does provide a hierarchical list of most of the elements that you can include in an expression. After looking at the list, you can either type your expression in the expression box, or you can select functions, operators, and other elements to copy them to the expression box, and then click **OK** to transfer them to the filter or query.

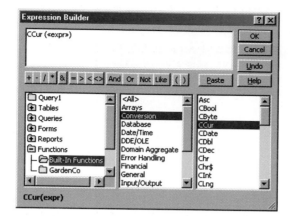

You've inserted the currency conversion function in the expression box. The *<<expr>>* inside the parentheses represents the other expressions that will eventually result in the number Access should convert to currency format.

12 Click **<<expr>>** to select it so that the next thing you enter will replace it.

13 The next element you want in the expression is the **UnitPrice** field from the Order Details table. Double-click **Tables**, click **Order Details**, and then double-click **UnitPrice**.

The Expression Builder now looks like this:

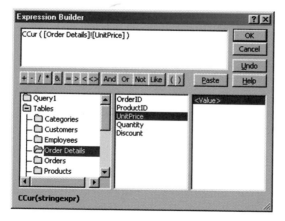

Your last action left the insertion point after UnitPrice, which is exactly where you want it.

14 Now you want to multiply the amount in the UnitPrice field by the amount in the Quantity field. Start by clicking the * (asterisk) button in the row of operator buttons below the expression box.

Access inserts the multiplication sign and another *<<expr>>* placeholder.

15 Click **<expr>>** to select it, and then insert the **Quantity** field by double-clicking it in the second column.

What you have entered so far multiplies the price by the number ordered, which results in the total cost for this item. However, The Garden Company offers discounts on certain items at different times of the year. The amount of the discount is entered by the sales clerk and stored in the Order Details table. In the table, the discount is expressed as the percentage to deduct—usually 10 to 20 percent. But it is easier to compute the percentage the customer will pay—usually 80 to 90 percent of the regular price—than it is to compute the discount and then subtract it from the total cost.

16 Type *(1-, then double-click **Discount**, and type).

The Expression Builder now looks like this (you will have to widen the window to see the whole expression):

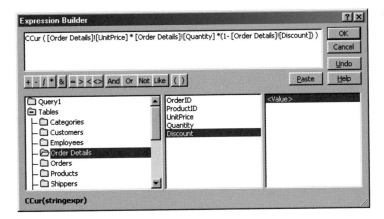

Remember that the discount is formatted in the datasheet as a percentage, but it is stored as a decimal number between 0 and 1. When you look at it you may see 10%, but what is actually stored in the database is 0.1. So if the discount is 10 percent, the result of *(1-Discount) is *.9. In other words, the formula multiplies the unit price by the quantity and then multiplies that result by 0.9.

17 Click **OK**.

Access closes the Expression Builder and copies the expression to the design grid.

18 Press Enter to move the insertion point out of the field, which completes the entry of the expression.

Tip

You can quickly make a column in the design grid as wide as its contents by double-clicking the line in the gray selection bar that separates the column from the column to its right.

19 Access has given the expression the name *Expr1*. This name isn't particularly meaningful, so rename it by double-clicking **Expr1** and then typing **ExtendedPrice**.

20 Click the **View** button to see these results in Datasheet view:

OrderID	Product Name	UnitPrice	Quantity	Discount	ExtendedPrice
11079	Crushed Rock	$62.50	1	0	$62.50
11079	Compost Bin	$58.00	1	0	$58.00
11080	Douglas Fir	$18.75	1	0	$18.75
11080	Fortune Rhododendron	$24.00	2	0.1	$43.20
11081	Golden Larch	$27.00	1	0	$27.00
11081	Lawn cart	$85.00	1	0.1	$76.50
11082	Bat Box	$14.75	3	0	$44.25
11083	Compost Bin	$58.00	1	0	$58.00
11083	GrowGood Potting Soil	$6.35	1	0	$6.35
11083	QwikRoot	$18.00	1	0	$18.00
11083	Grass Rake	$11.95	1	0	$11.95
11084	Gooseberries	$7.50	3	0	$22.50
11084	Ambrosia	$6.25	1	0	$6.25

Record: 1 of 215

The orders are now sorted on the **OrderID** field, and the extended price is calculated in the last field.

21 Scroll down to see a few records with discounts.

If you check the math, you will see that the query calculates the extended price correctly.

22 Close the query window, and when prompted to save the query, click **Yes**. Type **Order Details Extended** to name the query, and click **OK** to close it.

23 Close the database.

Creating a Query with a Wizard

Ac2002-3-1
Ac2002e-3-3

Approved Courseware

The process used to create a simple select query with the **Query Wizard** is almost identical to that for creating a form with the **Form Wizard.** With the **Query Wizard**, you can add one or more fields from existing tables or queries to the new query.

For Access to work effectively with multiple tables, it must understand the relationships between the fields in those tables. You have to create these relationships before using the **Query Wizard**, by clicking the **Relationships** button and then dragging a field in one table over the identical field in another table.

GardenCo

In this exercise, you will use the **Query Wizard** to create a new query that combines information from the Customers and Orders tables to provide information about each order. These tables are related through their common CustomerID fields. (This relationship has already been established in the GardenCo database files used in this chapter.) The working folder for this exercise is *SBS\Access\Queries\QueryWiz*. Follow these steps:

1   Open the **GardenCo** database located in the working folder.

2   On the **Objects** bar, click **Queries**, and then double-click **Create query by using wizard**.

The first page of the **Simple Query Wizard** opens.

Tip

You can also start the **Query Wizard** by clicking **Query** on the **Insert** menu or clicking the **New Object** button, and then double-clicking **Simple Query Wizard**.

3   Select **Table: Orders** from the **Tables/Queries** list.

4   Click the **>>** button to move all available fields to the **Selected Fields** list.

5   Select **Table: Customers** from the **Tables/Queries** list.

6   Double-click the **Address**, **City**, **Region**, **PostalCode**, and **Country** fields to move them to the **Selected Fields** list, and then click **Next**.

Tip

If the relationship between two tables hasn't already been established, you will be prompted to define it and then start the wizard again.

7   Click **Next** again to accept the default option of showing details in the results of the query.

8   Change the query title to **Orders Qry**, leave the **Open the query to view information** option selected, and then click **Finish**.

Access runs the query and displays the results in Datasheet view. You can scroll through the results and see that information is displayed for all the orders.

View

9   Click the **View** button to view the query in Design view.

Notice that the **Show** box is, by default, checked for each of the fields used in the query. If you want to use a field in a query—for example, to sort on, to set criteria for, or in a calculation—but don't want to see the field in the results datasheet, you can clear its **Show** check box.

10 Clear the **Show** check box for **OrderID**, **CustomerID**, and **EmployeeID**, and then click the **View** button to switch back to Datasheet view.

The three fields have been removed from the results datasheet.

11 Click the **View** button to return to Design view.

This query returns all record in the Orders table. To have this query match the records for a range of dates, you will convert it to a parameter query, which asks for the date range each time you run it.

12 In the **OrderDate** column, click in the **Criteria** cell, and type the following:

Between [Type the beginning date:] And [Type the ending date:]

Run

13 Click the **Run** button to run the query.

Access displays this dialog box:

Enter Parameter Value	☒
Type the beginning date:	
OK	Cancel

14 Type **1/1/01**, and press ⌷Enter⌷.

15 In the second **Enter Parameter Value** dialog box, type **1/31/01**, and press ⌷Enter⌷ again.

The datasheet is displayed again, this time listing only orders between the parameter dates.

16 Close the datasheet, clicking **Yes** to save the query.

17 Close the database.

Performing Calculations in a Query

AC2002e-3-5

Approved Courseware

You typically use a query to locate all the records that meet some criteria. But sometimes you are not as interested in the details of all the records as you are in summarizing them in some way. As an example, you might want to know how many orders have been placed this year or the total dollar value of all orders placed. The easiest way to get this information is to create a query that groups the necessary fields and does the math for you. To do this, you use **aggregate functions** in the query.

Access queries support the following aggregate functions:

Function	Calculates
Sum	Total of the values in a field
Avg	Average of the values in a field
Count	Number of values in a field, not counting Null (blank) values
Min	Lowest value in a field
Max	Highest value in a field
StDev	Standard deviation of the values in a field
Var	Variance of the values in a field

GardenCo

In this exercise, you will create a query that calculates the total number of products in The Garden Company's inventory, the average price of all the products, and the total value of the inventory. The working folder for this exercise is *SBS\Access \Queries\Aggregate*. Follow these steps:

1 Open the **GardenCo** database located in the working folder.

2 On the **Objects** bar, click **Queries**, and then double-click **Create query in Design view**.

Access first opens the query window in Design view and then displays the **Show Table** dialog box.

3 In the **Show Table** dialog box, double-click **Products**, and click **Close**.

Access adds the Products table to the query window and closes the **Show Table** dialog box.

4 In the list of fields in the Products table, double-click **ProductID** and then **UnitPrice**.

Access moves both fields to the design grid.

Totals

5 Click the **Totals** button on the toolbar.

A row named *Total* is added to the design grid, which should now look like this:

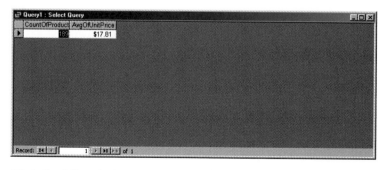

6 Click in the **Total** cell of the **ProductID** column, click the down arrow, and select **Count** from the drop-down list.

Access enters the word *Count* in the **Total** cell. When you run the query, this function will return a count of the number of records containing a value in the **ProductID** field.

7 In the **UnitPrice** column, set the **Total** cell to **Avg**.

When you run the query, this function will return the average of all the **Unit-Price** values.

Run

8 Click the **Run** button.

The result of the query is a single record containing the count and the average price, as shown here:

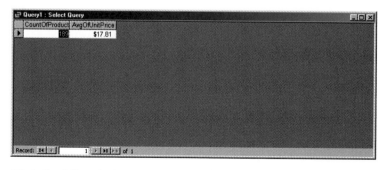

View

9 Click the **View** button to return to Design view.

10 In the **Field** cell of the third column, type **=UnitPrice*UnitsInStock** and press `Enter`.

The text you typed is changed to *Expr1: [UnitPrice]*[UnitsInStock]*. This expression will multiply the price of each product by the number of units in stock.

11 Set the **Total** cell of the third column to **Sum** to return the sum of all the values calculated by the expression.

12 Select **Expr1:**, and type **Value of Inventory:**.

13 Run the query again.

The results are shown here:

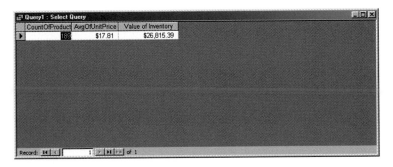

14 Close the query window, clicking **No** when prompted to save the query.

15 Close the database, and if you are not continuing on to the next chapter, quit Access.

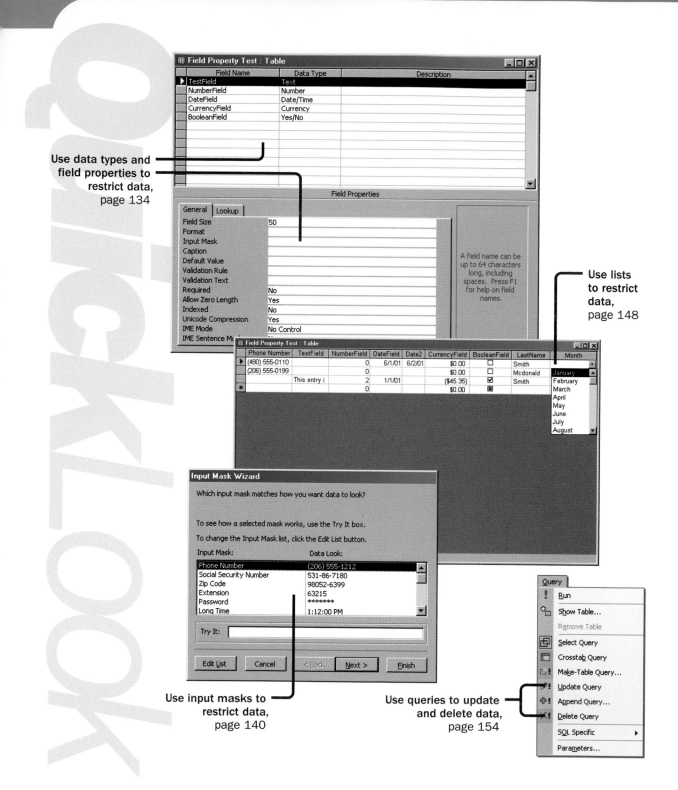

Use data types and field properties to restrict data, page 134

Use lists to restrict data, page 148

Use input masks to restrict data, page 140

Use queries to update and delete data, page 154

Chapter 6
Keeping Your Information Accurate

After completing this chapter, you will be able to:

✔ **Restrict the information entered in a database using the data type.**

✔ **Restrict the information entered in a database using various field properties.**

✔ **Update information in a table.**

✔ **Delete information from a table.**

Depending on how much information you have and how organized you are, you might compare a database to an old shoebox or a file cabinet, into which you toss items such as photographs, bills, receipts, and a variety of other paperwork for later retrieval. However, neither a shoebox nor a file cabinet restricts what you can place in it (other than how much you can place in it) or imposes any order on its content. It is up to you to decide what you store there and to organize it properly so that you can find it when you next need it. And neither a shoebox nor a file cabinet helps you with the task of updating your information when it changes or becomes obsolete.

When you create a database with Microsoft Access, you can set properties that restrict what can be entered in it, thereby keeping the database organized and useful. For example, The Garden Company wouldn't want its employees to enter text into fields that should contain numbers, such as price fields. Similarly, they wouldn't want to encourage employees to enter a long text description of something when a simple "yes" or "no" answer would work best. The field properties that control input are **Required**, **Allow Zero Length**, **Field Size**, **Input Mask**, and **Validation Rule**. The **Required** and **Allow Zero Length** properties are fairly obvious. If the **Required** property is set to **Yes**, the field can't be left blank. However, if **Allow Zero Length** is set to **Yes**, you can enter an empty **string** (two quotation marks with nothing in between), which looks like an empty field. The other properties are more complex, so you'll focus on them in the exercises in this chapter.

Tip

Each property has many options. For more information about how to use properties, search for *field property* in Access online Help.

To ensure the ongoing accuracy of a database, you can create and run action queries that quickly update information or delete selected records from a table. For example, The Garden Company might decide to increase the price of all products in one category by some percentage, or to remove one entire product line. This type of updating is easy to do with an action query. Not only does using a query save time, but it also avoids human input errors.

The exercises in this chapter demonstrate how to use the data type and some of the field properties to restrict the data that can be entered in a table or form. It is difficult to experiment with field properties in a table that is already filled with information, because changing a field's data type or properties can destroy or alter the data. For that reason, the first few exercises in this chapter use a new database that you will create just for the purpose of experimenting with data types and properties. Then you will resume working with sample GardenCo database files located in the following subfolders of the *SBS\Access\Accurate* folder: *DataType, FieldSize, InputMask, ValRules, Lookup, QueryUp,* and *QueryDel.*

Using the Data Type to Restrict Data

Ac2002-5-1
Ac2002e-1-1

Approved Courseware

The **Data Type** setting restricts entries to a specific type of data: text, numbers, dates, and so on. If, for example, the **data type** is set to **Number** and you attempt to enter text, Access refuses the entry and displays a warning.

In this exercise, you will create a brand new database, you will add fields of the most common data types, and then you'll experiment to see how the **Data Type** setting and **Field Size** property can be used to restrict the data entered into a table. The working folder for this exercise is *SBS\Access\Accurate\DataType.* Follow these steps:

1 In the **New File** task pane, click **Blank Database** in the **New** section to display the **File New Database** dialog box.

If the **New File** task pane is not displayed, click the **New** button on the toolbar.

2 Type **Field Test** in the **File name** box, browse to the working folder for this exercise, and then click **Create**.

Access opens the database window for the new database.

3   Double-click **Create table in Design view**.

A blank Table window opens in Design view so that you can define the fields that categorize the information in the table. You will define five fields, one for each of the **Text**, **Number**, **Date/Time**, **Currency**, and **Yes/No** data types.

4   Click in the first **Field Name** cell, type **TextField**, and press [Tab] to move to the **Data Type** cell.

5   The data type defaults to **Text**, which is the type you want. So press [Tab] twice to accept the default data type and move the insertion point to the next row.

6   Type **NumberField**, and press [Tab] to move to the **Data Type** cell.

7   Click the down arrow to expand the list of data types, click **Number**, and then press [Tab] twice.

8   Repeat steps 4 through 7 to add the following fields:

Field	Data Type
DateField	**Date/Time**
CurrencyField	**Currency**
BooleanField	**Yes/No**

Tip

The data type referred to as **Yes/No** in Access is more commonly called **Boolean** (in honor of George Boole, an early mathematician and logistician). This data type can hold either of two mutually exclusive values, often expressed as *yes/no*, *1/0*, *on/off*, or *true/false*.

Save

9   Click the **Save** button, type **Field Property Test** to name the table, and then click **OK**.

Access displays a dialog box recommending that you create a primary key.

10   You don't need a primary key for this exercise, so click **No**.

11   Click the row selector for **TextField** to select the first row.

Your table now looks like the one on the next page.

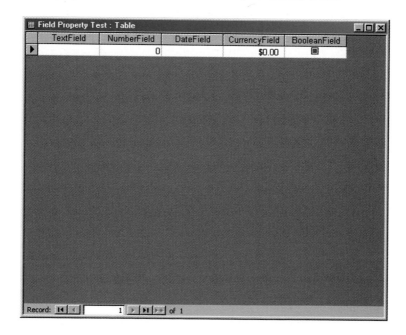

The properties for the selected field are displayed in the lower portion of the dialog box.

View

12 Click in each field and review its properties, and then click the **View** button to display the table in Datasheet view, as shown here:

13 The insertion point should be in the first field. Type **This entry is 32 charac-ters long**, and press [Tab] to move to the next field.

14 Type **Five hundred**, and press [Tab].

The data type for this field is **Number**. Access displays an alert box refusing your text entry.

15 Click **OK**, replace the text with the number **500**, and press [Tab].

16 Type a number or text (anything but a date) in the date field, and press [Tab]. When Access refuses it, click **OK**, type **Jan 1**, and press [Tab].

The date field accepts almost any entry that can be recognized as a date, and displays it in the default date format. Depending on the format on your computer, Jan 1 might be displayed as 1/1/2001 or 1/1/01.

Tip

If you enter a month and day but no year in a date field, Access assumes the date is in the current year. If you enter a month, day, and two-digit year from 00 through 29, Access assumes the year is 2000 through 2029. If you enter a two-digit year that is greater than 29, Access assumes you mean 1930 through 1999.

17 Type any text or a date in the currency field, and press [Tab]. When Access refuses the entry, click **OK**, type **–45.3456** in the field, and press [Tab].

Access stores the number you entered but displays ($45.35), the default for-mat for displaying negative currency numbers.

Tip

Access uses the regional settings in Microsoft Windows Control Panel to determine the display format for date, time, currency, and other numbers. If you intend to share database files with people in other countries, you might want to create custom for-mats to ensure that the correct currency symbol is always displayed with your values. Otherwise, the numbers won't change, but displaying them as dollars, pounds, marks, or lira will radically alter their value.

18 Try entering text or a number in the **Boolean** field. Then click anywhere in the field to toggle the check box between **Yes** (checked) and **No** (not checked), finishing with the field in the checked state.

This field won't accept anything you type; it only allows you to switch between two predefined values. Your datasheet now resembles the one shown on the next page.

⊞ Field Property Test : Table				_□×
TextField	NumberField	DateField	CurrencyField	BooleanField
✎ This entry is 32	500	1/1/01	($45.35)	☑
*	0		$0.00	▨

Record: ⏮ ◀ [1] ▶ ⏭ ▶* of 1

Tip

In Design view, you can use properties on the **Lookup** tab to display the Boolean field as a check box, text box, or combo box. You can also set the **Format** property on the **General** tab to use **True/False**, **Yes/No**, or **On/Off** as the displayed values in this field (though the stored values will always be -1 and 0).

19 Close the table, and then close the database.

Using the Field Size Property to Restrict Data

Ac2002e-1-1

Approved Courseware

You can set the **Field Size** property for the **Text**, **Number**, and **AutoNumber** data types. This property restricts the number of characters you can enter in a text field and the size of numbers that can be entered in a number or AutoNumber field. For text fields, the **Field Size** property can be set to any number from 0 to 255. AutoNumber fields are automatically set to **Long Integer**. Number fields can be set to any of the following values:

Setting	Description
Byte	Stores numbers from 0 to 255 (no fractions).
Integer	Stores numbers from –32,768 to 32,767 (no fractions).
Long Integer	(The default.) Stores numbers from –2,147,483,648 to 2,147,483,647 (no fractions).
Single	Stores numbers from –3.402823E38 to –1.401298E–45 for negative values and from 1.401298E–45 to 3.402823E38 for positive values.
Double	Stores numbers from –1.79769313486231E308 to – 4.94065645841247E–324 for negative values and from 1.79769313486231E308 to 4.94065645841247E–324 for positive values.
Decimal	Stores numbers from -10^28 -1 through 10^28 -1 (*.mdb*).

By setting the **Field Size** property to a value that allows the largest valid entry, you prevent the user from entering certain types of invalid information. If you try to type more characters in a text field than the number allowed by the **Field Size** setting, Access beeps and refuses to accept the entry. Likewise, a value that is below or above the limits of a number field is rejected when you try to move out of the field.

Field Test

In this exercise, you will change the **Field Size** property for several fields to see what impact this has on data already in the table and on new data you enter. The working folder for this exercise is *SBS\Access\Accurate\FieldSize*. Follow these steps:

1 Open the **Field Test** database located in the working folder.

2 Open the **Field Property Test** table in Design view.

3 Click in the **TextField** row, and in the **Field Properties** section, change the **Field Size** property to **12**.

4 Click in the **NumberField** row, click the **Field Size** property, click its down arrow, and then click **Byte** in the drop-down list.

You have just restricted the number of characters that can be entered in the text field to 12 and the values that can be entered in the number field to the range 0 to 255.

View

5 Click the **View** button to return to Datasheet view, clicking **Yes** when prompted to save the table.

The table contains data that doesn't fit these new property settings, so Access displays a warning, shown on the next page, that some data might be lost.

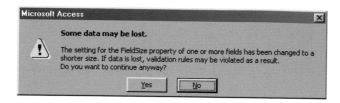

6 Click **Yes** to acknowledge the risk, and click **Yes** again to accept the deletion of the contents of one field.

Your datasheet now looks like this:

TextField now contains only 12 characters, rather than the 32 you entered. The other 20 characters have been permanently deleted. **NumberField** is empty. Because it is now limited to whole numbers from 0 through 255, the value of 500 that you entered has been deleted.

7 Type **2.5** as the **NumberField** entry, and press ⌷Enter⌷ to see what happens.

The number is rounded down to the nearest whole number.

8 Close the table, and then close the database.

Using an Input Mask to Restrict Data

Ac2002-2-2
Ac2002-2-4
Ac2002e-1-4

Approved Courseware

When you use **masks** in tables or forms, people entering information can see at a glance the format in which they should make entries and how long they should be. You can use the **InputMask** property to control how data is entered in text, number, date/time, and currency fields. This property has three sections, separated by semicolons, like the mask for a telephone number shown here:

!\(000") "000\-0000;1;#

The first section contains characters that are used as placeholders for the information to be typed, as well as characters such as parentheses and hyphens. Together, all these characters control the appearance of the entry. The following list explains the purpose of the most common input mask characters:

Character	Description
0	Required digit (0 through 9).
9	Optional digit or space.
#	Optional digit or space; blank positions are converted to spaces; plus and minus signs are allowed.
L	Required letter (A through Z).
?	Optional letter (A through Z).
A	Required letter or digit.
a	Optional letter or digit.
&	Required character (any kind) or a space.
C	Optional character (any kind) or a space.
<	All characters that follow are converted to lowercase.
>	All characters that follow are converted to uppercase.
!	Characters typed into the mask fill it from left to right. You can include the exclamation point anywhere in the input mask.
\	Character that follows is displayed as a literal character.
Password	Creates a password entry box. Any character typed in the box is stored as the character but is displayed as an asterisk (*).

Any characters not included on this list are displayed as literal characters. If you want to use one of the special characters in this list as a literal character, precede it with the \ character.

The second and third sections of the input mask are optional. Including a 1 or leaving nothing in the second section tells Access to store only the characters entered; including a 0 tells it to store both the characters entered and the mask characters. The character in the third section is displayed in a new record as the placeholder for the characters to be typed. This placeholder defaults to an underscore if the section is omitted.

The input mask !\(000") "000\-0000;1;# creates this display in a field in both a table and a form:

(###) ###-####

In this case, you are restricting the entry to ten digits—no more and no less. Access stores just the digits entered, not the parentheses, space, and dash (though those characters could be displayed in your table, form, or report if you set the correct format property).

Field Test

In this exercise, you will use the **Input Mask Wizard** to apply a predefined telephone input mask to a text field, forcing entered numbers into the (206) 555-0001 format. You will then create a custom mask to force the first letter of an entry to be uppercase (a capital letter). The working folder for this exercise is *SBS\Access\Accurate \InputMask*. Follow these steps:

1   Open the **Field Test** database located in the working folder.

2   Open the **Field Property Test** table in Design view.

3   Type **PhoneField** in the first blank **Field Name** cell, and leave the data type set to **Text**.

4   Click the row selector to select the row, and then drag the new field to the top of the field list so that it will appear at the left end of the table.

5   Save the table design, and with **PhoneField** still selected, click **Input Mask** in the **Field Properties** section.

6   Click the **...** button to the right of the cell to start the **Input Mask Wizard** and display the first page of the wizard, shown here:

> **Input Mask Wizard**
>
> Which input mask matches how you want data to look?
>
> To see how a selected mask works, use the Try It box.
>
> To change the Input Mask list, click the Edit List button.
>
> | Input Mask: | Data Look: |
> | --- | --- |
> | Phone Number | (206) 555-1212 |
> | Social Security Number | 531-86-7180 |
> | Zip Code | 98052-6399 |
> | Extension | 63215 |
> | Password | ******* |
> | Long Time | 1:12:00 PM |
>
> Try It: [   ]
>
> [Edit List] [Cancel] [< Back] [Next >] [Finish]

You can create an input mask by hand for text, number, date, or currency fields, or you can use this wizard to apply one of several standard masks for text and date fields.

7   With **Phone Number** selected in the **Input Mask** list, click **Next**.

The second page of the wizard displays the input mask and gives you the opportunity to change the placeholder character that will indicate what to type. The exclamation point causes Access to fill the mask from left to right with whatever is typed. The parentheses and hyphen are characters that Access will insert in the specified places. The 9s represent optional digits, and the 0s represent required digits, so you can enter a telephone number with or without an area code.

Tip

Because Access fills the mask from left to right, you would have to press the ➡ key to move the insertion point past the first three placeholders to enter a telephone number without an area code.

8   Change 999 to **000** to require an area code, and then change the place-holder character to **#**.

The dialog box now looks like this:

```
Input Mask Wizard

Do you want to change the input mask?

Input Mask Name:    User Defined
Input Mask:         !(000) 000-0000

What placeholder character do you want the field to display?
Placeholders are replaced as you enter data into the field.
Placeholder character:   #   ▼


Try It:   [                    ]

          Cancel    < Back    Next >    Finish
```

9   Click **Next**.

On the third page of the wizard, you specify whether you want to store the symbols with the data. If you store them, the data will always be displayed in tables, forms, and reports in this format. However, the symbols take up space, meaning that your database will be larger.

10   Leave the default selection—to store data without the symbols—and then click **Finish**.

Access closes the wizard and displays the edited mask as the **Input Mask** property, as shown on the next page.

11 Press [Enter] to accept the mask.

Access changes the format of the mask to !\(000") "000\-0000;;#. Notice the two semicolons that separate the mask into its three sections. Since you told Access to store data without the symbols, nothing is displayed in the second section of the mask.

12 Save your changes, and click the **View** button to return to Datasheet view.

13 Press the [↓] key to move to the new record, and type a series of at least ten digits and some letters to see how the mask works.

Any letters you type are ignored. The first ten digits are formatted as a telephone number. If you type more than ten digits, they are also ignored. If you type fewer than ten digits and press [Tab] or [Enter], Access warns you that your entry doesn't match the input mask.

View

Tip

An input mask can contain more than just the placeholders for the data to be entered. If, for example, you type **The number is** in front of the telephone number in the **Input Mask** property, the default entry for the field is *The number is (###) ###-####*. Then if you place the insertion point to the left of *The* and start typing numbers, the numbers replace the # placeholders, not the text. The **Field Size** setting is not applied to the characters in the mask, so if this setting is 15, the entry is not truncated even though the number of displayed characters (including spaces) is 28.

14 Return to Design view, and add a new field below **BooleanField**. Name it **LastName**. Leave the **Data Type** setting as the default **Text**.

15 Select the new field, click **Input Mask**, type **>L<?????????????????** (18 question marks), and press [Enter].

The > forces all following text to be uppercase. The *L* requires a letter. The <
forces all following text to be lowercase. Each *?* allows any letter or no letter,
and there is one fewer question mark than the maximum number of letters
you want to allow in the field (19, including the leading capital letter). The
Field Size setting must be greater than this maximum.

16 Save your changes, return to Datasheet view, type **smith** in the **LastName**
field of one of the records, and press ⎇. Try entering **SMITH**, and then
McDonald.

As you can see, this type of mask has its limitations. But it can be useful in
many situations.

17 Close the table, and then close the database.

Using Validation Rules to Restrict Data

A **validation rule** is an **expression** that can precisely define the information that
will be accepted in one or several fields in a record. You might use a validation rule
on a field containing the date an employee was hired to prevent a date in the future
from being entered. Or if you make deliveries to only certain local areas, you could
use a validation rule on the phone field or ZIP code field to refuse entries from
other areas.

You can type validation rules in by hand, or you can use the **Expression Builder** to
create them. At the field level, Access uses the rule to test an entry when you attempt
to leave the field. At the table level, Access can use the rule to test the content of several fields when you attempt to leave the record. If an entry doesn't satisfy the rule,
Access rejects the entry and displays a message explaining why.

Field Test

In this exercise, you will create and test several field validation rules and one table
validation rule. The working folder for this exercise is *SBS\Access\Accurate\ValRules*.
Follow these steps:

1 Open the **Field Test** database located in the working folder.

2 Open the **Field Property Test** table in Design view.

3 To add a validation rule to **PhoneField** that will prevent the entry of an area
code other than 206 or 425, start by selecting **PhoneField** and clicking in
the **Validation Rule** box.

A **...** button appears at the end of the **Validation Rule** box. You can click this
button to use the Expression Builder to create an expression, or you can
type an expression in the box.

4 Type the following in the **Validation Rule** box, and press ⏎:

Like "206*" Or Like "425*"

5 In the **Validation Text** box, type **Area code must be 206 or 425**.

You have set a rule for the first three digits typed in the **PhoneField** field and provided the text that Access should display if someone attempts to enter an invalid phone number.

6 Click in the **Caption** box, and type **Phone Number**.

The table window now looks like this:

7 Save the table.

Access warns you that data integrity rules have changed. The table violates the new rule because it contains blank phone number fields.

8 Click **No** to close the message box without testing the data.

Tip

You can test the validation rules in a table at any time by right-clicking the title bar of the table and clicking **Test Validation Rules** on the shortcut menu.

9 Return to Datasheet view, where the caption for the first field is now *Phone Number*.

10 Place the insertion point to the left of the first # of any **Phone Number** field, type **3605550009**, and press [Enter].

Tip

You can move the pointer to the left end of the **Phone Number** field and, when the pointer changes to a fat cross, click to select the entire field. The insertion point is then at the start of the area code when you begin typing.

146

The **Validation Rule** setting causes Access to display an alert box, warning you that the area code must be either 206 or 425.

11 Click **OK** to close the alert box, and type a new phone number with one of the allowed area codes.

12 Return to Design view, and add another date field. Type **Date2** as the field name, set the data type to **Date/Time**, and drag the new field to just below **DateField**.

13 Add a table validation rule to ensure that the second date is always later than the first one. Right-click the table window, and click **Properties** on the shortcut menu to open the **Table Properties** dialog box, shown here:

```
Table Properties                              X
 General
 Description . . . . . . . . . . . . . .
 Default View . . . . . . . . . . . . .  Datasheet
 Validation Rule . . . . . . . . . . . .
 Validation Text . . . . . . . . . . .
 Filter . . . . . . . . . . . . . . . . .
 Order By . . . . . . . . . . . . . . .
 Subdatasheet Name . . . . . . . .  [Auto]
 Link Child Fields . . . . . . . . . . .
 Link Master Fields . . . . . . . . . .
 Subdatasheet Height . . . . . . .  0"
 Subdatasheet Expanded . . . . .  No
 Orientation . . . . . . . . . . . . . .  Left-to-Right
```

Tip

This dialog box is not the one you see if you right-click the table in the database window and click **Properties**. The only point in common between the two is the **Description** property, which you can enter in either dialog box.

14 Click in the **Validation Rule** box, type **[DateField]<[Date2]**, and press `Enter`.

15 Type **Date2 must be later than DateField**, and close the dialog box.

16 Save the table (click **No** to close the data-integrity alert box), and return to Datasheet view.

17 In any record, type **6/1/01** in **DateField** and **5/1/01** in **Date2**, and then click in another record.

Access displays the **Validation Text** setting from the **Table Properties** dialog box, reminding you that **Date2** must be later than **DateField**.

18 Click **OK**, change **Date2** to **6/2/2001**, and click in another record.

19 Close the table and the database.

Using a Lookup List to Restrict Data

Ac2002-2-3
Ac2002e-1-3

Approved Courseware

It is interesting how many different ways people can come up with to enter the same items of information in a database. Asked to enter the name of their home state, for example, residents of the state of Washington will type *Washington*, *Wash*, or *WA*, plus various typos and misspellings. If you ask a dozen sales clerks to enter the name of a specific product, customer, and shipper in an invoice, the probability that all of them will type the same thing is not very high. In cases like this, where the number of correct choices is limited (to actual product name, actual customer, and actual shipper), providing the option to choose the correct answer from a list will improve your database's consistency.

Minor inconsistencies in the way data is entered might not be really important to someone who later reads the information and makes decisions. Most people know that *Arizona* and *AZ* refer to the same state. But a computer is very literal, and if you tell it to create a list so that you can send catalogs to everyone living in *AZ*, the computer won't include anyone whose state is listed in the database as *Arizona*.

You can limit the options for entering information in a database in several ways:

- For only two options, you can use a Boolean field represented by a check box. A check in the box indicates one choice, and no check indicates the other choice.

- For several mutually exclusive options on a form, you can use **option buttons** to gather the required information.

- For more than a few options, a **combo box** is a good way to go. When you click the down arrow at the end of a combo box, a list of choices is displayed. Depending on the properties associated with the combo box, if you don't see the option you want, you might be able to type something else, adding your entry to the list of possible options displayed in the future.

- For a short list of choices that won't change often, you can have the combo box look up the options in a list that you provide. Although you can create a lookup list by hand, it is a lot easier to use the **Lookup Wizard** to do it.

Field Test

In this exercise, you will use the **Lookup Wizard** to create a list of months from which the user can choose. You might use something like this to gather credit card information. The working folder for this exercise is *SBS\Access\Accurate\Lookup*. Follow these steps:

1   Open the **Field Test** database located in the working folder.

2   Open the **Field Property Test** table in Design view.

3 Add a new field below **LastName**. Name it **Month**, and set the data type to **Lookup Wizard**.

The first page of the **Lookup Wizard** is displayed:

You can use this wizard to create a combo box that provides the entry for a text field. The combo box list can come from a table or query, or you can type the list in the wizard.

Tip

If a field has a lot of potential entries, or if they will change often, you can link them to a table. (You might have to create a table expressly for this purpose.) If the field has only a few items and they won't change, typing the list in the wizard is easier.

4 Click **I will type in the values that I want**, and then click **Next**.

A combo box typically has only one column, but it can have more. On this page, you can set the number of columns and then enter the text that should appear in each one. If you specify more than one column, you also have to specify which column's text should be entered in the field when a selection is made from the list.

5 Leave the number of columns set to **1**, and click in the **Col1** box.

6 Enter the 12 months of the year, pressing ⟦Tab⟧ to create new rows as you need them. Then click **Next**.

7 Accept the *Month* default label, and click **Finish**.

8 Click the **Lookup** tab in the **Field Properties** section to view the **Lookup** information for the **Month** field, which looks as shown on the next page.

The wizard entered this information, but you could easily figure out what you would have to enter to create a lookup list by hand.

View

9   Click the **View** button to change to Datasheet view, saving your changes.

10   Adjust the column widths so that you can see all the fields, by dragging the vertical bars between columns in the header.

11   Click in the **Month** field of a record, and then click the down arrow to display the list, which looks like this:

12   Click **February** to enter it in the field.

13   Click in the next **Month** field, type **Jan**, and press [Enter].

As soon as you type the *J*, the combo box displays *January*. If you had typed *Ju*, the combo box would have jumped to *June*.

14 In the next **Month** field, type **jly**, and press ⏎.

The entry is accepted just as you typed it. Although there might be times when you want to allow the entry of information other than the items on the list, this isn't one of those times.

15 Return to Design view.

The last property on the **Lookup** tab is **Limit To List**. It is currently set to **No**, which allows people to enter information that isn't on the list.

16 Change **Limit To List** to **Yes**.

17 Save the table, return to Datasheet view, type **jly** in a new **Month** field, and press ⏎.

Access informs you that the text you entered is not on the list, and refuses the entry.

18 Click **OK**, press Esc to close the list, remove your entry, and then return to Design view.

A list of the names of months is convenient for people, but if your computer has to deal with this information in some mathematical way, a list of the numbers associated with each month is easier for it to use. There is a solution that will work for both humans and machines.

19 Create a new field named **Month2**, and again set the data type to **Lookup Wizard**.

20 Click **I will type in the values that I want**, and click **Next**.

21 Type **2** to add a second column, and then click in the **Col1** box.

22 Enter the following numbers and months in the two columns, pressing Tab to move from column to column:

Number	Month	Number	Month
1	January	7	July
2	February	8	August
3	March	9	September
4	April	10	October
5	May	11	November
6	June	12	December

The wizard now looks as shown on the next page.

23 Click **Next** to move to the next page.

24 Accept the default selection of **Col1** as the column whose data you want to enter when a selection is made from the list, and click **Finish**.

You return to the table, with the **Field Properties** section displaying the **Lookup** information, like this:

The wizard has inserted your column information into the **Row Source** box and set the other properties according to your specifications.

25 Change **Limit To List** to **Yes**.

26 Save your changes, switch to Datasheet view, and then click the down arrow in a **Month2** field to display this list:

DateField	Date2	CurrencyField	BooleanField	LastName	Month	Month2		
6/1/01	6/2/01	$0.00	☐	Smith	February		1	January
		$0.00	☐	Mcdonald	January		2	February
		$0.00	☐				3	March
1/1/01		($45.35)	☑	Smith			4	April
		$0.00	☑				5	May
							6	June
							7	July
							8	August

Record: |◄ ◄ 1 ► ►| ►* of 4

27 Click **January**.

Access displays the number *1* in the field, which is useful for the computer. However, people might be confused by the two columns and by seeing something other than what they clicked or typed.

28 Switch back to Design view, and in the **Column Widths** box, change the width for the first column to **0"** to prevent it from being displayed.

29 Save your changes, return to Datasheet view, and as a test, set **Month2** to **February** in two records and to **March** in one record.

Only the name of the month is now displayed in the list, and when you click a month, that name is displayed in the field. However, Access actually stores the associated number from the list's first column.

30 Right-click in the **Month2** column, click **Filter For** on the shortcut menu, type **2** in the box, and press ⏎.

Only the two records with *February* in the **Month2** field are now displayed.

Remove Filter

31 Click the **Remove Filter** button, and then repeat the previous step, this time typing **3** in the box to display the one record with *March* in the **Month2** field.

32 Close the **Field Text** database, clicking **Yes** when prompted to save your changes.

33 Close the database.

Updating Information in a Table

Ac2002e-3-1

Approved Courseware

As you use a database and as it grows, you might discover that errors creep in or that some information becomes out of date. You can tediously scroll through the records looking for those that need to be changed. But it is more efficient to use a few of the tools and techniques provided by Access for that purpose.

If an employee has consistently misspelled the same word, you can use the **Find** and **Replace** commands on the **Edit** menu to locate each instance of the misspelling and replace it with the correct spelling. This command works much like the same commands in Microsoft Word or Microsoft Excel.

However, if you decide to increase the price of some products or replace the content of a field only under certain circumstances, the **Find** and **Replace** commands won't be much use. For this task, you need the power of an **update query**, which is a select query that performs an action on the query's results.

GardenCo

In this exercise, you will use an update query to increase the price of all bulbs and cacti by 10 percent. The working folder for this exercise is *SBS\Access\Accurate\QueryUp*. Follow these steps:

1   Open the **GardenCo** database located in the working folder.

2   In the **Queries** pane, double-click **Create query by using wizard**.

3   In the **Tables/Queries** list, select **Table: Categories**.

4   Double-click **CategoryName** to move it to the **Selected Fields** list.

5   Select **Table: Products** in the **Tables/Queries** list.

6   Double-click **ProductName** and **UnitPrice** to move them to the **Selected Fields** list.

7   Click **Finish** to accept all defaults and create the query.

Access displays the query results in a datasheet. Only the **Category Name**, **Product Name**, and **Unit Price** fields are displayed, as shown here:

Category Name	Product Name	Unit Price
Bulbs	Bulb planter	$6.95
Bulbs	Magic Lily	$40.00
Bulbs	Autumn crocus	$18.75
Bulbs	Anemone	$28.00
Bulbs	Lily-of-the-Field	$38.00
Bulbs	Siberian Iris	$12.95
Bulbs	Daffodil	$12.95
Bulbs	Peony	$19.95
Bulbs	Lilies	$10.50
Bulbs	Begonias	$18.95
Cacti	Prickly Pear	$3.00
Ground Covers	Crown Vetch	$12.95
Ground Covers	English Ivy	$5.95

Record: 1 of 189

View

9 To check the accuracy of the query, click the **View** button.

Access displays a list of 18 discontinued products that will be deleted, but it hasn't actually changed the table yet. Scroll to the right to verify that all records display a check in the Products.Discontinued field.

10 Click the **View** button to return to Design view, confident that you have identified the correct records.

Tip

Before actually deleting records, you might want to display the Relationships window by clicking **Relationships** on the **Tools** menu. If the table you are deleting from has a relationship with any table containing order information that shouldn't be deleted, right-click the relationship line, click **Edit Relationship** on the shortcut menu, and make sure that **Enforce Referential Integrity** is selected and **Cascade Delete Related Records** is *not* selected.

Run

11 Click the **Run** button to run the delete query.

Access displays a warning to remind you of the permanence of this action.

12 Click **Yes** to delete the records.

Access displays another warning, stating it can't delete two of the records due to key violations. This is because two discontinued products have been ordered, and so are in the Order Details table. This table has a one-to-many relationship with the Products table, and **Enforce Referential Integrity** is set between the two tables.

13 Click **Yes** to run the query, and then click **View** to see the two discontinued products that were not deleted.

Save

14 If you think you might want to run the same delete query in the future, click the **Save** button and provide a name to save it. Then close the query.

Tip

If you are concerned that someone might accidentally run a delete query and destroy records you weren't ready to destroy, change the query back to a select query before saving it. You can then open the select query in Design view and change it to a delete query when you want to run it again.

15 Close the query, and then close the database.

16 If you are not continuing on to the next chapter, quit Access.

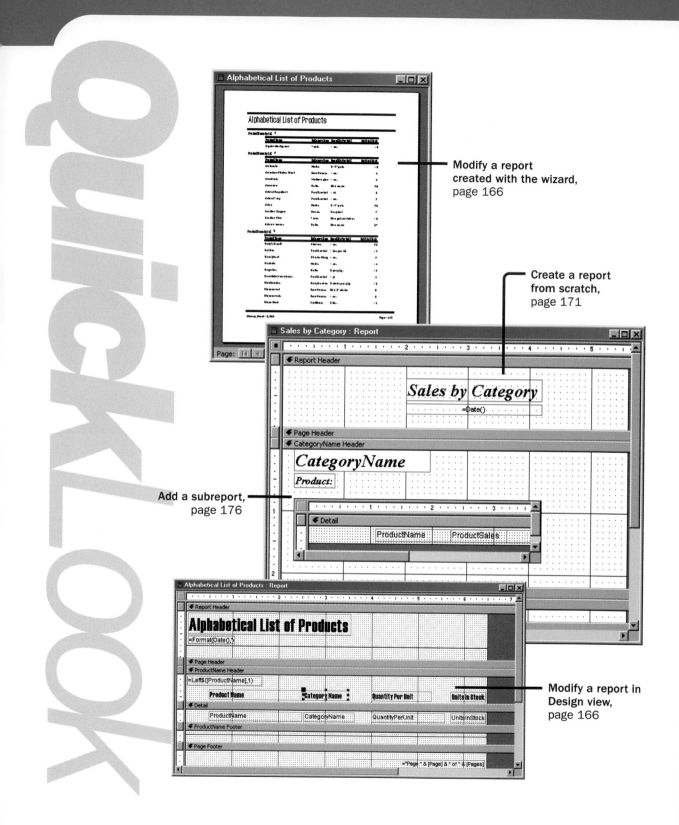

Modify a report created with the wizard, page 166

Create a report from scratch, page 171

Add a subreport, page 176

Modify a report in Design view, page 166

Chapter 7
Working with Reports

After completing this chapter, you will be able to:

✔ **Create a report using a wizard.**

✔ **Modify a report.**

✔ **Create a report from scratch.**

✔ **Add a subreport to a report.**

✔ **Preview and print a report.**

People generally think of **reports** as summaries of larger bodies of information. For example, The Garden Company's database might hold detailed information about thousands of orders. If you want to edit those orders or enter new ones, you do so directly in the table or via a form. If you want to summarize those orders to illustrate the rate of growth of the company's sales, you use a report.

Like a book report or the annual report of a company's activities, a report created in Microsoft Access is typically used to summarize and organize information in order to express a particular point of view to a specific audience. When designing a report, it is important to consider the point you are trying to make, the intended audience, and the level of information they will need.

In many ways, reports are like forms. You can use similar wizards to create them, and the design environment is much the same. Just as with a form, you can add label, text box, image, and other controls, and you can set their properties. You can display information from one or more records from one or more tables or queries, and you can have multiple sets of headers and footers.

In this chapter, you will learn how to generate and print reports that extract specific information from a database and format it in an easy-to-read style. You will be working with the GardenCo database files that are stored in the following subfolders of the *SBS\Access\Reports* folder: *RepByWiz*, *Modify*, *ByDesign*, *Subreport*, and *Print*.

Creating a Report Using a Wizard

Ac2002-7-1
Ac2002e-4-1
Ac2002e-4-3

The content of an Access report can be divided into two general categories: information derived from records in one or more tables, and everything else. The *everything else* category includes the title, page headers and footers, introductory and explanatory text, logo, background and graphics, and calculations based on database content.

You can use a wizard to get a jump-start on a report. The wizard creates a basic layout, attaches styles, and adds a text box control and its associated label for each field you specify. Depending on the report you want to produce, you might be able to do almost all the work in the wizard, or you might have to refine the report in Design view.

GardenCo

In this exercise, you will use the **Report Wizard** to create a simple report that displays an alphabetical list of The Garden Company's products. The working folder for this exercise is *SBS\Access\Reports\RepByWiz*. Follow these steps:

1 Open the **GardenCo** database located in the working folder.

2 On the **Objects** bar, click **Tables**, and then click the **Products** table to select it.

Forms vs. Reports

Forms and reports have one purpose in common: to give people easy access to the information stored in a database. The main differences between forms and reports are the following:

■ Forms are used to enter, view, and edit information. Reports are used only to view information.

■ Forms are usually displayed on the screen. Reports can be previewed on the screen, but they are usually printed.

■ Forms generally provide a detailed look at records and are usually for the people who actually work with the database. Reports are often used to group and summarize data and are often for people who don't actually work with the database but who use its information for other business tasks.

Forms and reports are sufficiently alike that you can save a form as a report when you want to take advantage of additional report refinement and printing capabilities.

Tip

If you select a table or query before starting the **Report Wizard**, that table or query becomes the basis for the report.

3   On the **Insert** menu, click **Report** to display the **New Report** dialog box.

Notice that **Products** is already selected as the table on which to base the new report.

4   Double-click **Report Wizard** to open the **Report Wizard**.

You use this page of the wizard to select the fields to be included in the new report.

Tip

You can also click **Report Wizard** in the **New Report** dialog box that appears when you click **Report** on the **New Object** button's list; or click the **New** button on the database window's toolbar; or double-click **Create report by using wizard** in the **Report** pane of the database window.

5   Double-click **ProductName**, **QuantityPerUnit**, and **UnitsInStock** to move them to the **Selected Fields** list.

Tip

Fields appear in a report in the same order they are listed in the wizard's **Selected Fields** list. You can save yourself the effort of rearranging the fields on the report if you enter them in the desired order in the wizard.

6   Select **Tables:Categories** in the **Tables/Queries** list to display the fields from the Categories table.

7   Click **ProductName** in the **Selected Fields** list to select it.

The next field you add will be inserted below the selected field.

8   Double-click **CategoryName**.

The **Report Wizard** now looks as shown on the next page.

Tip

If you are using more than two tables in a form or report, or if you will be using the same combination of tables in several places, it is more efficient to create a query based on those tables and use that query as the basis for the form or report.

9 Click **Next** to move to the wizard's second page, which looks like this:

When you include more than one table in a report, the wizard evaluates the relationships that exist between the tables and offers to group the records in any logical manner available. In this case, you can choose to group them by category or product. You can click either option to see it depicted in the right pane.

> If the relationships between the tables aren't already established in the Relationships window, you have to cancel the wizard and establish them now.

10 Accept the default to group **By Products**, and click **Next**.

On this page you can specify any fields you want to use to establish **grouping levels**. You want to group by the first letter of the product names.

11 Double-click **ProductName** to move it to the top of the simulated report on the right.

12 Click the **Grouping Options** button at the bottom of the page to open this dialog box:

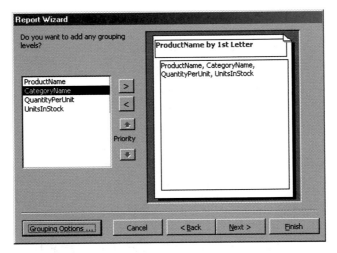

13 Display the **Grouping intervals** drop-down list, click **1st Letter**, and then click **OK**.

The wizard now looks like this:

14 Click **Next** to display a page where you can specify the sort order and summary options.

15 Specify **ProductName** as the first **Ascending** sort field.

You can use this page to specify up to four fields on which to sort. If any fields include numeric information, the **Summary Options** button becomes available. You can click it to display a list of the numeric fields, each with **Sum**, **Avg** (average), **Min** (minimum), and **Max** (maximum) check boxes. The only numeric field in this report is UnitsInStock, and there is no need to summarize it.

16 Click **Next** to display the next page of the wizard.

On this page, you can click the options in the **Layout** group to see what each one looks like. None of them is exactly what you are looking for, but **Outline 1** is close.

17 Click **Outline 1**, leave **Portrait** orientation selected, and then click **Next** to display a list of predefined styles.

18 Click **Compact**, and then click **Next** to display the wizard's final page.

19 Type **Alphabetical List of Products** as the title, and click **Finish** to preview the report, which looks like this:

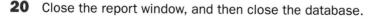

20 Close the report window, and then close the database.

Modifying a Report

Ac2002e-4-1

Approved Courseware

You can use the **Report Wizard** to get a quick start on a report, but you will usually want to use Design view to refine the report and add special touches. Refining a report is an iterative process: you switch back and forth between Design view and Print Preview to evaluate each change you make and to plan the next change. Fortunately, Design view for reports is very much like Design view for forms, so you should feel quite familiar in this environment.

GardenCo

In this exercise, you'll work with the Alphabetical List of Products report from the GardenCo database. The working folder for this exercise is *SBS\Access\Reports\Modify*. Follow these steps:

1 Open the **GardenCo** database located in the working folder.

2 On the **Objects** bar, click **Reports**.

3 Click **Alphabetical List of Products**, and then click the **Preview** button to open the report in Print Preview, like this:

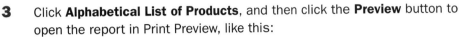

4 Enlarge the window, and then move the pointer over the page. The pointer changes to a magnifying glass with a plus sign in it to indicate that the page will zoom in if you click. Click once to zoom in, and notice some of the following problems with the report design:

- There is no date below the title.
- Some horizontal lines need to be removed, or added.
- There is some extraneous text.
- Labels and text boxes need to be rearranged.
- The list breaks in mid-group.
- There are a number of general formatting issues.

View

5 To fix some of these issues, click the **View** button to view the report in Design view, where it looks as shown on the next page.

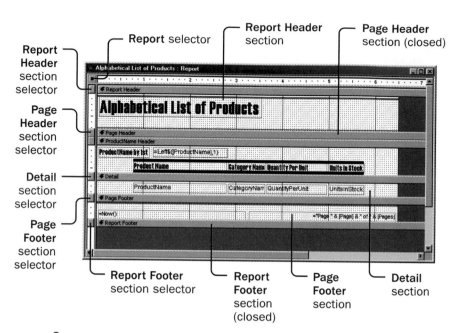

Report Header section selector

Report selector

Report Header section

Page Header section (closed)

Page Header section selector

Detail section selector

Page Footer section selector

Report Footer section selector

Report Footer section (closed)

Page Footer section

Detail section

6 Point to the top of the **Page Header** section selector. When the pointer changes to a two-headed vertical arrow, drag the selector down about a quarter inch.

You should now be able to see the double lines below the title. (The horizontal lines inserted by the wizard actually consist of sets of two lines.)

7 In the **Report Header** section, click one of the lines above the title (small black handles will indicate when a line is selected), and press ⌦ to delete it. Then repeat this step to delete the other line above the title and one of the lines below it.

Toolbox

8 If the toolbox is not already open, click the **Toolbox** button to open it.

9 Click the **Text Box** control in the toolbox, and then click in the blank area at the right end of the **Report Header** section to insert a text box and its label.

Text Box

10 Click the new label, and delete it.

11 Drag the text box to just below the title, aligned with its left edge. With the text box still selected, press the ⌨ key to open the **Properties** dialog box.

12 On the **Data** tab, click **Control Source**, and type the following:

=Format(Date(), "dd-mmm-yyyy")

You have just created a custom date format. The Date() function returns the current date and time. The Format() function determines the manner in which the date and time are displayed. Each time you preview or print the report, this expression will insert the current date in the text box and format it in this fashion: 17-Feb-2001.

13 Close the **Properties** dialog box.

Tip

You can quickly insert a text box that displays the date and/or time in one of several standard formats. While in Design view, click **Date and Time** on the **Insert** menu. A dialog box opens in which you can specify the format. When you click **OK**, Access inserts a text box in the **Header** section if it exists, or in the **Detail** section if it doesn't. You can then move the text box where you want it. For detailed information about date formats, search for *date formats* in Access online Help.

14 In the **ProductName Header** section, delete all of the bold lines above and below the labels. (Again, there are two sets of two.)

15 Delete the **Product Name by 1st** label, and drag the text box to the left edge of the section.

16 Click the text box containing **=Now()** in the **Page Footer** section, and then delete it.

17 Select all the labels in the **ProductName Header** section and the text boxes in the **Detail** section by dragging a rectangle around them.

Selection handles appear around the borders of all the controls, and you can now move them as a group.

18 Move the controls to the left until the left edge of **Product Name** lines up with the half-inch mark on the ruler at the top of the window.

The report window now looks like this:

19 Save your changes, and then switch to Print Preview to see what still needs to be changed in the report.

You still need to add a thin line at the bottom of each group, and you need to do something to prevent the groups from breaking across pages.

Sorting and Grouping

20 Switch back to Design view, and then click the **Sorting and Grouping** button on the toolbar to display this dialog box:

Sorting and Grouping	☒
Field/Expression	**Sort Order**
ProductName ▼	Ascending
ProductName	Ascending
ProductName	Ascending

Group Properties

Group Header	Yes	
Group Footer	No	Select a field or type an expression to sort or group on
Group On	Prefix Characters	
Group Interval	1	
Keep Together	No	

You use this dialog box to set group properties. The top field, which should already be selected, has an icon in its row selector indicating that it is the field on which records are grouped. Because **Group Header** is set to **Yes** and **Group Footer** to **No** in the **Group Properties** section, a ProductName header is displayed on your report, but a ProductName footer isn't. The footer is where you need to add the missing horizontal line.

21 In the **Group Properties** section, change **Group Footer** to **Yes**.

You will see a **ProductName Footer** section selector appear in the Design view window, above the **Page Footer** section.

22 Change the **Keep Together** setting to **Whole Group**, and close the **Sorting and Grouping** dialog box.

Line

23 Click the **Line** control in the toolbox, and then click near the top of the **ProductName Footer** section to insert a short horizontal line.

24 If the **Properties** dialog box isn't open, press ⌨F4 to open it, and then click the **Format** tab.

25 Type **0** as the **Left** property and **6.5** as the **Width** property.

26 Save your changes, and switch to Print Preview to see how the report looks.

You still need to remove the set of lines above the page number and realign the columns.

27 Switch to Design view, and delete the two lines at the top of the **Page Footer** section.

If you can't see the lines, drag a rectangle starting below the lines and moving upward to select them.

28 In the **ProductName Header** and **Detail** sections, select the label and text box for **Units In Stock**, and drag them to the right until their right edges touch the right edge of the background grid.

29 In the same two sections, move the label and text box for **Quantity Per Unit** to the right a bit—the left edge should be at about 3.75 inches.

30 Lengthen the label and text box for **CategoryName** and the text box for **QuantityPerUnit**.

The Design view window now looks something like this:

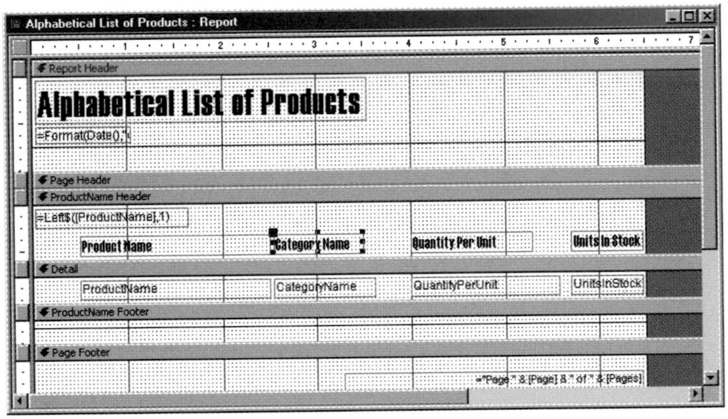

![Design view window showing the Alphabetical List of Products report with Report Header, Page Header, ProductName Header, Detail, ProductName Footer, and Page Footer sections. The Report Header contains the title "Alphabetical List of Products" and =Format(Date(),"..."). The ProductName Header has =Left$([ProductName],1) and column labels Product Name, Category Name, Quantity Per Unit, Units In Stock. The Detail section shows ProductName, CategoryName, QuantityPerUnit, UnitsInStock. The Page Footer contains ="Page " & [Page] & " of " & [Pages].]

31 Save your changes, and preview the report.

32 Close the report, and then close the database.

Creating a Report from Scratch

Ac2002e-4-1

Approved Courseware

When you want to create a report that displays records from one or more tables, using the **Report Wizard** is the fastest way to create the report and include all the desired field captions and contents. However, sometimes a **main report** simply serves as a shell for one or more subreports, and the main report displays little or no information from the underlying tables. In this case, it is often easier to create the main report by hand in Design view.

GardenCo

In this exercise, you will use a query as the basis for the shell for a report that lists sales by category. A CategoryName section will list the current category, but the **Page Header**, **Detail**, and **Page Footer** sections will contain no information. The working folder for this exercise is *SBS\Access\Reports\ByDesign*. Follow these steps:

1 Open the **GardenCo** database located in the working folder.

2 On the **Objects** bar, click **Queries**.

3 Click **Sales by Category** to select it.

4 On the **Insert** menu, click **Report**.

5 Double-click **Design View** to open a blank report.

Tip

The **Page Header**, **Detail**, and **Page Footer** sections you see in Design view are the default sections for a new report, but you don't have to use them all, and you can add others.

A small window also opens, displaying a list of the fields in the Sales by Category query.

6 On the **View** menu, click **Report Header/Footer**.

The sections are now enclosed in the **Report Header** and **Report Footer** sections.

7 On the **View** menu, click **Sorting and Grouping** to display the **Sorting and Grouping** dialog box.

You use this dialog box to specify the fields that will be used to group the records in the report.

8 Expand the **Field/Expression** drop-down list for the top row, and click **Category Name**.

9 In the **Group Properties** section, set **Group Header** to **Yes**.

An icon appears in the selector button to the left of Category/Name to indicate that it is a group heading, and the **Category/Name Header** section selector appears in the Design view window.

10 Close the **Sorting and Grouping** dialog box.

Toolbox

11 If the toolbox isn't displayed, click the **Toolbox** button on the toolbar.

12 Click the **Report** selector in the upper left corner of the report, and then press F4 to open the **Properties** dialog box.

Tip

If the report is already selected, the **Report** selector has a small black square in it.

13 In the **Properties** dialog box, click the **Format** tab, and set the **Grid X** and **Grid Y** properties to **10**.

The grid, which is represented by dots on the report background, becomes coarser and easier to use when aligning controls.

14 Set the height of each section by clicking the section selector and then setting the **Height** property on the **Format** tab in the **Properties** dialog box as follows:

Section	Setting
Report Header	1"
Page Header	0"
Category/Name Header	2.2"
Detail	0"
Page Footer	0.2"
Report Footer	0"

Tip

You can also set the height of a section by dragging the top of the section selector up or down.

The Design view window now looks like this:

Save

Label

15 Now that you have a little time invested in this report, click the **Save** button, type **Sales by Category** as the name of the report, and click **OK**.

16 To give the report a title, click the **Label** control in the toolbox and then click at the top of the **Report Header** section, about 2 inches from the left edge.

Access inserts a very narrow label.

17 Type **Sales by Category**, and press [Enter].

The label expands to hold the text you type, and when you press [Enter], Access selects the label control and displays its properties in the **Properties** dialog box.

18 Set the label's **Font** properties as follows:

Property	Setting
Font Name	Times New Roman
Font Size	20
Font Weight	Bold
Font Italic	Yes

The text in the label reflects each change. By the time you finish making all the changes, the text has outgrown its frame.

19 On the **Format** menu, point to **Size**, and then click **To Fit**.

20 Now you'll insert a date field. On the **Insert** menu, click **Date and Time** to display this dialog box:

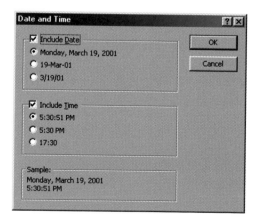

21 Make sure that **Include Date** and the first (long) date format are selected, clear the **Include Time** check box, and click **OK**.

A text box containing **=Date()** appears in the upper left corner of the **Report Header** section. If the report has no **Report Header** section, the text box appears in the **Detail** section.

Center

22 Drag the new text box below the title, adjust the width of the box to match the width of the title, and click the **Center** button on the Formatting toolbar to center the date in the box.

23 Drag the **CategoryName** field from the field list window to the top of the **CategoryName Header** section.

24 Delete the **Category Name** label that was inserted with the text box.

25 Select the text box, and set its **Font** properties to the same settings as those used for the report title.

26 On the **Format** menu, point to **Size**, and then click **To Fit**.

27 Position the text box with its top against the top of the section and its left edge 0.2 inch (two dots) in from the left, and then drag the right edge of the text box to about the 2.4-inch mark.

28 Click the **Save** button to save the report, and then take a look at it in Print Preview, where it looks like this:

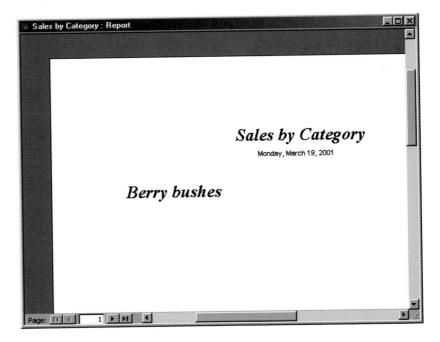

175

29 Return to Design view, and add a label below **CategoryName**. Click the **Label** button in the toolbox, click directly below the left edge of the text box, type **Product:**, and then press ⏎Enter⏎.

30 Set the **Font** properties that you set for **CategoryName**, except for **Font Size**, which should be **12**.

31 Right-click the label, point to **Size** on the shortcut menu, and then click **To Fit**.

32 Position the label against the bottom of the **CategoryName** text box, aligning their left edges.

33 Insert a page number in the **Page Footer** section by clicking **Page Numbers** on the **Insert** menu to display this dialog box:

Page Numbers	? X
Format	OK
● Page N̲	Cancel
○ Page N of M̲	
Position	
● T̲op of Page [Header]	
○ B̲ottom of Page [Footer]	
A̲lignment:	
Center ▼	
☑ S̲how Number on First Page	

34 Click **Page N of M** in the **Format** group and **Bottom of Page [Footer]** in the **Position** group. Set **Alignment** to **Center**, and leave **Show Number of First Page** checked. Then click **OK**.

Access centers a text box containing the expression =*"Page " & [Page] & " of " & [Pages]* in the **Page Footer** section.

35 Save the report, preview the results, and then close it.

36 Close the database.

Adding a Subreport to a Report

You can use a wizard to quickly create a report that is bound to the information in one table or in several related tables. However, reports often include multiple sets of information that are related to the topic of the report but are not necessarily related to each other. A report might, for example, include charts, spreadsheets, and other forms of information about several divisions or activities of a company. Or it might include information about production, marketing, sales, compensation, and the company's 401(K) plan. All these topics are related to running the business, but they don't all fit nicely into the structure of a single Access report.

One solution to this problem is to create separate reports, print them, and put them in one binder. But an easier solution is to use **subreports**. A subreport is simply a report that you insert in a subreport control that you have placed in another report. You can create the subreport as you would any other report and then use a wizard to insert it, or you can use a wizard to insert a subreport control in the main report and then let the wizard guide you through the process of creating the subreport in the control. In either case, you end up with both the main report and the subreport listed as objects in the **Reports** pane of the database window.

Often you will use queries as the basis for reports that require summary calculations or statistics. But you can also enhance the usefulness of both regular reports and subreports by performing calculations in the reports themselves. By inserting **unbound** controls and then using the Expression Builder to create the expressions that tell Access what to calculate and how, you can make information readily available in one place instead of several.

Tip

Assuming that the correct relationships have been established, you can quickly add an existing report as a subreport by opening the main report in Design view and then dragging the second report from the **Reports** pane to the section of the main report where you want to insert it.

GardenCo

In this exercise, you will add a subreport to a main report. This subreport will display the total sales for each of the products in the category that is selected on the main report, as well as a calculated control for the total sales for the category. The working folder for this exercise is *SBS\Access\Reports\Subreport*. Follow these steps:

1 Open the **GardenCo** database located in the working folder.

2 Open the **Sales by Category** report in Design view.

Subform/
Subreport

3 Click **Subform/Subreport** in the toolbox, and then click a point even with the left edge of the Product label and about two grid intervals below it.

Access opens a blank, unbound subreport on the main report and displays the first page of the **SubReport Wizard**, shown on the next page.

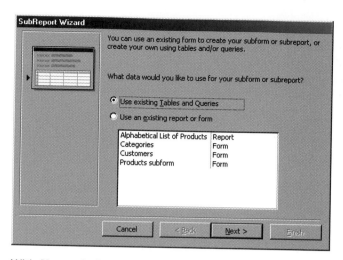

4. With **Use existing Tables and Queries** selected, click **Next**.

5. Select **Query: Sales by Category** from the **Tables/Queries** list.

6. Double-click **CategoryID**, **ProductName**, and **ProductSales** to move them to the **Selected Fields** list, and then click **Next**.

7. Accept the default **Choose from a list** selection by clicking **Next**.

8. Accept the suggested name, *Sales by Category subreport*, and click **Finish**.

   The **Sales by Category** subreport takes the place of the unbound subreport in the main report.

9. If the **Properties** dialog box for the subreport isn't displayed, click the subreport control and press ⌸ to display the dialog box.

10. On the **Format** tab, change the width of the subreport to **4"** and the height to **1"**. Then press ⌷.

11. In the subreport, right-click the **Report Header** section selector, and click **Report Header/Footer** on the shortcut menu to delete the header and footer. Click **Yes** in the alert box.

12. In the subreport, right-click the **Page Header** section selector, click **Page Header/Footer** on the shortcut menu, and click **Yes** in the alert box.

    The subreport now has only a **Detail** section.

13. In the **Detail** section, delete the **CategoryID** text box.

14 Click the **ProductName** text box, and change its width to **2.125"**.

15 Click the **ProductSales** text box, and change its **Left** property to **2.3"** and its **Width** property to **1"**.

16 On the main report, click the partially hidden **Sales by Category** subreport label, and delete it.

Tip

If you accidentally delete something, press [Ctrl]+[Z] to undo the deletion.

The subreport now looks like this:

17 Now you'll add a section in which to calculate the total product sales for each category. Click the selector in the upper left corner of the subreport, and then click **Report Header/Footer** on the **View** menu to display those sections.

Text Box

18 Scroll the subreport to display the **Report Footer** section, click the **Text Box** control in the toolbox, and then click anywhere in the footer grid.

Access inserts an unbound control and its label. You will use this control to perform the calculation.

19 Change the label's text to **Total:**, and set the **Font Name** property to **Arial**, the **Font Size** property to **9**, and the **Font Weight** property to **Bold**.

20 Now click the text box control, click the **Data** tab in the **Properties** dialog box, and click the ... button to open the **Expression Builder**.

21 Double-click **Functions**, and click **Built-In Functions** in the first column. Then scroll the third column, and double-click **Sum**.

Access displays *Sum (<<expre>>)* in the expression box.

22 Select **<<expr>>**, click **Sales by Category subreport** in the first column, and double-click **ProductSales** in the second column.

The Expression Builder now looks like this:

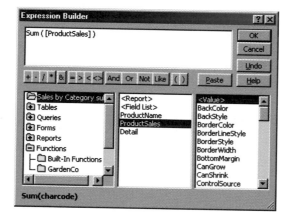

23 Click **OK** to close the **Expression Builder**, and then press ⏎ Enter to enter the calculation in the unbound text box.

24 Click the **Format** tab of the **Properties** dialog box, and format the control as **Arial**, **9**, and **Bold**. Then click the **Format** property, and click **Currency** in the drop-down list.

Now the results of the calculation will be displayed as currency.

25 Position and size the calculated control and its label to match those in the **Detail** section above.

Your report now looks like this:

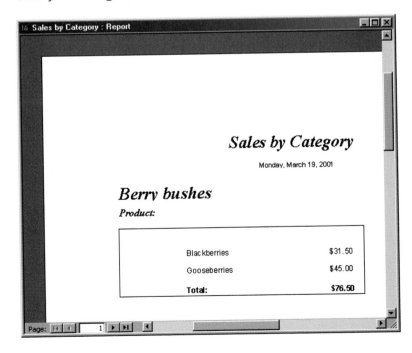

26 Save your changes, and switch to Print Preview to see these results:

This looks pretty close to what you want, but to make the report look cleaner, you need to remove the border around the subreport.

27 Return to Design view, and click the subreport to select it.

28 On the **Format** tab of the **Properties** dialog box, change the **Border Style** property to **Transparent**.

Tip

Several factors affect the layout of the subreport on the main report when it is displayed in Print Preview. The width of the subreport sets the width of the space available for the display of text. The height of the subreport sets the minimum height of the area where product information is displayed (because the **Can Shrink** property for the subreport is set to **No**). The maximum height of the product display area is the length of the list (because the **Can Grow** property is set to **Yes**) plus the space between the bottom of the subreport and the bottom of the **Detail** section.

29 Save your changes, preview the report, and then close it.

30 Close the database.

Previewing and Printing a Report

Ac2002-7-3

Approved Courseware

Print Preview in Access is very similar to Print Preview in other Microsoft Office products. If you check out your reports carefully in Print Preview, you won't be in for any major surprises when you print them. But Access also provides a "quick and dirty" preview option called Layout Preview that displays only enough of the report for you to see all the elements. This view often produces a shorter report that provides just enough information to help you refine the layout but is faster to print.

GardenCo

Most people don't spend a lot of time studying the preview and print options, so in this exercise you will review them, in case there are a few you haven't tried yet. Then you'll print a report. The working folder for this exercise is *SBS\Access\Reports\Print*. Follow these steps:

1 Open the **GardenCo** database located in the working folder.

2 Open the **Alphabetical List of Products** report in Design view.

View

3 Click the **View** button's arrow to display this list of possible views:

Each of the three choices—Design view, Print Preview, and Layout Preview—has an associated icon. The Design view icon has a border, indicating it is the current view. The Print Preview icon is duplicated on the **View** button, indicating that it is the default view if you simply click the button rather than display this menu and choose a view. When you are in Design view, both Print Preview and Layout Preview are available.

4 Click **Print Preview**.

In the preview environment, the Formatting and Report Design toolbars are hidden, the toolbox is hidden, and an image of how the report will look when it is printed is displayed, along with the Print Preview toolbar, as shown here:

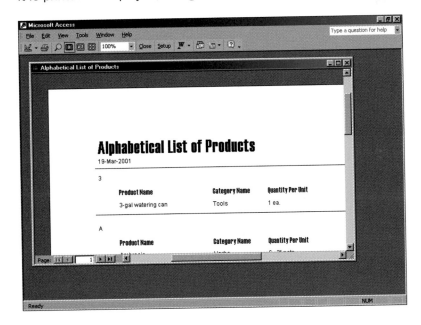

Zoom

5 Click the **Zoom** button to toggle the page magnification so that an entire page fits in the report window.

Next Page

6 Repeatedly click the **Next Page** button on the Navigation bar to view each of the 10 pages of this report.

7 Move the pointer over a page, and when the pointer changes to a magnifying glass with a plus sign in it, click to zoom in for a closer look.

The plus sign changes to a minus sign, meaning that you can click to zoom out again.

8 Click the **Close** button on the Print Preview toolbar.

9 Display the **View** button's arrow, and click **Layout Preview** in the list.

The same Print Preview toolbar is displayed, and the report looks similar to the way it does in Print Preview. However, not all products are listed in each group. (If you can't see the page clearly, zoom in.)

10 Click the **Next Page** button.

In Layout Preview, the report has only two pages.

11 Click the **Close** button to return to Design view.

12 On the **File** menu, click **Print** to display the **Print** dialog box:

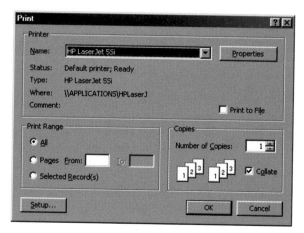

This is a standard Microsoft Windows **Print** dialog box. You can click the **Setup** button to open the **Page Setup** dialog box, or **Properties** to open a dialog box where you can set properties specific to the printer specified in the **Name** box. You can also specify which pages to print and the number of copies of each.

13 Click **Cancel** to close the **Print** dialog box.

14 Close the report and the database.

15 If you are not continuing on to the next chapter, quit Access.

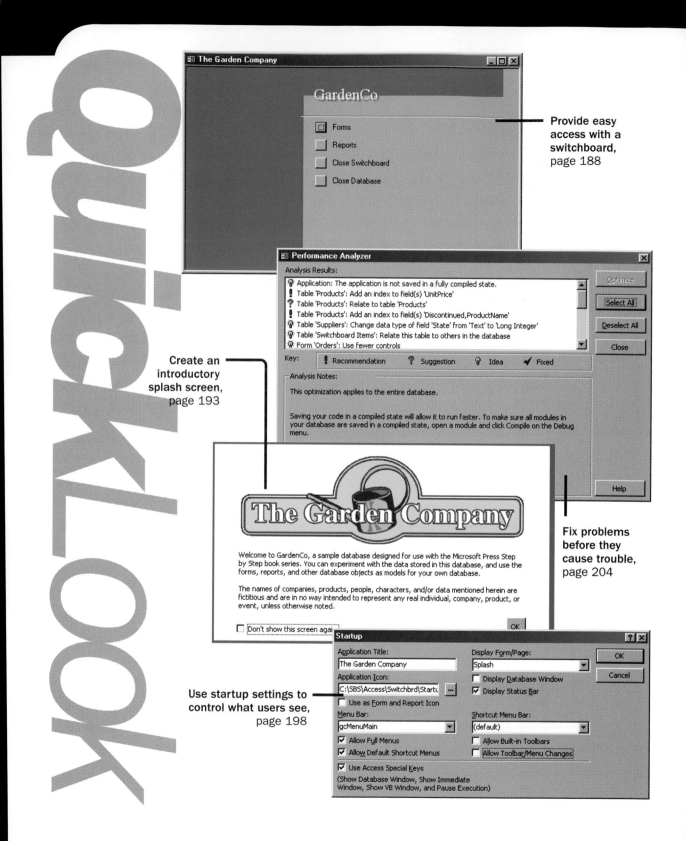

Provide easy
access with a
switchboard,
page 188

The Garden Company

GardenCo

Forms

Reports

Close Switchboard

Close Database

Performance Analyzer

Analysis Results:

Application: The application is not saved in a fully compiled state.

Table 'Products': Add an index to field(s) 'UnitPrice'

Table 'Products': Relate to table 'Products'

Table 'Products': Add an index to field(s) 'Discontinued,ProductName'

Table 'Suppliers': Change data type of field 'State' from 'Text' to 'Long Integer'

Table 'Switchboard Items': Relate this table to others in the database

Form 'Orders': Use fewer controls

Key: ! Recommendation ? Suggestion 💡 Idea ✔ Fixed

Analysis Notes:

This optimization applies to the entire database.

Saving your code in a compiled state will allow it to run faster. To make sure all modules in your database are saved in a compiled state, open a module and click Compile on the Debug menu.

Optimize

Select All

Deselect All

Close

Help

Create an
introductory
splash screen,
page 193

The Garden Company

Welcome to GardenCo, a sample database designed for use with the Microsoft Press Step by Step book series. You can experiment with the data stored in this database, and use the forms, reports, and other database objects as models for your own database.

The names of companies, products, people, characters, and/or data mentioned herein are fictitious and are in no way intended to represent any real individual, company, product, or event, unless otherwise noted.

☐ Don't show this screen again

OK

Fix problems
before they
cause trouble,
page 204

Startup

Application Title:
The Garden Company

Application Icon:
C:\SBS\Access\Switchbrd\Startu...
☐ Use as Form and Report Icon

Menu Bar:
gcMenuMain

✔ Allow Full Menus

✔ Allow Default Shortcut Menus

✔ Use Access Special Keys
(Show Database Window, Show Immediate
Window, Show VB Window, and Pause Execution)

Display Form/Page:
Splash
☐ Display Database Window
✔ Display Status Bar

Shortcut Menu Bar:
(default)

☐ Allow Built-in Toolbars

☐ Allow Toolbar/Menu Changes

OK

Cancel

Use startup settings to
control what users see,
page 198

QuickLook

Chapter 8
Making It Easy for Others to Use Your Database

After completing this chapter, you will be able to:

✔ Create a switchboard for easy access to forms and reports.

✔ Create a splash screen to convey useful information.

✔ Set startup options to control what users can do.

✔ Keep your database application in good repair.

A database created with Microsoft Access is a complex combination of objects and information and the tools required to manage and manipulate them. With a little effort, you have learned how to work with these components to enter, organize, retrieve, and display information. You have become a database developer. You can create databases that you, or others familiar with Access, can use.

However, if information will be entered and retrieved from your database by people who aren't proficient with Access, the information will be safer and the users happier if you take some steps to insulate them from the inner workings of Access. You need to turn your collection of objects and information into an application that organizes related tasks. Then users can focus on the job at hand, not on the program used to develop the application. With a little extra effort on your part, you can add features that make it much easier for others to access and manipulate your data, and much more difficult to unintentionally change or delete it. The most common ways to control access to a database application are through switchboards and startup options.

In this chapter, you will learn how to create and customize your own switchboard, create a splash screen, set various startup options, and use several Access utilities to help maintain the health of a database. You will be working with the GardenCo database files and a few other sample files that are stored in the following subfolders of the *SBS\Access\Switchbrd* folder: *SBManager*, *Splash*, *Startup*, and *Health*.

Creating a Switchboard with Switchboard Manager

Ac2002e-2-2

Approved Courseware

A **switchboard** appears as a hierarchy of pages containing buttons that the user can click to open additional pages, display dialog boxes, present forms for viewing and entering data, preview and print reports, or initiate other activities. For example, a switchboard for The Garden Company's database might allow salespeople to display a form for quickly entering orders or adding new customers.

You can create switchboards by hand or with the help of **Switchboard Manager**. A switchboard created by hand is made up of multiple forms (pages) of your own design that are linked together by macros and Microsoft Visual Basic for Applications (VBA) code. A switchboard created with **Switchboard Manager** consists of a Switchboard Items table and one generic form containing eight hidden buttons. You can use Design view to change the location of buttons and add other visual elements (such as pictures), but unlike with a switchboard created by hand, you can change the number of active buttons and what happens when each one is clicked only by editing information in the Switchboard Items table, either directly or with **Switchboard Manager**.

Tip

Although you don't need to know how switchboards created with **Switchboard Manager** work to be able to use one, it helps to know what's going on behind the scenes in case you need to make changes. When the switchboard is opened, Access runs VBA code that reads information stored in the Switchboard Items table and uses it to set form properties that determine which buttons are visible on the generic form. Code also assigns labels and actions to the visible buttons. If you click a button to go to a second level in the switchboard hierarchy, the code reads the table again and resets the properties for the generic form to create the page for the new level.

GardenCo

In this exercise, you will use **Switchboard Manager** to create a simple switchboard for the GardenCo database. This switchboard has two levels. The first level is a page with buttons the user can click to edit or enter information in the database's forms, preview or print reports, close the switchboard, close the database, or quit Access. Clicking the **Forms** button at the first level opens a second-level page that lists the forms that can be viewed. Clicking the **Reports** button opens a second-level page that lists reports. Both second-level pages include a button to return to the first-level page. The working folder for this exercise is *SBS\Access\Switchbrd\SBManager*. Follow these steps:

1 Open the **GardenCo** database located in the working folder.

2 On the **Tools** menu, point to **Database Utilities**, and click **Switchboard Manager**. Click **Yes** when Access asks if you would like to create a switchboard.

This first page of **Switchboard Manager** is displayed:

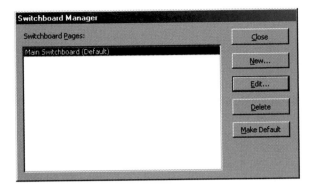

This dialog box lists any existing switchboard pages. (It lists only pages created by **Switchboard Manager**; if you created any pages by hand, they are not listed here.) This database doesn't currently have any switchboard pages, but Access lists a default page to get you started.

3 With **Main Switchboard** selected in the **Switchboard Pages** list, click **Edit**.

4 In the **Switchboard Name** box, replace *Main Switchboard* with **The Garden Company**, and click **Close**.

The Garden Company switchboard is now the default for this database.

5 Click **New** to display the **Create New** dialog box.

You use this dialog box to name new pages you want to add to the switchboard. You will create the two second-level pages now so that you can reference them later, when you add buttons to the first page.

6 Type **Forms** to replace the text that is already selected in the **Switchboard Page Name** box, and then click **OK**.

7 Click **New** again, name the new page **Reports**, and click **OK**.

The **Switchboard Manager** dialog box now displays your new pages.

8 With **The Garden Company** selected, click **Edit**.

Access displays this **Edit Switchboard Page** dialog box:

9 Click **New** to display the **Edit Switchboard Item** dialog box, shown here:

Edit Switchboard Item		
Text:	New Switchboard Command	OK
Command:	Go to Switchboard ▾	Cancel
Switchboard:	▾	

This is where you assign properties to one of the buttons on the generic switchboard page. In the first box, you enter the text that will be the label for a button. In the second box, you enter the command Access should run when the button is clicked. In the third box, you enter any information (parameters) required by the command. This information will be stored in the Switchboard Items table.

10 Type **Forms** in the **Text** box.

The second box already contains the **Go to Switchboard** command, which is what you want for this example.

11 In the **Switchboard** box, display the list of switchboard pages, click **Forms**, and then click **OK**.

The label and list of items in the third box vary depending on the command chosen in the second box.

12 Click **New** again, type **Reports** in the **Text** box, select **Reports** from the **Switchboard** drop-down list, and click **OK**.

13 Click **New** again, and type **Close Switchboard**.

You want the switchboard to close when this button is clicked. To do this, you will use a macro.

14 Display the list of commands in the **Command** box, and click **Run Macro**.

The label for the third box changes to **Macro**.

15 Display the list of macros, scroll down, click **Switchboard.closeSB**, and then click **OK** to close the dialog box and save the changes.

Tip

The **Switchboard.closeSB** macro does not come with Access; it was written specifically for this exercise. If you want, you can review this macro, and several others in the GardenCo database, by clicking **Macros** on the **Objects** bar and then opening a macro in Design view.

You have specified that Access should open the macro group called *Switchboard* and start running the macro at the line named *closeSB*.

16 Click **New** again, type **Close Database**, and select the **Exit Application** command. This command does not require a parameter, so click **OK** to close the dialog box and save the changes.

The **Edit Switchboard Page** dialog box now looks like this:

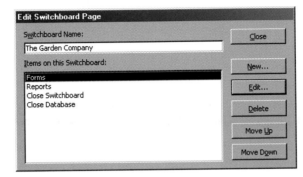

17 Click **Close** to return to **Switchboard Manager**.

18 Click **Forms**, and then click **Edit**.

19 Add five new buttons with the following properties:

Text	Command	Third Box
Edit/Enter Categories	Open Form in Edit Mode	Categories
Edit/Enter Orders	Open Form in Edit Mode	Orders
Edit/Enter Products	Open Form in Edit Mode	Products
Edit/Enter Suppliers	Open Form in Edit Mode	Suppliers
Return	Go to Switchboard	The Garden Company

20 Click **Close** to return to **Switchboard Manager**.

21 Select **Reports**, click **Edit**, and add five buttons with these properties:

Text	Command	Third Box
Preview/Print Catalog	Open Report	Catalog
Preview/Print Customer Labels	Open Report	Customer Labels
Preview/Print Invoices	Open Report	Invoice
Preview/Print Products	Open Report	Alphabetical List of Products
Return	Go to Switchboard	The Garden Company

22 Click **Close** twice to close **Switchboard Manager**.

23 Now click **Forms** on the **Objects** bar, and double-click **Switchboard**.

Your new switchboard opens in Form view, where it looks like this:

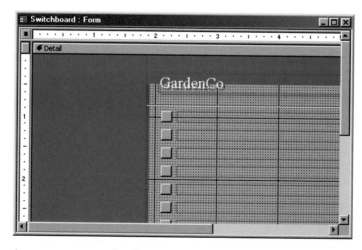

24 Click **Forms**, and then click **Edit/Enter Categories** to look at the Categories form. When you are finished, close the form.

25 Click **Return** to return to the first-level switchboard window.

View

26 Click the **View** button to view the switchboard in Design view, as shown here:

As you can see, the form has eight buttons and no label text.

27 Click the first button, press F4 to open the **Properties** dialog box, click the **Format** tab, and look at the **Visible** property.

The first button and label are both set to **Yes**.

28 Click the rest of the buttons on the form, one at a time.

The rest of the buttons are set to **No** (not visible). When the form is displayed in Form view, it reads the Switchboard Items table and uses the data there to set the **Visible** property of the buttons and labels.

29 Click the **Event** tab, and then look at the **On Click** event for the buttons and labels.

Each event is associated with a variable. In the Switchboard Items table, created by the **Switchboard Manager** to store information about the switchboard's buttons, this variable is in turn associated with the command and parameters (if any) you specified. When you click a button in Form view, Access checks the **On Click** property, looks up the variable in the Switchboard Items table, and carries out the associated command.

30 Close the **Switchboard** form, and then close the database.

Tip

You can reopen **Switchboard Manager** to add more pages or commands, and you can open the Switchboard form in Design view to add graphics or other objects. Because everything needed to produce the working switchboard is contained in the Switchboard form and its underlying Switchboard Items table, you can copy or import the form and the table to any other database in which you might want a similar switchboard, modifying them as needed with **Switchboard Manager**.

Creating a Splash Screen

Ac2002e-2-1

Approved Courseware

Many applications display a **splash screen** upon starting. This screen is sometimes an animation or piece of artwork, sometimes an advertisement for the company that created the database application, and occasionally a useful dialog box that provides information or instructions. The hidden purpose of a splash screen is often to divert the user's attention while the rest of the application loads into the computer's memory. The Access applications that you create probably won't take a long time to load, but a splash screen can still be useful.

Because the splash screen is the first thing users see each time they open the application, you can use it to remind them of important points, such as how to get help or how to contact you. This is also a good place to display a randomly selected tip—as long as the tip is more useful than irritating. To avoid having users get annoyed at anything that stands between them and the use of your application, you should always provide the option of not having the splash screen appear in the future.

A splash screen that users can interact with in some manner—by clicking buttons or entering text—is a specialized type of dialog box. You create this type of dialog box in Access by adding controls to a form.

193

GardenCo
tgc_logo1
Paragraphs

In this exercise you will create a simple splash screen for the GardenCo database. The working folder for this exercise is *SBS\Access\Switchbrd\Splash*. Follow these steps:

1 Open the **GardenCo** database located in the working folder.

2 On the **Objects** bar, click **Forms**, and then double-click **Create form in Design view**.

Save

3 Click the **Save** button, name the form **Splash**, and click **OK**.

4 If the **Properties** dialog box is not already displayed, press F4.

The **Form** object should already be selected in the list at the top of the dialog box.

5 Click the **Format** tab, and set the following properties:

Property	Setting
Scroll Bars	Neither
Record Selectors	No
Navigation Buttons	No
Dividing Lines	No
Auto Center	Yes
Border Style	None
Control Box	No
Min Max Buttons	None
Close Button	No
Width	5.5"

Toolbox

6 If the toolbox is not displayed, click the **Toolbox** button.

You will use the tools in the toolbox to create a box to hold The Garden Company's logo.

Rectangle

7 In the toolbox, click the **Rectangle** tool, and then click anywhere in the **Detail** section.

A small rectangle appears where you clicked.

8 On the **Format** tab of the **Properties** dialog box, set the following properties for the rectangle:

Property	Setting
Left	0
Top	0
Width	5.5"
Height	3.25"
Back Style	Normal
Special Effect	Flat
Border Style	Solid
Border Color	32768
Border Width	6 pt

Image

9   In the toolbox, click the **Image** tool, and then click somewhere near the top of the rectangle.

Access inserts an image frame and displays the **Insert Picture** dialog box.

10   Change **Files of type** to **Graphics Interchange Format**, and in the *SBS\Access\Switchbrd\Splash* folder, double-click **tgc_logo1**.

Access inserts The Garden Company's logo in the image control.

11   Drag the image to center the logo along the top of the form, just below the border, like this:

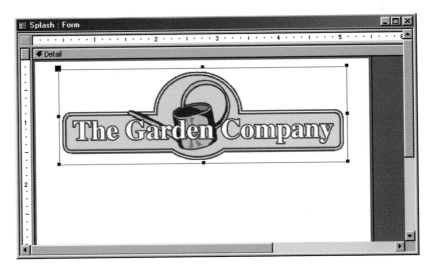

Label

12 Click the **Label** tool in the toolbox, and then click below the left corner of the logo to insert a label. Type **Placeholder** in the label, and press [Enter].

13 Align the left edge of the label with the left edge of the logo, and set the top just below the bottom of the logo.

14 Drag the handle at the bottom right corner of the label down and to the right until the label is as wide as the logo and about an inch high.

15 Open any text editor, such as Microsoft Notepad, browse to the *SBS\Access \Switchbrd\Splash* folder, and double-click **Paragraphs**. Copy the two paragraphs in that file, and then paste them in the label, replacing the *Placeholder* text.

Your form now looks like this:

Check Box

16 Click the **Check Box** tool, and click about a quarter inch below the label, aligned with its left edge, to insert a check box.

17 In the **Properties** dialog box, click the **Other** tab, and name the control **chkHideSplash**. Then on the **Data** tab, set the **Default Value** property to **0** (meaning *No*).

18 Click the label associated with the check box, and on the **Format** tab, type **Don't show this screen again** as its **Caption** property.

19 With the label still selected, click the **Format** menu, select **Size**, and then click **To Fit**.

The entire caption is now displayed.

Control
Wizards

20 If the **Control Wizards** button is not active in the toolbox, click it.

Command
Button

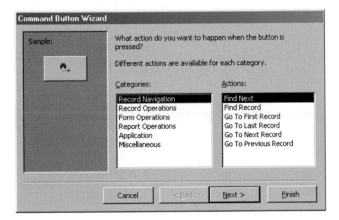

21 Click the **Command Button** tool, and insert a command button near the right edge of the form, opposite the check box.

Access adds a button to the form and starts the **Command Button Wizard**, whose first page looks like this:

Command Button Wizard

Sample:

What action do you want to happen when the button is pressed?

Different actions are available for each category.

Categories:

Record Navigation
Record Operations
Form Operations
Report Operations
Application
Miscellaneous

Actions:

Find Next
Find Record
Go To First Record
Go To Last Record
Go To Next Record
Go To Previous Record

Cancel   < Back   Next >   Finish

22 In the **Categories** list, click **Form Operations**.

23 In the **Actions** list, click **Close Form**, and click **Next**.

24 Click **Text**, change the caption text to **OK**, and then click **Next**.

25 Name the button **OK**, and click **Finish**.

Your form now looks like this.

26 Save the design, and then switch to Form view.

The form has a gray border because it doesn't quite fill the design grid.

27 Return to Design view, and drag the borders of the gray grid horizontally and vertically so that the grid disappears behind the form.

Tip

You can also close the Splash form and reopen it in Form view to resize the design grid to fit the form.

Here's how the form looks in Form view:

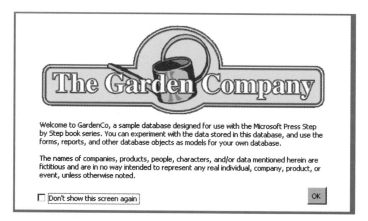

28 Save your changes, and then switch back to Form view.

29 Click **OK** on the form to close the splash screen.

30 Close the database.

Setting Startup Options

Ac2002e-2-2

Approved Courseware

You can start Access and open a database in a variety of ways. Here are the most common ways:

- Click **Start**, point to **Programs**, and click **Microsoft Access**.
- Double-click a shortcut to **MSACCESS**.
- Double-click a shortcut to a database file.
- Double-click a database file name in Windows Explorer.

With the first two methods, Access starts, displaying a blank window from which a new database can be created or an existing one opened. With the last two methods, Access starts, and then it opens the specified database.

Tip

When you start a program by clicking a command on the **Start** button's **Programs** submenu, you are in fact clicking a shortcut. The entire **Start** menu is a hierarchical arrangement of shortcuts.

If your database will be used by inexperienced users, you might want to control which features are available when a database opens. Access provides several ways to do this. If you want users to be able to open only one database, you can add one or more options to the shortcut used to start Access. These options can open a specific database, run macros, and perform other tasks. A more common way to control the user's environment is to set startup options in each database. You can use startup options to control the menus and toolbars available to the user, the form displayed (such as a splash screen or switchboard), and other features. The startup form can include macros and VBA procedures that run automatically to set other conditions.

Tip

This exercise uses custom toolbars and menus that were created specially for the sample database. For information about how to create this type of item, search for *toolbar* in Access online Help. Also, the Orders form in this exercise uses several custom macros. You can review these macros by clicking **Macros** on the **Objects** bar and then opening **orderForm** in Design view. The exercise also uses VBA code attached to the splash screen. You can review this code by selecting the Splash form and then clicking the **Code** button on the Access window's toolbar.

GardenCo

In this exercise, you will set startup options that tie together a splash screen, a switchboard, and some custom menus to create a version of the GardenCo database that is appropriate for inexperienced users. The goal is to remove all commands and objects that could be confusing or that might allow users to accidentally damage a table, form, query, or other object. The working folder for this exercise is *SBS\Access \Switchbrd\Startup*. Follow these steps:

1 Open the **GardenCo** database located in the working folder.

2 On the **Tools** menu, click **Startup** to display the dialog box shown on the next page.

When Access opens a database, it looks at these settings and configures the database accordingly.

3 With the insertion point in the **Application Title** box, type **The Garden Company**, and press Tab.

The text you just entered will be displayed in the Access title bar, replacing the usual *Microsoft Access* title.

4 Click the **...** button at the end of the **Application Icon** box, and browse to *SBS\Access\Switchbrd\Startup*. Click **icon_tgc**, and then click **OK** to enter it as the application icon.

This icon will appear in the left corner of the title bar, followed by *The Garden Company*.

Troubleshooting

The full path to the icon is recorded. As long as you don't move the icon, you can move the database to another folder on the same computer, and Access will still find the icon. If you plan to move the database to a different computer, you should instead use the icon's **Universal Naming Convention (UNC)** path.

5 Click the arrow at the right end of the **Menu Bar** box, and then select **gcMenuMain**.

This is a menu bar created specifically for this exercise. The alternative, **(default)**, is the standard menu bar.

6 In the **Display Form/Page** box, display the list of forms, and select **Splash**.

This database's splash screen will be displayed each time the database is opened.

7 Clear the **Display Database Window** check box, but leave **Display Status Bar** checked.

Tip

For experienced users, the database window is like a home page: it is where everything starts. But having this window available could be confusing for someone whose only job is entering orders and could be disastrous if inexperienced people make changes to critical data.

8   Leave the **Shortcut Menu Bar** box set to **(default)**.

9   Clear both the **Allow Built-in Toolbars** and the **Allow Toolbar/Menu Changes** check boxes.

Clearing these check boxes prevents any of the built-in toolbars from being displayed, and prevents the user from making changes to custom toolbars and menus.

10   For the time being, leave **Use Access Special Keys** selected.

If this option is selected, several special key combinations are available. You will use $\boxed{\text{Ctrl}}+\boxed{\text{F11}}$ to toggle the standard menu on while you are testing the database.

The dialog box now looks like this:

11   Click **OK** to close the **Startup** dialog box.

Most startup options don't go into affect until you close and restart the database. The only changes you should see now are the icon and the name in the Access window's title bar.

12   Close and reopen the **GardenCo** database.

The startup options go into effect: you see the new title bar, the custom menu bar, and the splash screen.

13   On the splash screen, click **OK**.

Troubleshooting

> If you get an error when you click **OK** on the splash screen, click the **Reset** button. The Visual Basic Editor will be displayed. Click **References** on the **Tools** menu, scroll down, click **Microsoft DAO 3.6 Object Library**, and click **OK**. Then repeat your tests.

The VBA code attached to the Splash form in the GardenCo database causes the switchboard to be displayed.

14 On the switchboard, click **Forms**, and then click **Edit/Enter Orders** on the second-level switchboard page.

The Orders form and its associated custom toolbar appear, as shown here:

15 On the **View** menu, click **Customers**.

The Customers form opens on top of the Orders form, and because your custom toolbar is associated only with the Orders form, it disappears.

16 Close the **Customers** form.

The custom toolbar reappears.

17 Right-click the **Orders** form.

The standard shortcut menu appears.

Tip

Being able to display the shortcut menu could be a problem if you don't want to give users the means to alter the form's design. You could solve this problem by creating a custom shortcut menu and specifying it in the form's properties.

18 Press `Esc` to close the menu, and then close the **Orders** form.

19 Press `Ctrl`+`F11`.

The standard menu bar replaces the custom one. (If you missed that change, you can press `Ctrl`+`F11` again to toggle between the standard menu bar and the custom one.)

Tip

Toggling between the menu bars is possible because you did not clear the **Use Access Special Keys** check box in the **Startup** dialog box. It is handy to have this option available while you are developing a database, but you might want to disable it when the database is ready to put into service.

20 Press `F11`.

This Access Special Key displays the database window—another reason why the Access Special Keys probably should not be available to users.

21 Close the database window, which closes the GardenCo database.

22 While holding down the `Shift` key, open **GardenCo** again, using any method.

Holding down the `Shift` key while you start the database bypasses all of the startup options, so the database starts the same way it did before you set these options.

Tip

The only way to prevent a user from bypassing your startup options is to write and run a VBA procedure that creates the **AllowByPassKey** property and sets it to **False**. There is no way to set this property through Access. For information about how to do this, search for *AllowByPassKey* in the Help file available when you are working in the Visual Basic Editor.

23 Close the **GardenCo** database.

Keeping Your Application Healthy

In the day-to-day use of an Access database—adding and deleting records, modifying forms and reports, and so on—various problems can develop. This is especially true if the database is stored on a local area network and is accessed by multiple users. Access monitors the health of database files as you open and work with them. If it sees a problem developing, it attempts to fix it. If Access can't fix a problem, it usually displays a message suggesting that you take some action. But Access doesn't always spot problems before they impact the database, and sometimes database performance seems to slow down or become erratic. Even if no serious errors creep in, simply using a database causes its internal structure to become fragmented, resulting in a bloated file and inefficient use of disk space.

You don't have to wait for Access to spot a problem. There are various things you can do to help keep your database healthy and running smoothly. Your first line of defense against damage or corruption in any kind of file is the maintenance of backups. Database files rapidly become too large to conveniently back up to floppy disk, but you have many other options: you can copy the file to another computer on the network, send it as an e-mail attachment to another location, use a tape backup, burn a CD-ROM, or copy it to some other removable media.

Access provides several utilities that you can use to keep your database running smoothly. The following list describes a few of these utilities:

- **Compact and Repair Database**. Compacting the database rearranges how the file is stored on your hard disk, which optimizes performance. The repair portion of this utility attempts to repair corruption in tables, forms, reports, and modules.

- **Performance Analyzer**. This utility analyzes the objects in your database and offers feedback divided into three categories: ideas, suggestions, and recommendations. If you would like to follow through on any of the suggestions or recommendations, you can click a button to have Access optimize the file.

- **Documenter**. This tool, which is part of the **Performance Analyzer**, produces a detailed report that can be saved and printed. It includes enough information to rebuild the database structure if that were ever necessary.

- **Detect and Repair**. This command, which appears on the **Help** menu, is not a command to be clicked casually. Running this utility might make changes to files and registry settings that affect all Office programs.

GardenCo

In this exercise, you will compact and repair the GardenCo database. You will then run the **Performance Analyzer** and **Documenter**. The working folder for this exercise is *SBS\Access\Switchbrd\Health*. Follow these steps:

1 Open the **GardenCo** database in the working folder.

2 On the **File** menu, click **Database Properties** to open this dialog box:

![GardenCo Properties dialog box showing the Summary tab with fields: Title GardenCo, Subject blank, Author Catherine Turner, Manager Catherine Turner, Company The Garden Company, Category blank, Keywords blank, Comments blank, Hyperlink base blank]

This dialog box contains five tabs that display interesting information about your database.

3 Click the **General** tab, and note the size of the database.

4 Click **OK** to close the dialog box.

5 On the **Tools** menu, point to **Database Utilities**, and then click **Compact and Repair Database**.

The utility takes only a few seconds to run, and you will see no difference in the appearance of the database.

Troubleshooting

If you don't have enough space on your hard disk to store a temporary copy of the database, if you don't have appropriate permissions, or if someone else on your network also has the database open, **Compact and Repair Database** will not run properly.

6 Display the **Database Properties** dialog box again, and compare the current size to its previous size.

You can expect a 10 to 25 percent reduction in the size of the database if you have been using it for a while.

Tip

It is a good idea to compact and repair the database often. You can have Access do this automatically each time the database is closed, by clicking **Options** on the **Tools** menu, selecting the **Compact on Close** option on the **General** tab of the **Options** dialog box, and clicking **OK**.

7 Click **OK** to close the **Database Properties** dialog box.

8 On the **Tools** menu, point to **Analyze**, and then click **Performance**.

This **Performance Analyzer** dialog box is displayed:

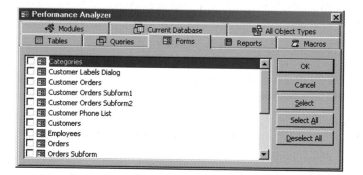

This dialog box contains a tab for each type of object that can be analyzed and a tab that displays objects of all types.

9 Click the **All Object Types** tab.

10 Click **Select All**, and then click **OK** to start the analyzer.

You will see quite a bit of action on your screen as the analyzer opens and closes windows. (If the splash screen is open, the analyzer skips it.) When it finishes, the analyzer displays its results in this dialog box:

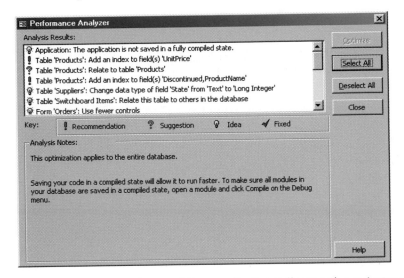

An icon in the left column of the results list indicates the category of each entry: **Recommendation**, **Suggestion**, **Idea**, and **Fixed**. (When you first run the **Performance Analyzer**, there will be no **Fixed** entries in the list.) Clicking an entry displays information about it in the **Analysis Notes** section.

11 Scroll through the list, click each entry in turn, and read through all the analysis notes.

Most of the suggestions are valid, though some, such as the one to change the data type of the PostalCode field to **Long Integer**, are not appropriate for this database.

12 Click one of the entries that recommends adding an index to one or more fields, and then click the **Optimize** button.

The index is added (you can check the table, if you want), and the category of the item is changed from **Recommendation** to **Fixed**.

13 Close the **Performance Analyzer** dialog box.

14 On the **Tools** menu, point to **Analyze**, and then click **Documenter** to open the dialog box shown on the next page.

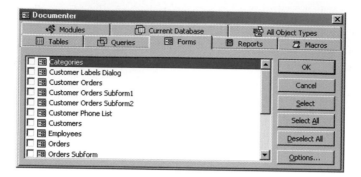

The **Documenter** dialog box is similar to the **Performance Analyzer** dialog box, in that it contains a tab for each object type that it can document. You can select individual objects on one or more tabs, or click **All Object Types** and make your selections.

15 Click the **Tables** tab, and then click the **Options** button.

The **Options** dialog box offers print options associated with the current tab, as shown here:

The options differ for each tab, but all are similar to these, in that they allow you to specify what to include in the documentation for each type of object.

16 Click **Cancel** to close the dialog box.

17 Click the **All Object Types** tab.

18 Click **Select All**, and then click **OK** to start the documentation process.

As the documenter runs, objects are opened and closed, and the status bar displays the progress through the objects. When the process finishes, a report is displayed in Print Preview. A typical page is shown here:

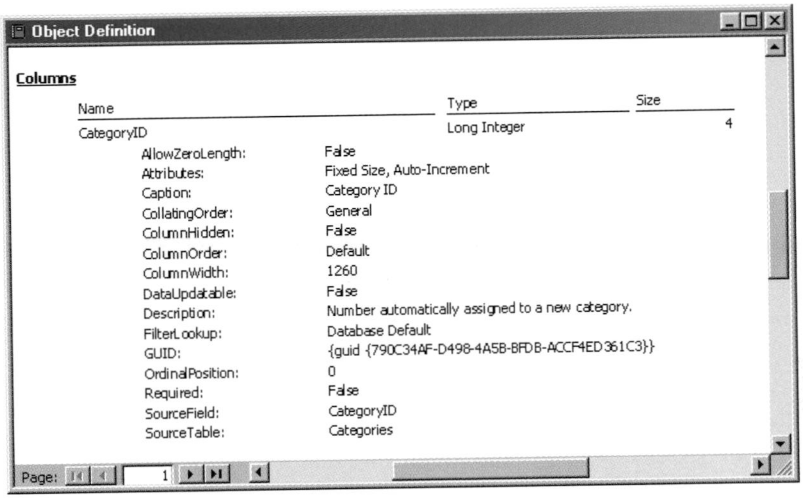

This report can run to hundreds of pages, so you probably don't want to click the **Print** button right now. However, it is a good idea to save a report such as this for your own databases, in case you ever need to reconstruct them.

Tip

You can't save the report generated by the documenter, but you can export it. On the **File** menu, click **Export**, and then select a format. The best format is probably RTF, which can be opened in Microsoft Word.

19 Close the report, and then close the **GardenCo** database.

20 If you are not continuing on to the next chapter, quit Access.

Update SBS Briefcase ? ✕

The following files need to be updated. To change the update action, use the right mouse button to click the file you want to change.

GardenCo

In Briefcase
Modified
3/22/01 4:23 PM

⇒
Replace

In C:\Sbs\Access\S...
Unmodified
3/22/01 4:18 PM

Update   Cancel

Synchronize different
replicas of a database,
page 218

Set Database Password ? ✕

Password:

Verify:

OK
Cancel

Split a database to
protect underlying data,
page 223

Database Splitter

This wizard moves tables from your current database to a new back-end database. In multi-user environments, this reduces network traffic, and allows continuous front-end development without affecting data or interrupting users.

It could be a long process. Make a backup copy of your database before splitting it.

Would you like to split the database now?

Split Database

Require a
password,
page 214

User and Group Permissions ? ✕

Permissions | Change Owner

User/Group Name:

Admin
AmyA
CatherineT
KimY
LaniC
MichaelE
MikeG

Object Name:

Customer Phone List
Customer Orders
Customer Orders Subform1
Customer Orders Subform2
Customer Labels Dialog
Switchboard
Splash

List: ◉ Users ○ Groups   Object Type: Form

Permissions

☐ Open/Run   ☐ Read Data
☐ Read Design   ☐ Update Data
☐ Modify Design   ☐ Insert Data
☐ Administer   ☐ Delete Data

Current User: CatherineT

OK   Cancel   Apply

Assign permissions to
members of workgroups,
page 232

Chapter 9
Keeping Your Information Secure

After completing this chapter, you will be able to:

✔ Encrypt and decrypt a database.

✔ Control who can open a database and what they can change.

✔ Distribute copies of a database and merge changes into a master copy.

✔ Create and maintain workgroups for multi-user databases.

✔ Prevent changes to a database.

The need for **database security** is an unfortunate fact of life. As with your house, car, office, or briefcase, the level of security required by your database depends on the value of what you have and whether you are trying to protect it from curious eyes, accidental damage, malicious destruction, or theft.

The security of a company's business information can be critical to its survival. For example, The Garden Company's owners might not be too concerned if a person gained unauthorized access to their products list, but they would be very concerned if a competitor managed to see—or worse, steal—their customer list. And it would be a disaster if someone destroyed their critical order information.

Your goal as a database developer is to provide adequate protection without imposing unnecessary restrictions on the people who should have access to your database. The type of security required to protect a database depends to a large extent on how many people are using it and where it is stored. If your database is never opened by more than one person at a time, you don't have to worry about the potential for corruption if several people try to update the same information at the same time. If many people access the database to work with different types of information, you will want to consider setting up workgroups and assigning permissions to restrict the information each group can see and the actions they can perform. If your database is sold as part of an application, you will want to take steps to prevent it from being misused in any way.

In this chapter, you will explore various ways to protect data from accidental or intentional corruption and to make it difficult for curious eyes to see private information. The sample files for the exercises in this chapter can be found in the following subfolders of the *SBS\Access\Secure* folder: *Encrypt, Password, Share, Replicate, Split, Multi, Maintain, VBA,* and *MDE.*

Hiding Database Content from Prying Eyes

Ac2002e-7-3

Approved Courseware

A database created with Microsoft Access is a **binary file**, meaning that it is composed of mostly unreadable characters. If you open it in a word processor or a text editor, at first glance it looks like gibberish. However, if you poke around in the file long enough, you will discover quite a bit of information in plain text. Most likely, not enough information is exposed to allow someone to steal anything valuable. But if you are concerned that someone might scan your database file with a utility that looks for key words, you can **encrypt** the file to make it really unreadable.

Encrypting a file doesn't prevent it from being opened and viewed in Access. It does not add password protection or any other kind of security. But it does keep people who don't have a copy of Access from being able to read and perhaps make sense of the data in your file. The only difference you may see when opening an encrypted database in Access is that some tasks may take slightly longer. If this is an issue, you will want to **decrypt** it to work with it.

GardenCo

In this exercise, you will encrypt and decrypt the GardenCo database. This is not just an idle exercise. If you ever need to send your database to someone via e-mail or on a physical disk, encrypting it will protect it while it is in transit. Once the file arrives safely, it can be decrypted to restore the database to its original state. The working folder for this exercise is *SBS\Access\Secure\Encrypt.* Follow these steps:

1 Open the **GardenCo** database located in the working folder.

2 On the **Tools** menu, point to **Security,** and then click **Encrypt/Decrypt Database** to open the **Encrypt Database As** dialog box.

3 In the *SBS\Access\Secure\Encrypt* folder, type **GardenCo_Encrypt** as the name of the encrypted file you want to create, and click **Save.**

Access creates an encrypted version of the database but leaves you working in the original GardenCo database. You could have saved the encrypted database with the same name (you would be warned that you were overwriting an existing file), but this way you can compare the two versions.

4 Close the database, start a text editor such as Microsoft Notepad or Helios TextPad, and open the **GardenCo** database.

Here is a small section of the GardenCo database in a text editor:

```
TextPad - [C:\SBS\Access\Secure\Encrypt\GardenCo.mdb]
File  Edit  Search  View  Tools  Configure  Window  Help

1AD60:  6F 72 69 65 73 2E 43 61   74 65 67 6F 72 79 4E 61   ories.Cate
1AD70:  6D 65 36 00 11 00 11 00   11 00 0D 00 04 00 67 08   me6........
1AD80:  00 3E 00 00 80 06 00 00   00 00 00 00 00 00 00 01   .>...........
1AD90:  16 00 00 80 00 00 00 00   00 00 00 00 FF FE 50 72   ..........Pr
1ADA0:  6F 64 75 63 74 73 2E 50   72 6F 64 75 63 74 4E 61   oducts.Prc
1ADB0:  6D 65 33 00 11 00 11 00   11 00 0D 00 04 00 67 08   me3........
1ADC0:  00 3E 00 00 80 05 00 00   00 00 00 00 00 00 00 02   .>...........
1ADD0:  50 00 72 00 6F 00 64 00   75 00 63 00 74 00 73 00   P.r.o.d.u.
1ADE0:  21 00 21 00 21 00 11 00   0D 00 04 00 0F 08 00 3E   !.!.!......>
1ADF0:  00 00 80 05 00 00 00 00   00 00 00 00 01 43 00      .............C.
1AE00:  61 00 74 00 65 00 67 00   6F 00 72 00 69 00 65 00   a.t.e.g.o.
1AE10:  73 00 25 00 25 00 25 00   11 00 0D 00 04 00 0F 08   s.%.%.%...
1AE20:  00 3E 00 00 80 FF 00 00   00 00 00 00 00 00 00 01   .>...Iÿ...
1AE30:  11 00 11 00 11 00 11 00   0D 00 04 00 07 08 00 3E   ...........
1AE40:  00 00 80 00 00 00 00 00   00 00 00 00 00 01 11 00   ...I....
1AE50:  11 00 11 00 11 00 0D 00   04 00 47 08 00 3D 00 00   .........=..
1AE60:  80 05 00 00 00 00 00 00   00 00 01 53 00 77 00 00   I.......S.w..
1AE70:  69 00 74 00 63 00 68 00   62 00 6F 00 61 00 72 00   i.t.c.h.b.
1AE80:  64 00 20 00 49 00 74 00   65 00 6D 00 73 00 33 00   d. .I.te.
1AE90:  33 00 33 00 11 00 0D 00   04 00 0F 08 00 3D 00 00   3.3.......=..
1AEA0:  80 03 09 00 00 00 00 00   00 00 00 00 00 00 00 00   I..........
1AEB0:  04 00 00 00 00 00 00 00   00 00 00 00 00 00 00 00   ............

                                          0    0   Read Ovr Block Sync  Caps
```

5   Close the **GardenCo** database, and then open **GardenCo_Encrypt** in the same text editor. Here is the same section of the database, in the encrypted version:

```
TextPad - [C:\SBS\Access\Secure\Encrypt\GardenCo_Encrypt.mdb]
File  Edit  Search  View  Tools  Configure  Window  Help

1AD60:  E8 92 F5 8B D8 0A FE B0   71 05 CD 68 E4 B1 1E 71   è'õ‹Ø.þ°q.
1AD70:  68 02 87 6B 37 E1 87 38   9F 4E B4 E0 94 77 B9 10   h.‡k7á‡8ƒN
1AD80:  23 21 69 19 B0 C0 E1 EA   A8 4F C4 1D 41 33 F5 88   #!i.°Àáê¨O
1AD90:  0C 5C 2C D3 D5 62 9E 5A   3C 07 6A E0 2B 72 E5 68   .\,ÓÕbžZ<.
1ADA0:  4F 06 34 55 1D 14 2E BE   A5 A3 D9 7A 61 81 97 51   O.4U...¾¥£
1ADB0:  D7 3E 04 3B 82 96 DC 3D   42 7C 58 6D 8A 45 E0 D6   ×>.;‚–Ü=B|
1ADC0:  2C 64 3C 33 85 DA 48 62   FF 7E 94 48 7B EE DD 66   ,d<3…ÚHbÿ~
1ADD0:  DC B6 8C 52 61 73 A7 6A   A8 11 F5 80 A2 64         Ü¶ŒRas§j¨.
1ADE0:  00 EB 36 81 F8 07 C3 A6   F7 14 A7 04 82 A4 2F A6   .ë6.ø.Ã¦÷
1ADF0:  A8 FB 69 66 99 A6 90 06   D6 F3 F3 D6 E2 95 53 3D   ¨ûif™¦..Ö
1AE00:  17 F5 39 E5 AA 43 02 CD   8D 15 7D 44 F7 02 5A 39   .õ9åªC.Í.
1AE10:  5A E7 CF 5C E8 BD 6C E0   EF F5 D4 72 A6 AE 86 C3   ZçÏ\è½là
1AE20:  4A 43 0B 8D E8 90 20 7D   EC A8 FE 50 97 8B 36 00   JC.è. }ì¨
1AE30:  89 DB CD 43 89 19 A8 AB   C3 EF 54 83 5E 64 5E B3   ‰ÛÍC‰.¨«
1AE40:  09 81 A3 DF A2 AA C7 40   4B AC A4 F0 DB 4A 7E 98   .£ß¢ªÇ@K
1AE50:  56 C2 46 33 38 5C 17 D3   40 06 36 24 6F 13 FD 1F   VÂF38\.Ó
1AE60:  6A EF 1C 2C AC 41 D7 18   DA 16 B6 A1 6F 12 B5 C0   jï.,¬A×.
1AE70:  A5 EC 3B EC CD E1 31 CA   EB B6 3C 8B 20 2D 18 F0   ¥ì;ìÍá1Ê
1AE80:  C8 5F 1A 00 1C C7 9B 35   49 D8 58 C0 0B 0B A6 4F   È_...Ç›5I
1AE90:  69 68 F6 D2 66 C1 4F 73   C0 E5 EA DF E2 C6 AE 57   ihöÒfÁOsÀ
1AEA0:  44 14 81 84 92 03 FF 21   D4 1B 7E 46 5D 6B 67 2D   D..„'.ÿ!Ô
1AEB0:  1B 96 0B 94 2A DB 2F DE   7D 36 A9 CA B9 0F C4 64   .–.”*Û/Þ}6

                                          0    0   Read Ovr Block Sync  Caps
```

You can see that it would be difficult to make much sense of the original file, but the encrypted version is even less meaningful.

6   Close the text editor.

7 In Access, open the **GardenCo_Encrypt** file located in the *SBS\Access \Secure\Encrypt* folder.

The encrypted file looks identical to the original.

Tip

Encrypting a database compresses it, but the amount of **compression** is minimal. Using the Compact and Repair utility provides more compaction. Using a third-party compression program such as WinZip provides far more compression than either of the other methods and has the added benefit of effectively encrypting the database.

8 To decrypt the database, first close the **GardenCo_Encrypt** database.

9 On the **Tools** menu, point to **Security**, and click **Encrypt/Decrypt Database**.

In the **Encrypt/Decrypt Database** dialog box, browse to the *SBS\Access \Secure\Encrypt* folder, select **GardenCo_Encrypt**, and click **OK**.

The **Decrypt Database As** dialog box opens.

10 Type **GardenCo_Decrypt** in the **File name** box, and click **Save**.

11 Quit Access.

12 Start Microsoft Windows Explorer, browse to the *SBS\Access\Secure \Encrypt* folder, and compare the size of the three files.

Decrypting a database doesn't uncompress it, so usually the difference in size between the encrypted file and the decrypted file, if any, is minimal.

13 Close Windows Explorer.

Controlling Who Can Open Your Database

Ac2002e-7-5

Approved Courseware

You can prevent unauthorized users from opening a database by assigning it a **password**. Anyone attempting to open the database will then be asked for the password. If they enter it correctly, they will have full access to the database; if they don't, the database won't open.

Tip

You can use anything as a password, as long as you remember these rules. Passwords are case-sensitive and can range from 1 to 20 characters. You can include letters, accented characters, numbers, spaces, and most symbols. A password can't start with a space, and it can't include any of the following: \ [ ] : | < > + = ; , . ? *. A good password should not be a word found in a dictionary, and it should include uppercase and lowercase letters, and punctuation or numbers.

A database password is easy to set, and it is better than no protection at all in that it keeps most honest people out of the database. However, many inexpensive password recovery utilities are available, theoretically to help people recover a lost password. Anyone can buy one of these utilities and "recover" the password to your database. Also, the same password works for all users, and nothing prevents one person from giving the password to many other people. As a result, simple password protection is most appropriate for a single-user database. If your database is on a **network server** and can be opened by more than one person at a time (multi-user), you should consider setting up a workgroup and assigning a security account password.

When setting or removing a password, you must open a database for **exclusive use**, meaning that nobody else can have the database open. This won't be a problem for the database used in the exercise, but if you want to set or remove a password for a real database that is on a network, you will need to make sure nobody else is using it.

GardenCo

In this exercise, you will assign a password to the GardenCo database. You start this exercise with Access and all databases closed. The working folder for this exercise is *SBS\Access\Secure\Password*. Follow these steps:

1   Start Access.

Open

2   On the Access toolbar, click the **Open** button to display the **Open** dialog box.

3   Browse to the *SBS\Access\Secure\Password folder*, select **GardenCo**, and then click the **Open** button's down arrow to display the list of options shown in the lower right corner of this screen:

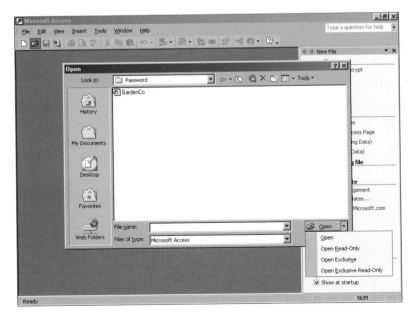

4   Click **Open Exclusive**.

5 On the **Tools** menu, point to **Security**, and click **Set Database Password**. This **Set Database Password** dialog box appears:

6 Type **Nos!Len**, and press `Tab` to move the insertion point to the **Verify** box.

7 Type **Nos!Len** again, and click **OK** to assign the password to the database.

Tip

To remove the password, repeat steps 2 through 4 to open the database exclusively (you will have to enter the password), point to **Security** on the **Tools** menu, and then click **Unset Database Password**. Type the password in the dialog box that appears, and press `Enter`. Access removes the password, and anyone can then open the database.

8 Close and reopen the database.

This dialog box appears:

9 Type something other than the correct password, and click **OK**.

Access warns you that the password is not valid.

10 Click **OK** to close the message, type the correct password (**Nos!Len**), and then click **OK** again.

The database opens, and you can use it as you normally would.

11 Close the database again.

Sharing a Database

When a limited number of people are working on a local area network (LAN), **sharing a database** is easy. You simply place the database file in a folder that everyone can access, and then limit who can do what to the database by using the same **network security** you use to protect other information on the network. The number of people who can share a database in this manner depends on how many access it at the same time and what they want to do.

Access manages multiple users fairly well, but you will want to take precautions to prevent potential corruption of your database if multiple users attempt to update the same record at the same time. For example, if more than one employee at The Garden Company tried to change the same record in the Products table at exactly the same time, the results would be unpredictable if no precautions were in place. For small groups of people, you might want to implement **pessimistic locking**, which locks a record for the entire time it is being edited. For larger groups, you might want to implement **optimistic locking**, which locks a record only for the brief time that Access is saving the changes.

Important

When sharing a database on a LAN, each workstation on which the database will be opened must have a copy of Access installed.

GardenCo

In this exercise, you will explore several options that are designed to ensure that a database can be shared without any problem. The working folder for this exercise is *SBS\Access\Secure\Share*. Follow these steps:

1 Open the **GardenCo** database located in the working folder.

2 On the **Tools** menu, click **Options** to display the **Options** dialog box.

3 Click the **Advanced** tab to display these options:

4 In the **Default open mode** section, make sure that **Shared** is selected.

If the **Exclusive** option is selected, only one person at a time can open the database. If **Shared** is selected, more than one person can have the database open. (The **Shared** option can be overridden by selecting **Open Exclusive** in the **Open** dialog box.)

5 In the **Default record locking** section, click **Edited record**.

This action locks only the record that is being edited.

6 Make sure the **Open database using record-level locking** check box is selected.

7 Confirm that the following **properties** are still set to their default values, which should be appropriate for most situations:

Property	Setting
Refresh interval (sec)	60
Number of update retries	2
ODBC refresh interval (sec)	1500
Update retry interval (msec)	250

Tip

These properties work together to determine what happens when two users attempt to update a record at the same time. For more information about these properties, click the **Help** button (**?**) in the upper right corner of the dialog box, and then, with the question-mark pointer, click the box containing a setting.

8 Click **OK** to close the dialog box.

Now when someone is editing a record in this shared database, no one else will be able to make a change to that same record.

9 Close the database, and then quit Access.

Replicating a Database

Ac2002e-7-6

Approved Courseware

Database **replication** is the process of converting your database to a new version, called a **Design Master**, and then creating **replicas** of that master database that can be distributed to different people, who can then edit the data. Each person working on the database must have his or her own replica.

To create a replica of a database, you open the database, point to **Replication** on the **Tools** menu, and click **Create Replica**. Access closes the database and creates a master and a replica (named *Replica of <database>*). To create the next replica, you choose the **Create Replica** command again. The name of each replica is made unique by the addition of a number. After users have made changes to their replicas, the modified replicas are returned to you. You then use the other commands on the **Replication** submenu to synchronize the versions and resolve conflicts. For more information on this process, display the *replication* topic in Access online Help.

Database **synchronization** is the process of comparing the information between two members of the replica set (two versions of the master database) and merging any changes. If changes to the same field in the same record cause any conflicts, a winner and a loser are determined by priorities assigned to the members of the set. (For example, the replica that was edited by The Garden Company's sales manager would probably have a higher priority than the one edited by a sales clerk.) The winning change is applied to the master database, and the losing change is recorded as a conflict. After the master database has been compared to each replica, all changes have been recorded, and all conflicts have been resolved (you can use the **Conflict Resolution Wizard** to help with this process), all the replicas are updated with the current information from the Design Master and are sent back to the remote locations.

Tip

This process sounds complex, and it is. If you think you have a need for replication, you should look into acquiring Microsoft Office XP Developer (MOD). Several of the more difficult tasks are made much easier with the help of the **Replication Manager**, which is included with MOD.

The primary use of replication is in **data warehouses** where, for example, daily database updates might be sent from branch stores to be synchronized with a master database at night. Updated information about stock levels and specials would then be returned to the branch stores in the morning.

A full-scale exercise demonstrating database replication is too complex for the simple format of this book, but one fairly simple form of database replication can be useful to the average user. Microsoft Windows comes with **Briefcase**, which uses replication to keep files in sync when you work on different computers in different locations. For example, the owner of The Garden Company might want to take the GardenCo database home at night to work with it on her laptop.

GardenCo

In this exercise, you will replicate a database to Briefcase on the desktop of your computer. You start this exercise with Access and all databases closed. The working folder for this exercise is *SBS\Access\Secure\Replicate*. Assuming that you don't currently have a Briefcase folder on your computer, follow these steps:

New Briefcase

1 Right-click the desktop, point to **New**, and then click **Briefcase**.

A **New Briefcase** icon appears on your desktop.

Tip

If the Briefcase program isn't installed on your computer, you will need to install it by using the **Add/Remove Programs** icon in Control Panel.

2   Rename *New Briefcase* to **SBS Briefcase** by clicking the icon, clicking its name, replacing *New* with **SBS**, and pressing ⏎.

3   Start Windows Explorer, and browse to the *SBS\Access\Secure\Replicate* folder.

4   Reduce the size of the Windows Explorer window and arrange Explorer so that you can see both the GardenCo database file and SBS Briefcase on your desktop.

Tip

The Briefcase folder doesn't have to be on the desktop. You can follow these steps from within any folder selected in Windows Explorer to create a folder named *New Briefcase* in that folder.

5   Drag **GardenCo** to **SBS Briefcase**.

The **Updating Briefcase** alert box displays the message *Copying from 'Replicate' to 'SBS Briefcase'*, and after a moment, this message appears:

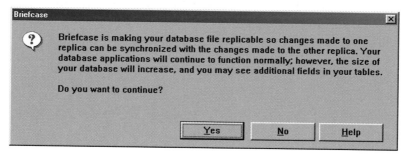

6   Click **Yes** to continue.

Access displays this dialog box:

7   Click **Yes** to have Briefcase make a backup copy of your database.

Another dialog box informs you that Briefcase has converted your database to a Design Master and placed a replica in the SBS Briefcase folder.

8   Click **OK** to accept the option to allow design changes only in the original copy of the database and to finish the replication process.

9   Click **Finish** to close the **Welcome to the Windows Briefcase** dialog box.

In Windows Explorer, notice the difference in size between the Design Master (GardenCo) and the backup (GardenCo.bak). Replication substantially increases the size of the database.

You now have the Design Master and a backup copy of the database in the working folder and a replica of the database in the SBS Briefcase folder. If you want to work on the database on a different computer that is not connected to this one via a LAN, you can copy the replica (or the entire SBS Briefcase folder) to removable media, such as a Zip disk or CD-ROM. (It's almost certainly too big for a floppy disk.)

Tip

If you want to work on a laptop connected via a LAN to the computer containing the GardenCo database, you can drag the database to the Briefcase on your laptop.

10 To simulate the editing and synchronizing process, start by double-clicking the **SBS Briefcase** folder to open it.

As you can see on the next page, the Briefcase is similar to a normal Explorer folder. Notice that the **Sync Copy In** column has a path to the Design Master, and the setting in the **Status** column is **Up-to-date**.

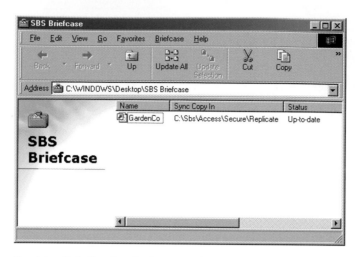

11 Double-click **GardenCo** to start Access and open the database.

A replication symbol appears to the left of each table, form, and other object name. Note that design changes can be made only in the original file.

12 On the **Objects** bar, click **Forms**, and then double-click **Products** to open the Products form.

13 Change the name of the first product from *Magic Lily* to **Mystic Lily**.

14 Close the form and the database.

15 Quit Access, and then close the SBS Briefcase window.

If you were working on a different computer, at this point you would be ready to synchronize the replica with the master database stored on the office computer.

16 Double-click **SBS Briefcase**.

The setting in the **Status** column has changed to **Needs updating**.

Tip

You changed the replica stored on the same computer as the master database, so rather than closing and opening the SBS Briefcase folder, you could have pressed F5 to refresh the status.

17 On the **Briefcase** menu, click **Update All**.

This **Update SBS Briefcase** dialog box opens:

Update SBS Briefcase

The following files need to be updated. To change the update action, use the right mouse button to click the file you want to change.

| GardenCo | In Briefcase
Modified
3/22/01 4:23 PM | ⇒
Replace | In C:\Sbs\Access\S...
Unmodified
3/22/01 4:18 PM |

Update   Cancel

This dialog box shows the condition of both databases. Because only the replica has changed, an arrow pointing toward the master database suggests that the changes in the replica replace the information in the master. If only the master had changed, or if both databases had changed, the arrows would be different. You can accept the suggestion, or you can right-click an entry and select another option to override the suggestion.

18 Click **Update** to update the master database.

A status message indicates that the update is being performed, and when it is finished, the status in the folder changes to **Up-to-date**.

19 Close the SBS Briefcase window.

20 Start Access, open the original **GardenCo** database in the *SBS\Access \Secure\Replicate* folder, open the **Products** form, and confirm that the change you just made appears there.

21 Close the **Products** form, and close the database.

Splitting a Database

Ac2002e-8-2

Approved Courseware

In a large organization, different people will have different uses for the information in a large database. They might want to develop their own variations of your queries, forms, and reports, or even create their own. Allowing dozens of people to edit the objects in a database leads at best to confusion and at worst to disaster.

One easy solution to this problem is to split the database into a **back-end database**, containing the tables, and a **front-end database**, containing the other database objects. You can store the back-end database on a server and distribute the front-end database to all the people who work with the data. They can use the queries, forms, reports, pages, macros, and Microsoft Visual Basic for Applications (VBA) code that you developed, or they can write their own. Although everyone still has access to the data in the tables, and there is still the potential for corrupting the data, the rest of your database objects are secure.

Tip

Before splitting a database, you should make a backup copy of it. The easiest way to make a backup is to browse to the database in Windows Explorer, click the database file, and press Ctrl+C to copy it. You can then press Ctrl+V to paste it in the same folder, or open a different folder and paste it there. The name of the copy will be the same as the original with *Copy of* to the left of it; you can rename the file if you like.

GardenCo

In this exercise, you will split the GardenCo database into back-end and front-end **components**. The working folder for this exercise is *SBS\Access\Secure\Split*. Follow these steps:

1 Open the **GardenCo** database located in the working folder.

2 On the **Tools** menu, point to **Database Utilities**, and click **Database Splitter**.

You are presented with this dialog box:

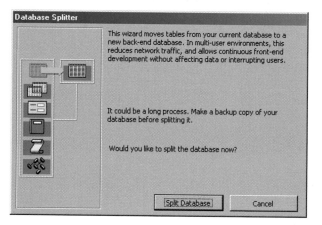

3 Click **Split Database**.

Access displays the **Create Back-end Database** dialog box so that you can specify where the back-end database should be stored and provide a name.

4 In the *SBS\Access\Secure\Split* folder, click **Split** to accept the default name of **GardenCo_be.mdb**.

5 After the database is successfully split, click **OK** to return to the database window.

In the list of tables, each table name is preceded by an arrow, indicating that it is linked to a table in a different database.

6 Open the **Categories** table in Design view.

Access informs you that some properties can't be modified.

7 Click **Yes** to open the table, and then click each field name in the top section of the Design view window.

A message displayed in red in the **Field Properties** section informs you that the properties for the selected field cannot be modified.

8 Close the table.

9 Click the other object types on the **Objects** bar.

Each type appears to be intact, and you can modify the object if necessary.

10 Close **GardenCo**, and open **GardenCo_be**.

This database contains only tables. Other types of objects are listed on the **Objects** bar but do not exist in the database.

11 Open the **Categories** table in Design view.

You'll see that you can modify the properties of the fields in the table.

12 Close the table, and then close the **GardenCo_be** database.

Setting Up a Workgroup

Ac2002e-7-5

Approved Courseware

As you develop a database and it grows in size, it can contain an enormous amount of interrelated information about your company. Different departments might need to view different parts of this information. For example, The Garden Company's management group might need to see financial information, the marketing and sales groups might need to see order information, and the human resources group might need to see employee and timekeeping information. Although representatives of each group might need access to some of the information in the database, it is not appropriate for everyone to be able to see everything. In fact, it might not be appropriate for some employees to open the database at all.

You can control the access of individuals or groups to the entire database or to specific objects in it by implementing user-level security. The Access user-level security model is based on the following four elements:

- **Objects**: The tables, queries, forms, reports, and so on that make up the structure of a database.

- **Permissions**: A set of attributes that specify the kind of access a user has to data or objects in a database.

- **Users**: The individual people authorized to access a database. You can assign each user a unique user name and password and grant explicit permission to view or change specific objects in the database.

- **Groups**: Sets of users authorized to access a database. If multiple users require the same permissions, you can create a group, assign permissions to it, and add the users to the group. Once added, they "inherit" the permissions of the group.

Information about these four elements is stored in a **workgroup information file (WIF)**. When you install Access, the setup program creates a default **workgroup** and sets up two groups, Admins and Users, within that workgroup. Until you take over management of database security, Access assigns everyone to both groups, with a default user name of *Admin* and a blank password. Because of the blank password, nobody has to log in, and everyone has permission to open, view, and modify all data and objects in any new database created while the default workgroup is active. All information about the security setup of the default workgroup is stored in the default WIF.

If you want to set up some kind of security for a database, you could modify the default WIF to change the default setup, but it is wiser to create a new workgroup by creating a new WIF. If you need many groups and permission levels, setting up a user-level security system by hand can be quite a chore. But if your needs are relatively simple, the **Security Wizard** will guide you through the process and set up a system that you can later modify.

Tip

Access user-level security is conceptually similar to the security systems that can be set up for Microsoft Windows NT or Microsoft Windows 2000 servers. If you have any experience with those systems, implementing security for a database will be relatively easy.

GardenCo

In this exercise, you will use the **Security Wizard** to secure the GardenCo database by creating a new workgroup and adding groups, users, passwords, and permissions. The working folder for this exercise is *SBS\Access\Secure\Multi*. Follow these steps:

1   Open the **GardenCo** database located in the working folder.

2   On the **Tools** menu, point to **Security**, and then click **User-Level Security Wizard** to display the page shown here:

```
Security Wizard

The Security Wizard creates an unsecured backup copy of the
current Microsoft Access database and secures the current
database.

The workgroup information file contains the names of users and
groups that will develop or use your application. To modify your
current workgroup information file, you must have administrator
permissions. Don't use the default workgroup information file.

Do you want to create a new workgroup information file or
modify the current one?

  ( •) Create a new workgroup information file.

  ( ) Modify my current workgroup information file.

  Help          Cancel       < Back      Next >       Finish
```

3   Click **Next** to create a new workgroup information file (WIF).

Creating a new WIF creates a new workgroup, to which you can assign the users or groups you want to be able to use this database.

4   Replace the text in the **WID** box by selecting it and typing **sbsTGC1234**.

It is a good idea to create a new workgroup ID, but if you do, it is important that you record this ID in a safe place.

5   In the **Your name** box, type **Catherine Turner** (the owner of The Garden Company).

6   In the **Company** box, type **The Garden Company**.

7   Leave the default selection to create a shortcut to open the secured database, and click **Next**.

You use the page shown here to specify which objects should be secured:

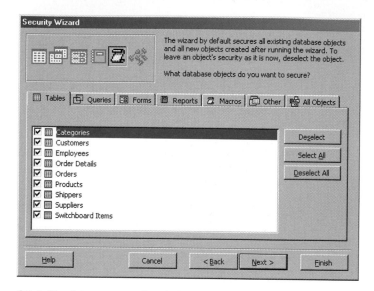

8   Click **Next** to accept the default selections and secure all objects.

On the next page of the **Security Wizard**, you can specify the additional groups to create, as shown here:

You can click a group's name (not its check box) and see what permissions it has in the **Group Permissions** box.

9 Select the check boxes for **Full Data Users** and **New Data Users**, and then click **Next** to display this page:

You use this page to assign permissions to the default Users group, but you don't need to do this because nobody will be assigned to this group.

10 Click **Next** to move on to the next page, where you can add new users.

11 In the **User name** box, type **CatherineT**, in the **Password** box, type **pw0**, and then click **Add This User to the List**.

CatherineT is added to the list of users.

Tip

When securing a real database, you should use more complex passwords, or you can leave them blank and have each user set his or her own password later.

12 Repeat step 11 to add the following users:

Name	Password
KimY	pw1
MikeG	pw2
LaniC	pw3
SteveD	pw4
AmyA	pw5

(continued)

Name	Password
MichaelE	**pw6**
SusanF	**pw7**
RichardK	**pw8**

Your screen now looks like this:

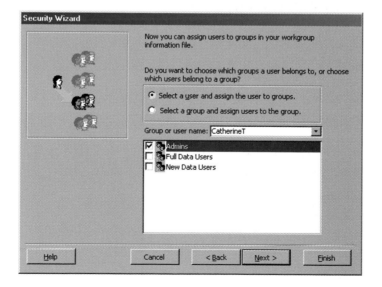

13 Click **Next** to move to this page, which you use to assign users to groups:

14 Click **Select a group and assign users to the group**.

Existing groups can be selected from the **Group or user name** list, and all users are listed in the large box below it. Currently **Admins** is the selected group, and a check mark in the **CatherineT** check box indicates that she is the only user assigned to this group.

15 In the **Group or user name box**, select **New Data Users**, and then add **AmyA** to this group.

16 In the **Group or user name box**, select **Full Data Users**, and add **KimY**, **LaniC**, **MichaelE**, **SusanF**, and **RichardK** to this group.

17 Click **Next**, and then click **Finish** in the wizard's final page to accept the default name for the backup copy of your unsecured database.

Access displays a report listing all the settings you have made. You can print the report, or export it to a text file and store it in a secure location.

18 Close the report, declining the offer to save it.

The **Security Wizard** encrypts and closes the database.

19 When a message informs you that you must reopen Access to use the new workgroup, click **OK** to close the message box.

20 Quit Access.

21 On the desktop, double-click the new **GardenCo.mdb** shortcut icon.

The properties of the shortcut icon include information that starts Access with the database's workgroup active. You are presented with this **Logon** dialog box:

Your user name might appear in the **Name** box.

22 In the **Name** box, type **CatherineT**, and in the **Password** box, type **pw0**. Then click **OK**.

The database opens as usual. As long as you use the shortcut icon, you will be able to open this database.

23 Close the database, and quit Access.

Tip

If you move a secured database and want to continue using the desktop shortcut to open it, you can edit the shortcut's properties. Right-click the shortcut icon, and click **Properties**. Press the ⌷Home⌷ key to move the insertion point to the left end of the **Target** box, and then hold down the →| key to scroll through the target setting, which consists of three sections. The first starts Access, the second specifies the path of the database Access should open, and the third specifies the path of the WIF. To update this target, change the second and third paths to point to the current locations of the database file and the WIF. (The latter has an extension of *.mdw*.) Then change the path in the **Start in** box, and click **OK**.

Maintaining a Workgroup

Ac2002e-7-5

Approved Courseware

When you want to secure a multi-user database, the **Security Wizard** guides you through the process of creating a workgroup, adding groups and users, and assigning passwords and permissions. After the workgroup has been created, you can either use workgroup commands to maintain it or run the wizard again to modify the WIF.

The following workgroup commands are grouped together on the **Security** submenu of the **Tools** menu:

Command	Purpose
Workgroup Administrator	Change the current workgroup.
User and Group Permissions	Change the permissions that groups or users have for all database objects.
User and Group Accounts	Add and delete users and groups. Assign users to groups. Clear any password or change the logon password for the user currently logged on.
User-Level Security Wizard	Create and modify workgroups.

What users can do with these commands is determined by their permissions.

GardenCo
Secure.mdw

In this exercise, you will explore these commands and change a user password. To complete this exercise, you must first work through the previous exercise. The working folder is *SBS\Access\Secure\Maintain*. Follow these steps:

1 Start Access.

Open

2 Try to open the GardenCo database by clicking the **Open** button on the Access toolbar, browsing to the working folder, and double-clicking **GardenCo**.

Access tells you that you don't have the permissions necessary to open this database.

3 Click **OK** to close the alert box.

Access remains on your screen, but no database is open.

4 On the **Tools** menu, point to **Security**, and then click **Workgroup Administrator** to open this dialog box:

Tip

Your dialog box will not display the same user, company, and path information that you see above.

You can use this dialog box to manually create a new workgroup or to join a different workgroup.

5 Write down the name and path of the current workgroup. You will need this information later.

6 Click **Join** to display this dialog box:

7 Click **Browse**, browse to the *SBS\Access\Secure\Maintain* folder, select **Secured** (this WIF file was already created and named by the wizard), and click **Open**.

8 Click **OK** to accept the path and name for the selected WIF.

An alert box informs you that you have joined the selected workgroup.

9 Click **OK** to close the alert box, and click **OK** again to close the **Workgroup Administrator** dialog box.

10 Try again to open **GardenCo** by double-clicking its file name in the *SBS\Access\Secure\Maintain* folder.

This time, Access displays the **Logon** dialog box.

11 In the **Name** box, type **CatherineT**, and in the **Password** box, type **pw0**. Click **OK**.

The database opens.

Important

Access to different secured databases can be controlled by different WIFs, and you can have multiple WIFs on one computer. However, only one workgroup can be active on a computer at any time. After you join a workgroup, you remain in that workgroup until you join a different one. The current workgroup is stored in the computer's registry as an attribute of Access. Because this workgroup requires users to log on, any user trying to open any Access database from this computer will be asked for a user name and password. (A user on a different computer could connect through the LAN and open any non-secured database stored on this computer without logging on, but that user could not open a secured database.)

12 On the **Tools** menu, point to **Security**, and click **User and Group Permissions**.

This dialog box is displayed:

Any member of the Admins group can use this dialog box to set permissions for an individual user or a group. Permissions are set separately for each user and each object type. You select the user in the **User/Group Name** box, select the object in the **Object Type** drop-down list, and then select one or more of the objects of that type in the **Object Name** list. Finally, click each permission you want to assign.

13 Click **Groups** in the **List** section.

When this workgroup was created, permissions for groups were set and users were assigned to the groups. Users inherit the permissions of the groups they belong to, so this is a quick way to set permissions for several people at one time.

14 Click each group name, and watch the permissions change.

Note that New Data Users cannot modify table design.

15 Click **Cancel** to close this dialog box, and then quit Access.

16 Start Access again, and open the **GardenCo** database located in the *SBS\Access\Secure\Maintain* folder, this time logging on as **AmyA** with a password of **pw5**.

Amy is a member of the New Data Users group.

17 Attempt to open any table in Design view.

Access warns that you don't have permission to modify the table and asks if you want to open it as read-only. You would see a similar message if you tried to delete a record, but not if you tried to add a record.

18 Click **No** to close the alert box, and then quit Access.

19 Start Access, and reopen the same database as **CatherineT**, with the password **pw0**.

20 On the **Tools** menu, point to **Security**, and then click **User and Group Accounts** to display this dialog box:

As a member of the Admins group, Catherine can add and remove users and groups. She can also clear the password of any user so that the user can log on and set a new password.

Tip

Any user can change his or her own password. Members of the Admins group can clear the password of any user, but they can't change any password except their own.

21 Click the **Change Logon Password** tab to display these options:

User and Group Accounts	? X
Users Groups Change Logon Password	
User Name: CatherineT	
Old Password:	
New Password:	
Verify:	
OK Cancel Apply	

Catherine can use this dialog box to change her own password.

22 In the **Old Password** box, type **pw0** (the current password), press ⎚, type **Nos27Len** (the new password), press ⎚ again, and verify the new password by typing it again. Then click **OK**.

The next time Catherine logs on, she will have to use the new password.

23 On the **Tools** menu, point to **Security**, and then click **User-Level Security Wizard**.

You can use the wizard to modify the current workgroup. You can change anything you set when you used this wizard to create the workgroup, except the user names and passwords of existing users.

24 Click **Cancel**.

25 Quit Access, start Windows Explorer, and then try to open any non-secured database by clicking its file name in one of the *SBS\Access* subfolders.

Access asks you to log on because the active workgroup requires it.

26 Click **Cancel**, and then click OK.

27 Browse to the *SBS\Access\Secure\Maintain* folder, and open the **GardenCo** database, logging on as **CatherineT** with the new password **Nos27Len**.

28 Now you will rejoin your original workgroup. On the **Tools** menu, point to **Security**, and then click **Workgroup Administrator**.

Troubleshooting

If you are using Microsoft Windows 2000, one of the folders in the path to your original workgroup might be hidden. In order to browse to it, you will have to set Windows Explorer to show hidden files and folders. To do this, start Windows Explorer, click **Folder Options** on the **Tools** menu, click the **View** tab, click **Show hidden files and folders**, and click **OK**.

29 Click **Join**.

30 Click **Browse**, browse to the WIF whose name and path you wrote down in step 5, and click **Open**.

31 Click **OK** to close the **Workgroup Information File** dialog box, and click **OK** twice more to close the message box and the dialog box.

Access again informs you that you don't have permission to open this database. (It is a secured database and you are no longer a part of its workgroup.)

32 Click **OK**.

33 Try to open any non-secured database in one of the *SBS\Access* subfolders.

The database opens without asking you to log on because the default workgroup doesn't require it.

You can now open any non-secured database using any method. If you want to experiment further with a secured database, use the desktop shortcut to open the version of GardenCo stored in the *SBS\Access\Secure\Multi* folder.

Preventing Changes to VBA Code

Ac2002e-8-3

Approved Courseware

If you have added VBA procedures to a database, you certainly don't want users who aren't qualified or authorized to make changes to your code. You can prevent unauthorized access in two ways: you can protect your VBA code with a password, or you can save the database as a Microsoft Database Executable (MDE) file. If you set a password for the code, it remains available for editing by anyone who knows the password. If you save the database as an MDE file, people using the file can run your code, but they can't view or edit it.

GardenCo

In this exercise, you will secure the VBA code in a database by assigning a password to it. The working folder for this exercise is *SBS\Access\Secure\VBA*. Follow these steps:

1 Open the **GardenCo** database in the working folder, and then press [Alt]+[F11] to open the Visual Basic Editor.

2 On the Visual Basic Editor's **Tools** menu, click **GardenCo Properties**.

3 In the **GardenCo Project Properties** dialog box, click the **Protection** tab to display these options:

```
┌─────────────────────────────────────────────────────┐
│ GardenCo - Project Properties                    [X] │
│ ┌─────────┬────────────┐                             │
│ │ General │ Protection │                             │
│ ├─────────┴────────────────────────────────────────┐ │
│ │ ┌ Lock project ──────────────────────────────────┐│ │
│ │ │                                                ││ │
│ │ │  ☐ Lock project for viewing                    ││ │
│ │ │                                                ││ │
│ │ │                                                ││ │
│ │ └────────────────────────────────────────────────┘│ │
│ │ ┌ Password to view project properties ───────────┐│ │
│ │ │  Password         [                          ] ││ │
│ │ │                                                ││ │
│ │ │  Confirm password [                          ] ││ │
│ │ └────────────────────────────────────────────────┘│ │
│ │                                                    │ │
│ │            [   OK   ]  [ Cancel ]  [  Help  ]      │ │
│ └────────────────────────────────────────────────────┘ │
└─────────────────────────────────────────────────────┘
```

4 Select the **Lock project for viewing** check box.

5 In the **Password** box, type **2002!VBA**, and press [Tab] to move the insertion point to the **Confirm Password** box.

6 Type the password again, and then click **OK**.

You have set the password, but it won't be active until the next time you open the database.

7 Press [Alt]+[F11] to return to Access, and then close the database.

8 Open the database again, and then press [Alt]+[Tab] to switch to the Visual Basic Editor.

The editor opens, but all that is displayed in the Project Explorer is the name of the project. The Code window is closed.

9 Click the plus sign to the left of the GardenCo project name to expand the project.

This dialog box opens:

10 Type **2002!VBA**, and click **OK**.

The project expands to display its components.

Tip

You have to enter the password only once per database session. In other words, you won't have to enter it again unless you close and reopen the database.

11 To remove the password, click **GardenCo Properties** on the **Tools** menu to open the **GardenCo Project Properties** dialog box.

12 Click the **Protection** tab, clear the **Lock project for viewing** check box, remove the asterisks in the two password boxes, and click **OK**.

Tip

The lock and password settings operate independently. Clicking the **Lock project for viewing** check box requires the user to enter the password to view the project. If a password has been set and the **Lock project for viewing** check box is cleared, the user can view the project code but has to enter the password to open the **Project Properties** dialog box.

13 Close the Visual Basic Editor, and then close the database.

Securing a Database That Will Be Publicly Distributed

Ac2002e-8-3

Approved Courseware

When a database is used only in one office or on a local area network (LAN) or wide area network (WAN), you have considerable control over who has access to it. But if you send the database out into the world—on its own or as part of a larger application—you lose that control. There is no way you can know who is using it or what tools they might have available to hack into it. If thinking about this keeps you awake at night, you should distribute your database as a **Microsoft Database Executable (MDE)** file.

Suppose the owners of The Garden Company want to make their database available for use by gardening clubs in the area, but they don't want people to be able to change its objects and perhaps "break" things. Saving a database as an MDE file compiles all modules, removes all editable source code, and compacts the destination database. Users of the MDE file can view forms and reports and update information, as well as run queries, macros, and VBA code. They *cannot* do the following:

■ View, edit, or create forms, reports, or modules in Design view.

■ Add, delete, or change references to other objects or databases.

■ Change VBA code.

■ Import or export forms, reports, or modules.

GardenCo

In this exercise, you will secure a database by saving it as a distributable MDE file. You start this exercise with the GardenCo database closed. The working folder for this exercise is *SBS\Access\Secure\MDE*. Follow these steps:

1 If you are working in a multi-user environment, make sure that all other users close the database for which you want to create an MDE file.

Important

> You cannot convert a database back from the MDE format, so before you save a database as an MDE file, create a backup copy. If you need to make changes to forms, reports, or VBA code, you will have to make them in the original database and then save it as MDE again.

2 On the **Tools** menu, point to **Database Utilities**, and click **Make MDE File**.

Important

> Access 2002 can save a database as an MDE file only if it is in Access 2002 format. Although Access 2000 is the default format for databases created with Access 2002, Access 2002 can't save an Access 2000 database as MDE: you first have to convert it to 2002 format. If necessary, you can use the **Convert Database** command under **Database Utilities** on the **Tools** menu.

3 In the **Database To Save As MDE** dialog box, browse to the *SBS\Access\Secure\MDE* folder, select **GardenCo**, and then click **Make MDE**.

This dialog box opens:

4   Type **TGC** in the **Edit name** box, and click **Save**.

The process only takes a moment; no message alerts you when it is completed.

5   Click the **Open** button, browse to the *SBS\Access\Secure\MDE* folder, and double-click **TGC**.

6   Click each of the object types on the **Objects** bar while watching the **Design** button at the top of the database window.

The **Design** button is available for tables, queries, and macros, but unavailable for all other object types.

7   Close the database, and if you are not continuing on to the next chapter, quit Access.

Tip

If you intend to distribute your database for installation on systems where the setup is unknown, you should look into the **Package and Deployment Wizard** in Microsoft Office XP Developer.

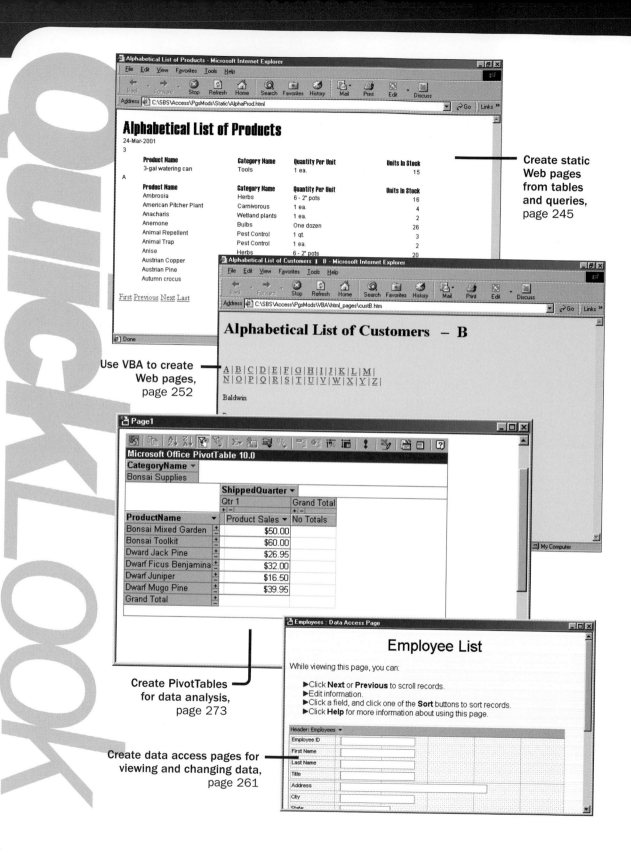

Create static
Web pages
from tables
and queries,
page 245

Use VBA to create
Web pages,
page 252

Create PivotTables
for data analysis,
page 273

Create data access pages for
viewing and changing data,
page 261

Chapter 10
Working with Pages and Modules

After completing this chapter, you will be able to:

✔ Create static Web pages for viewing data on the Web.

✔ Create static Web pages using VBA code.

✔ Create dynamic Web pages for modifying data on the Web.

✔ Create PivotTables and PivotCharts for analyzing data on the Web.

The World Wide Web is the largest public clearinghouse of information in the world. It has become *the* place to publish and distribute books, software, and data of all types. If your organization has an Internet presence, you will want to take advantage of features in Microsoft Access that can be used to publish your database information so that it is accessible via an intranet or the Internet.

Important

This discussion assumes that you are already familiar with the Internet, the World Wide Web, Internet service providers, and methods of placing HTML pages on a Web site for publication. If this is not the case, you should still be able to follow along and work through the exercises, but you might need help moving your files to the Web. A good source of information about creating and publishing a Web site is *Microsoft FrontPage Version 2002 Step by Step* (Microsoft Press, 2001).

Information on the Web is viewed with a **Web browser**. The two most popular Web browsers are Microsoft Internet Explorer and Netscape Navigator; however, these browsers are available in many versions, and other browsers are also available. All browsers are capable of viewing files based on a simple set of **Hypertext Markup Language (HTML)** tags. Newer versions of the popular browsers also recognize non-standard HTML tags and other file formats, such as **Dynamic Hypertext Markup Language (DHTML)** and **Extensible Markup Language (XML)**.

Important

If you intend to place database information on the Web, give careful thought to what operating system and browser will be used by people viewing your site. If you would like your site to be available to the general public, then you will have to forgo cutting-edge technology, such as data access pages, in favor of static Web pages or Active Server Pages (ASP).

You can use Access to create two types of Web pages:

- **Static HTML pages,** which provide a snapshot of some portion of the database contents at one point in time. These pages can be viewed by any modern browser and can be stored on a server running any server software.

- **Dynamic Web pages**, which are created in response to some action on the part of each user.

There are two main types of dynamic Web pages:

- **Data access pages** allow users to directly manipulate data in your database. You can allow users to add, edit, and delete records, and change their view of the data, in much the same way as they would in a form. To take full advantage of data access pages, users must be running Internet Explorer version 5.0 or later.

- **Active Server Pages** are stored on a **network server** and generate different views of the data in response to choices users make on a Web page. The pages can be viewed with any modern browser, but the server where the pages are stored must be running Microsoft Windows NT 4 or Microsoft Windows 2000. Although Access can export a form or report as an Active Server Page, you will not do that in this chapter. Search for *ASP* in Access online Help for more information.

In this chapter, you will create static and dynamic Web pages. You will get an overview of Microsoft Visual Basic for Applications (VBA) and see how VBA procedures stored in Access modules can be used to create Web pages. You will also add controls to data access pages to allow other people to view your data, add and edit records, make projections, and analyze your data. You will be working with the GardenCo database files and several other sample files that are stored in these subfolders of the *SBS\Access\PgsMods* working folder: *Static, VBA, AutoPage, Wizard,* and *Analyze.*

Creating Static Web Pages

The most basic form of an HTML page is a static page. If you want any Web browser that supports HTML 3.2 or later to be able to view your data, you should display the data in static HTML pages. Static pages are downloaded and displayed in their entirety; the user can't edit them, and there are no tricky bits that pop up or change format as users move through the page.

Access can export tables, queries, forms, and reports as static HTML pages. Exported tables, queries, and forms are displayed in datasheet format. (If you have a lot of data, the Web page might be very long.) Exported reports are displayed on a series of short pages, similar to reports in Access.

GardenCo

In this exercise, you will export the Alphabetical List of Products report from the GardenCo database to a set of static HTML pages. The working folder for this exercise is *SBS\Access\PgsMods\Static*. Follow these steps:

1   Open the **GardenCo** database located in the working folder.

2   On the **Objects** bar, click **Reports**.

3   Open the **Alphabetical List of Products** report in Print Preview, just to see what it looks like.

4   Close the report.

5   On the **File** menu, click **Export** to display the **Export** dialog box.

6   Browse to the *SBS\Access\PgsMods\Static* folder, type **AlphaProd** in the **File name** box, select **HTML Documents** as the **Save as type** setting, select the **Autostart** check box, and then click **Export**.

7   In the **HTML Output Options** dialog box, make sure the **Select a HTML Template** check box is not selected, and then click **OK**.

Access displays its progress as it exports the report to HTML pages. Because you clicked **Autostart**, when the export process is complete, the first HTML page opens in your Web browser. (It may appear as a blinking button on the taskbar.)

8   If you don't see the HTML page, click **Alphabetical List of Products** on the taskbar to display it.

The first HTML page looks like this:

Title

Navigation links

Page number

When Access created these pages, it placed a title in the title bar, put the data in the body of the page, and added navigation links and a page number at the bottom.

9 Start Microsoft Windows Explorer, and browse to the working folder.

Access created a file named *AlphaProd*, which is the first page of the report, and nine more files named *AlphaProd2* through *AlphaProd10*, which are the remaining pages.

10 Return to the HTML page, and repeatedly click the **Next** hyperlink to scroll through the 10 pages of the report.

Tip

If you are interested in seeing the HTML code that makes this page look the way it does, you can view it in Internet Explorer by right-clicking the body of the page and clicking **View Source**. If you are running Netscape Navigator, click **View Document Source** or **View Page Source** on the **View** menu, depending on the version of Netscape you are using.

11 Close the HTML report and the **GardenCo** database.

Exploring Visual Basic for Applications

Ac2002e-8-1

Approved Courseware

Microsoft Visual Basic for Applications (VBA) is a high-level programming language developed for the purpose of creating Windows applications. A common set of VBA instructions can be used with all Microsoft Office products, and each product also has its own set. VBA includes hundreds of commands and can be extended indefinitely with third-party controls and routines you write yourself.

You can use VBA to integrate features of Microsoft Word, Microsoft Excel, Microsoft Outlook, and other applications, as well as Access. If you work with Office applications and have any interest in programming, VBA is well worth learning. This topic provides an overview of VBA. For more information about this subject, see the VBA online Help file and other books from Microsoft Press.

Tip

The VBA online Help file is not installed in the default Office setup. However, if you attempt to use it by clicking **Microsoft Visual Basic Help** on the **Help** menu displayed from within the Visual Basic Editor, you will be prompted to insert the installation CD, and the files will be installed.

VBA programs are called **procedures** or simply **code**. Access refers to VBA procedures as **modules** and represents them with the **Modules** object on the **Objects** bar. In VBA itself, there are two types of modules: **class modules**, which are associated with a specific form or report, and **standard modules**, which contain general procedures that are not associated with any object. When you use the **Switchboard Manager** or the **Command Button** tool in the toolbox, VBA code is automatically attached to your forms, so you may have already used VBA without realizing it.

Code

When you write or edit VBA code, you do so in the **Visual Basic Editor,** sometimes referred to as the **Visual Basic Integrated Development Environment (IDE)**. If you are working in Access and you have selected a form, report, or module in the database window, a **Code** button becomes available on the Access window's toolbar. Clicking this button opens the Visual Basic Editor and places the insertion point in the code for the highlighted object. If you are working in Access without having selected an object and want to switch to the Visual Basic Editor, press [Alt]+[F11]. (This method works for all Microsoft Office applications.)

Shown on the next page is the Visual Basic Editor as it would look if you selected the Switchboard form in the GardenCo database and clicked the **Code** button.

Object box   **Procedure** box

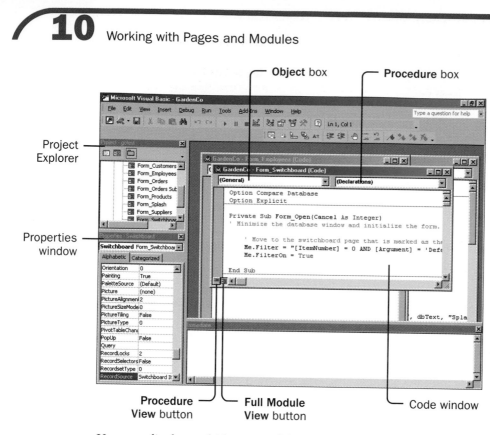

Project Explorer

Properties window

Procedure View button   Full Module View button   Code window

You can display or hide most of the VBE components by clicking the appropriate button or a command on the **View** menu. You can also use the following buttons to change how information is displayed:

Project Explorer

■ Click the **Project Explorer** button. The pane for the Project Explorer is displayed. You use the Project Explorer to find and display the VBA objects in the active database.

Toggle Folders

■ Click the **Toggle Folders** button at the top of the Project Explorer. When the button is active, the VBA objects are categorized in the Class Objects and Modules folders. When it is inactive, the objects are listed without being categorized.

Full Module View

■ Click the **Full Module View** button at the bottom of the Code window. All the procedures from the module selected in the Project Explorer pane are displayed.

Procedures View

■ Click the **Procedures View** button. Only the active procedure—the one containing the insertion point—is displayed.

The **Object** box, on the upper left side of the Code window, lists all the objects, such as command buttons, labels, and text boxes, that appear on the form. Even the form itself is an object. When you select an object in this list, a placeholder for the most common event associated with that object is created in the code pane below.

The **Procedure** box, on the upper right side of the Code window, lists all the procedures associated with the currently selected object. These procedures are associated with **events**, such as a mouse click on a command button. When you select a procedure in this list, the name of the event is added to the first line of the object's placeholder in the code pane below.

In the code pane itself, everything above the first horizontal line is the **Declarations** section of the module. This section sets the module's requirements and defaults. Two declarations, Option Compare Database and Option Explicit, are usually included by default. You can add others.

Important

Using Option Explicit forces you to explicitly declare all variables before using them. If you attempt to use an undeclared variable, an error occurs when the code is compiled. Variables are discussed on the next page.

Below the **Declarations** section, the code pane displays the procedures included in the module. Procedures can be categorized as follows:

- **Sub procedures**, which are a series of VBA statements enclosed by Sub and End Sub statements that perform actions but don't return a value.

- **Function procedures**, which are enclosed in Function and End Function statements and return a value.

Each procedure is a block of code that accomplishes a specific purpose. In the previous graphic, each procedure was created by the **Switchboard Manager** to respond to requests to create a switchboard and respond to the click of a button on the switchboard page.

The VBA statements in a procedure are often interspersed with **comments**. These are notes that help the programmer or someone reading the code understand the code's purpose. Comments are defined by an apostrophe; anything after an apostrophe on a line of code is a comment. The Visual Basic Editor makes comments obvious by formatting them as green text.

Within each line of code, you will see that some words are blue and others are black. The blue words are **keywords**, reserved as part of the VBA programming language. The black words are variables or values supplied by the programmer.

One of the first things done in many procedures is to use Dim (dimension) statements to define (declare) the **variables** that will be used in the procedure. Declaring a variable sets its type. (VBA supports the data types used for Access fields and other types.) Declaring a variable also sets the exact appearance of the word representing the variable—the combination of uppercase and lowercase characters.

Tip

If you always include at least one uppercase character in variable declarations and then always type the variable name in lowercase, you can take advantage of the fact that when VBA recognizes a variable or keyword, it changes it to the capitalization style of its definition. So if you misspell a word, you won't see it changed, which is a hint to check your spelling.

Every programming language has certain formatting conventions. Most of them have no impact on whether or not the code runs, but many make it easier to visually follow what is going on in the code and locate problems. Indenting is one such convention. When typing VBA code, use a tab to indent lines that are part of a larger element. In the switchboard code shown earlier, everything between the beginning and end of the procedures is indented by one tab, and the code for some statements, such as For…Next loops and If…Then…Else statements, are indented another tab.

As you type words that are part of the VBA programming language (keywords), the Visual Basic Editor often offers hints and autocomplete options. If, for example, you are using the DoCmd statement, when you type the period after DoCmd, a list of all possible methods appears, like this:

You can either continue to type, or scroll in the list and select the method you want. When you complete the command and press `Space`, a box displays the syntax for the rest of the command, like this one for DoCmd.OpenForm:

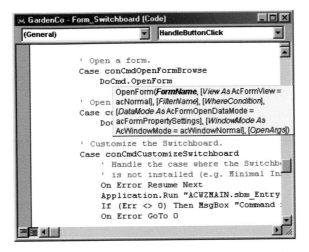

If a line of code extends beyond the edge of the screen, it will still run, but it is hard to read. You can break a long line of code by typing a space and an underscore and then pressing `Enter`. (You can press `Tab` to set the second line of code off from the first, but that's not a requirement.) Although the code will continue on the next line, it will be treated as one line of code. Here is an example:

```
 GardenCo - Form_Switchboard (Code)
(General)                    HandleButtonClick

           ' Open a Data Access Page
           Case conCmdOpenPage
               DoCmd.OpenDataAccessPage _ ———————— Manual line break
               rs![Argument]

           ' Any other command is unrecognized.
           Case Else
               MsgBox "Unknown option."

      End Select

      ' Close the recordset and the database.
      rs.Close

HandleButtonClick_Exit:
On Error Resume Next
      Set rs = Nothing
```

You can get more information about any VBA command by highlighting it in the Visual Basic Editor and pressing `F1` to open Visual Basic Help.

Using VBA to Create a Web Page

Ac2002e-8-1

Approved Courseware

Exporting an Access object to static Web pages is quick and easy, but if you want to manipulate the data as you create the static pages, the export process won't be of much use. A better way is to create a module containing VBA code that manipulates the data.

As an example, suppose The Garden Company wants to use data in the Customers table to create a set of 26 Web pages, one for each letter of the alphabet. Each page will list the customers whose last names start with the correlating letter and will contain links to all the other pages in the set. All the legwork for setting up the pages can be done with VBA code.

The sample GardenCo database for this exercise includes HTML_final, a finished and fully commented version of the HTML module you will be creating. If you don't want to type the code as instructed, you can copy it from each Step# module provided in the sample database, paste it into your new HTML module, and then delete the comment from the copied code.

Tip

The more complex a program is, the more ways there are to write it. This exercise doesn't pretend to illustrate the best programming methods and doesn't take the time to explain every code detail. You can learn more about each VBA command by clicking it and then pressing [F1] to read about it in Access online Help.

GardenCo

In this exercise, you will follow the typical programming process of writing a module in stages, testing each stage before moving on to the next. In the first stage, you will write code to open the database and look at each record in the Customers table. In the second stage, you will figure out how to spot the change in the first letter of each person's last name. In the third stage, you will open a new text file for each letter and add some HTML code to it. In the fourth and final stage, you'll do some housekeeping and close all the files. The working folder for this exercise is *SBS\Access\PgsMods\VBA*. Follow these steps:

1   Open the **GardenCo** database located in the working folder.

2   On the **Objects** bar, click **Modules**.

3   Click the **New** button on the database window's toolbar.

The Visual Basic Editor opens, with a new module highlighted in the Project Explorer.

Save

4   Click the **Save** button on the Visual Basic Editor's toolbar, name the module **HTML**, and click **OK**.

5   On the **Insert** menu, click **Procedure** to display this dialog box:

Add Procedure	
Name: [＿＿＿＿＿＿]	OK
	Cancel
Type	
⦿ Sub	
○ Function	
○ Property	
Scope	
⦿ Public	
○ Private	
☐ All Local variables as Statics	

6   In the **Name** box, type **createHTML**, and then click **OK** to accept the default settings.

A new sub procedure is inserted in the code pane.

7   If Option Explicit isn't in the **Declarations** section at the top of the code pane, position the insertion point at the end of Option Compare Database, press ⏎Enter, type **Option Explicit**, and press ⏎Enter again.

You will now be forced to declare any variables before running the program. If you don't, the program won't run, and you will have to stop and declare the variables.

Tip

To have the editor add Option Explicit to every new module, click **Options** on the **Tools** menu. On the **Editor** tab of the **Options** dialog box, click **Require Variable Declaration**. It is a good idea to select all the options on this tab. Press the F1 key with the tab visible to read information about the options.

8 Click the empty line below Public Sub, press the [Tab] key, and then either copy and paste the following lines from Step08, or type them, pressing [Enter] at the end of each line:

```
Dim con As Object
Dim rs As Object
Dim stSql As String
Dim firstRec As Boolean
Dim activeDir As String
Dim curWord As String
Dim curLtr As String
Dim oldLtr As String
Dim skipLtr As String
Dim qt As String
Dim i As Integer
```

Important

If you want to copy and paste a code block from the Step# modules, double-click the module name in the Project Explorer, select the code in the code pane, press [Ctrl]+[C], click the Code window to activate it, position the insertion point where you want the copied code to appear, and press [Ctrl]+[V]. Close the Step# Code window. You will then need to remove the comments so that the code will actually be run with the rest of the procedure. To do this, right-click a blank area on the Visual Basic Editor's toolbar, click **Edit** to display the **Edit** toolbar, select the commented code block, and click the **Uncomment Block** button. Then make any necessary adjustments to the indents to make the lines match what you see in the instructions.

You have just used the Dim (dimension) statement to declare all the variables you will use in this procedure. You would normally do this as you found a need for each variable.

9 Press [Enter] twice to leave a couple of blank lines. (You will add code here later.) Then either copy and paste the following lines from Step09, or type them, pressing [Enter] at the end of each line:

```
qt = Chr(34)
Set con = Application.CurrentProject.Connection
stSql = "SELECT * FROM [Customers] ORDER BY LastName"
Set rs = CreateObject("ADODB.Recordset")
rs.Open stSql, con, 1    ' 1 = adOpenKeyset
```

The first line sets the value of the variable *qt* to represent a quotation mark. You use this trick to print a quotation mark, because simply typing the quotation mark in the code would be interpreted as part of the code. The rest of the lines connect to the current database and run a query that selects all records from the Customers table, after first sorting it by LastName.

Tip

When you press ⌷Enter⌷ after typing a line of code, the line is analyzed, its **syntax** is checked, and all variable names and keywords are set to the appropriate capitalization style. If you get in the habit of declaring variables with mixed case and typing all code in lowercase, you will be able to spot typos more easily.

10 Add a few more blank lines, and then copy and paste the following lines from Step10, or type them. (Press ⌷Tab⌷ to indent the second line, and press the ⌷Backspace⌷ key to remove the indent before typing the last line.)

```
Do Until rs.EOF
    curWord = rs!LastName
    Debug.Print curWord
    rs.MoveNext
Loop
```

This segment (called a *Do...Loop statement*) opens the first record in the Customers table, sets the variable *curWord* to the value of the LastName field, prints the value of *curWord*, and then moves to the next record. This set of steps is repeated until the last record is printed.

11 Add a few more blank lines, and copy and paste the following lines from Step11, or type them:

```
rs.Close
Set rs = Nothing
Set con = Nothing
```

These lines close the database and free up the object variables by disassociating them from the actual objects, which in turn frees up memory and system resources.

Your code window should now look like this:

```
GardenCo - HTML (Code)                              _□×
(General)                 ▼    createHTML            ▼
    qt = Chr(34)
    Set con = Application.CurrentProject.Connec
    stSql = "SELECT * FROM [Customers] ORDER BY
    Set rs = CreateObject("ADODB.Recordset")
    rs.Open stSql, con, 1    ' 1 = adOpenKeyset


    Do Until rs.EOF
        curWord = rs!LastName
        Debug.Print curWord
        rs.MoveNext
    Loop

    rs.Close
    Set rs = Nothing
    Set con = Nothing
```

Tip

You should save your work often by clicking the **Save** button on the toolbar.

12 On the **View** menu, click **Immediate Window**.

The Immediate window is displayed below the Code window. You can use the Immediate window to test a line of code or to change the value of a variable. But in this case, you will use it as an output window to view the results of the Debug.Print command.

Run Sub/
UserForm

▶

13 Click anywhere within your sub procedure, and then click the **Run Sub/User-Form** button on the toolbar.

The procedure runs, and the last name of each customer from the Customers table is printed in the Immediate window.

14 Click in the Immediate window, press [Ctrl]+[A] to select all its content, and press the [Del] key to delete the selection.

15 Click your code to shift the focus to the procedure, and press [F8] to begin stepping through the code.

The first line of the sub procedure is highlighted in yellow, indicating that it will be the next line of code processed.

16 Press [F8] again.

The highlight skips the Dim statements and moves to the *qt = Chr(34)* line.

17 Continue pressing F8 and watching the highlight until it has passed *Loop* and returned to *Do Until rs.EOF*.

This loop is the core of the program. It will execute one time for each record in the table. The first time through, it sets *curWord* to the value of the last name in the first record of the table, prints that value in the Immediate window, and then moves to the next record.

18 Press F8 to move the highlight to *curWord = rs!LastName*.

19 Hold the pointer over *curWord* for a few seconds, and then do the same over *rs!LastName*.

As you hover over each expression, its current value is displayed in a Screen-Tip. The variable *curWord* displays the name from the first record in the table, and *rs!LastName* displays the value of the current record.

20 Press F8 again, and check the values displayed on both sides of the expression on the line above.

Now they are the same.

21 Press F8 to finish running the procedure.

Your procedure now opens the database and gets the last name from each record in the Customers table.

22 Replace the *Debug.Print* line in your code with the following code, by either copying and pasting it from Step22 or typing it:

```
curLtr = UCase(Left(curWord, 1))
If curLtr <> oldLtr Then 'we have a new letter
    Debug.Print curLtr
    oldLtr = curLtr
End If
```

The first line gets the leftmost character of *curWord*, changes it to upper-case if it isn't already, and sets it as the value of *curLtr*. The If statement compares the value of *curLtr* to *oldLtr*. (At this point *oldLtr* will be blank, because its value hasn't been set.) If the value is different, it is printed, and then *oldLtr* is set to the current value of *curLtr;* otherwise, the flow of code passes to the next line after the If statement, which moves to the next record.

23 Press F5 to run the program.

This time the letters of the alphabet are printed in the Immediate window, below the list of customer names. If you scroll the window's contents, you will see that several letters are missing, not because something is wrong with your code, but because no customers have last names beginning with those letters.

24 In the blank lines you left below the last Dim statement, copy and paste these lines of code from Step24, or type them:

```
activeDir = Application.CurrentProject.path
If Dir(activeDir & "\html_pages", vbDirectory) = "" Then
    MkDir activeDir & "\html_pages"
End If
```

The first line sets the value of *activeDir* to the path of the folder (or directory) containing the database. The If statement checks to see if that directory has a subdirectory named *html_pages* in which to store the HTML pages you create. If it doesn't, the MkDir command creates the subdirectory.

25 Insert a line above the Do...Loop statement, and then copy or paste this line from Step25, or type it:

```
firstRec = True
```

You need to differentiate between the first record of a letter and all remaining records. Variables such as *firstRec* are often referred to as **flags** that can be set to true or false.

26 Delete the *Debug.Print* line above the line that compares *oldLtr* to *curLtr*.

27 Click at the end of the line that compares *oldLtr* to *curLtr*, press ⏎ to insert a new line, press ⇥ to indent, and copy and paste the following code from Step27, or type it:

```
If Not firstRec Then 'end the previous page
    Print #1, "</body>"
    Print #1, "</html>"
    Close #1
Else
    firstRec = False
End If

Open activeDir & "\html_pages\" & "cust" & curLtr & ".htm" _
    For Output As #1
Print #1, "<html>"
Print #1, "<head><title>Alphabetical List of Customers  " _
    & "&ndash;   " & curLtr & "</title></head>"
Print #1, "<body bgcolor=yellow link=red>"
Print #1, "<h1>Alphabetical List of Customers   &ndash;" _
    & "  " & curLtr & "</h1>"
Print #1, "<br>"
Print #1, "<br>"
```

In the previous step, and in some of the following steps, lines of code have been broken to fit the width of this book. When you break a line of code in the Visual Basic Editor, use a space followed by an underscore, as shown on the previous page.

This code checks to see if the record being processed is the first one: if not, it writes the tags to close out the previous HTML file. It then opens a new HTML file and writes tags to it.

28 Insert a line above *rs.MoveNext*, and copy and paste from Step28, or type:

```
Print #1, "<p>" & rs!FirstName & " " & rs!LastName
```

This creates a paragraph in the HTML file containing the first and last names of the customer, separated by a space.

29 Insert a line after *Loop*, and then insert this code from Step29, or type it:

```
Print #1, "</body>"
Print #1, "</html>"
Close #1
```

This adds the closing HTML tags to the last file, and closes it.

30 Click the **Save** button, and then click the **Run Sub/UserForm** button to run the program, which will create a series of HTML files in a new folder called *html_pages* in the working folder for this exercise. It should take only a few seconds.

Troubleshooting

A typo or a misplaced instruction can cause a program to go into an endless loop. If your program seems to be running far too long, you can press [Ctrl]+[Pause Break] to switch to debug mode, where you can run the program one step at a time to try to locate the problem.

31 In Windows Explorer, browse to the *html_pages* folder in the *SBS\Access \PgsMods\VBA* folder.

The folder contains a series of HTML files, one for almost every letter of the alphabet.

32 Double-click **custA** to open it in your browser.

33 View the HTML source code for the page. (If you are using Internet Explorer, right-click the body of the page, and click **View Source**.)

The source looks like this:

```
custA - Notepad
File  Edit  Search  Help
<html>
<head><title>Alphabetical List of Customers  &ndash;   A</tit
<body bgcolor=yellow link=red>
<h1>Alphabetical List of Customers   &ndash;  A</h1>
<br>
<br>
<p>Ackerman
<p>Akers
<p>Alboucq
<p>Atkinson
</body>
</html>
```

Your VBA code wrote the HTML tags and database information to the file.

34 Close the source window and your browser, and then return to the Visual Basic Editor.

35 If necessary, insert a line betweeen *Print #1, "<br>"* and *End If*, and copy and paste the following code from Step35, or type it:

```
For i = 65 To 77
    Print #1, "<font color=" & qt & "purple" & qt & "size=+1><a href=" _
        & qt & "cust" & Chr(i) & ".htm" & qt & ">" & Chr(i) & _
        "</a> | </font>"
Next i
Print #1, "<br>"
For i = 78 To 90
    Print #1, "<font color=" & qt & "purple" & qt & "size=+1><a href=" _
        & qt & "cust" & Chr(i) & ".htm" & qt & ">" & Chr(i) & _
        "</a> | </font>"
Next i
Print #1, "<p>"
```

This code prints the letters *A* through *M* on one row at the top of each page, and *N* through *Z* on the next row. Each letter is a link to the HTML page for that letter.

36 Save your changes, and run the program again. Then return to the *html_files* folder, and open **custB**.

The Web page looks like this:

The Web page screenshot shows Microsoft Internet Explorer displaying:

Alphabetical List of Customers – B

A|B|C|D|E|F|G|H|I|J|K|L|M|
N|O|P|Q|R|S|T|U|V|W|X|Y|Z|

Baldwin

Benson

Berglund

Berry

Boseman

Bremer

Browne

37 Click **F** to jump to the page containing last names starting with *F*.

The appropriate page is displayed.

38 Click **X**.

An error tells you that the page you requested cannot be displayed. No customers have a last name starting with *X*, so your VBA code didn't create a page for it. This is true of several other letters, too.

39 Close your browser, close the Visual Basic Editor, and close the **GardenCo** database.

Creating a Data Access Page with AutoPage

Ac2002-8-3

Approved Courseware

If you are confident that everyone who will need to access your data on the Internet or an intranet will be using Internet Explorer version 5.0 or later, and that they will have Microsoft Office XP Web Components installed, you can take advantage of the special capabilities of **data access pages**. (Office XP Web Components is a set of ready-made controls that allow you to work interactively with information in a data access page.)

A data access page is similar to a form, in that it can be used to view, enter, edit, or delete data from a Microsoft Access or a Microsoft SQL Server database. Like a form, a data access page is an Access object. Unlike a form, a page is not stored as part of your database: it is an external HTML file that is linked to your database in such a way that it makes the information in the database available over an intranet or the Internet. The window displayed when you click **Pages** on the **Objects** bar contains shortcuts to any pages you have created, and each page contains code that connects it to the appropriate database when the page is opened in Internet Explorer.

In Design view, a data access page looks somewhat like a form or report in Design view, but there are several differences.

■ In a form or report, the entire object is contained within the sections. In a data access page, the sections contain and control data that is **bound** to the database. The space above and below the sections is also part of the page, and you can place text and other controls in it.

■ The Field List for a form or report displays only the fields in the specific table or query to which the object is bound. The Field List for a data access page displays fields from all available tables and queries.

You can view a data access page in Access or in Internet Explorer. For example, suppose The Garden Company's head buyer is visiting suppliers and she wants to check the store's stock of particular kinds of gardening tools. She can connect to the Internet, start Internet Explorer, open an Inventory data access page, check current stock levels, and change the On Order field to show the number of items she is about to order from the supplier.

Important

In order to interact with and use the full functionality of a data access page, users must have Office XP installed on their computers. If they don't, they can view the data but they can't add, delete, or edit data.

There are four ways to create a data access page: in Design view, from an existing Web page, with the **Page Wizard**, or with AutoPage. AutoPage is the simplest method. Like AutoForm and AutoReport, AutoPage creates a simple page using all the available fields and minimal formatting.

GardenCo

In this exercise, you will create a data access page that allows people to update entries in the Employees table in the GardenCo database via the Internet. The working folder for this exercise is *SBS\Access\PgsMods\AutoPage*. Follow these steps:

1   Open the **GardenCo** database located in the working folder.

2   Click **Pages** on the **Objects** bar.

3   Click the **New** button on the database window's toolbar to display this **New Data Access Page** dialog box:

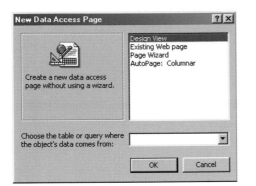

4   Click **AutoPage: Columnar**, select **Employees** from the list of tables and queries, and then click **OK**.

This simple data access page is created and displayed in Page view:

Every field in the underlying Employees table, along with its caption, is listed in one column. (AutoPage creates only columnar pages.) Below the **fields** is a navigation bar, which is included by default in all data access pages. (You might have to increase the size of the window to see this bar.)

5   Click the **Save** button on the toolbar to save your new page.

6 In the **Save As Data Access Page** dialog box, click **Save** to save the file in the *SBS\Access\PgsMods\AutoPage* folder with the suggested name of *Employees*.

7 If Access warns that the connection string for this page uses an absolute page, click **OK** to dismiss the message.

Since you are using a file on your own computer and not a network computer, a **UNC path** is not appropriate.

Next

▶

8 Hold the pointer over each navigation button until a ScreenTip displays the name of the button.

9 Click the **Next** button on the navigation bar to move to the next record.

Lost Database or Data Access Page?

A data access page is an HTML file that is connected to a **data source**—in this case, an Access database. The data source can be located on the same computer as the data access page or on some other computer on an intranet or the Internet. Where it's located is not important as long as the data access page can locate and open the database.

The page's **ConnectionString** property, which is stored in the HTML file, includes a path to the data source and other information that allows it to connect to the source. If you create a data access page while you have the data source open on your own computer, the **ConnectionString** property includes a path to your hard drive, in the usual C:\ path format. When the page is opened on another computer, the page is downloaded to that computer. The **ConnectionString** information is read, the computer attempts to follow the path to the data source, and the attempt fails. Using a UNC path ensures that the data source can be found because it specifies the computer on which the data source is stored, as well as the drive and folders.

Just as you can "lose" a data source, you can also "lose" data access pages. If you create a data access page and later move it or rename the folder where it is stored, you will get an error when you attempt to open it in either Access or Internet Explorer. To fix this problem, try to open the page in Page view. When you see the message that the file can't be found, click the **Update Link** button, and locate the HTML file. You will then be able to open the page, but you will get another error stating that the page can't find the database. Switch to Design view, click the title bar to select the page, and then click **Properties** on the **View** menu to open the **Properties** dialog box for the page. On the **Data** tab, click **ConnectionString**, and then click its ... button. In the **Data Link Properties** dialog box, click the **Connection** tab, edit or browse to the correct path in the first box, and then click **OK**.

Help

Help

10 Click the **Help** button.

Access online Help opens to the topic *About data access pages*.

11 Close Help.

12 In Windows Explorer, browse to the *SBS\Access\PgsMods\AutoPage* folder, and open **Employees** in Internet Explorer by double-clicking it.

The page should look and function identically to the way it did in Access.

Tip

You can view data access pages only in Internet Explorer 5.0 or later. (You must also have Internet Explorer 5.0 or later installed on your computer to create data access pages.) These exercises were developed using Internet Explorer 5.5. If you are using Internet Explorer 5.0, you might notice slight differences in the screens and in the options available.

Sort Ascending

13 Click the **Last Name** field, and then click the **Sort Ascending** button on the navigation bar.

The records are sorted in ascending order, based on the last name.

View

14 Minimize Internet Explorer (don't close it). Then click the **View** button on the Access window's toolbar to view the Employees page in Design view.

Your screen looks like this:

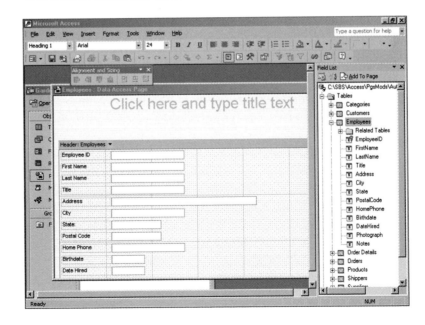

15 Click the **Close** button in the upper right corner of the Field List so that you can see the entire page window.

16 Click where you see *Click here and type title text*, and type **Employee List**.

As you can see in the **Style** box on the Formatting toolbar, the words you typed are styled as Heading 1.

17 Press the ↓ key to move to the line below the heading.

The **Style** box shows that this paragraph is styled as Normal.

18 Type the following:

While viewing this page, you can:

Bullets

19 Press Enter, click the **Bullets** button on the Formatting toolbar, and type the following lines, pressing Enter after each:

Click Next or Previous to scroll records.

Edit information.

Click a field, and click one of the Sort buttons to sort records.

Click Help for more information about using this page.

Here are the results:

266

Bold

20 Double-click the word *Next* in the first bulleted item, and click the **Bold** button on the Formatting toolbar.

21 Do the same for the words *Previous*, *Sort*, and *Help*.

22 Scroll down the page, click below the navigation bar, and type:

Copyright 2001, The Garden Company.

Tip

You can add a © symbol by clicking where you want the symbol to appear, and then with [Num Lock] turned on, holding down the [Alt] key and typing **0169** on the numeric keypad. When you release the [Alt] key, the copyright symbol is inserted.

23 Select the line you just typed, click the down arrow next to the **Font Size** box on the Formatting toolbar, and click **8**.

The size of the text changes to 8 points.

24 Save the page, and then click the **View** button.

The bottom part of the page now looks like this:

Employees	‑ □ ×
Title	Owner
Address	507 - 20th Ave. E.
City	Seattle
State:	WA
Postal Code	34569
Home Phone	(206) 555-0100
Birthdate	12/8/68
Date Hired	5/1/92
Photograph	EmpID1.bmp
Notes	Catherine is the owner of The Garden Company. Her education includes a degree in Accounting and an MBA from the University of Washington. She completed "The Master Gardener" program at Edmonds Community College and is a

Employees 1 of 9

Copyright 2001, The Garden Company.

25 Return to Design view.

26 Delete the **Last Name** label, drag the **LastName** text box to the right, and then drag both the **FirstName** text box and its label down until the text box is in line with the **LastName** text box.

27 Double-click the **First Name** label, click the **Other** tab to open its **Properties** dialog box, and change the **InnerText** property to **Name**.

As you have just seen, the process for changing the layout and properties of a data access page is almost identical to that for a form or report.

Tip

You can also view the properties for an element of a data access page by clicking it and then clicking **Properties** on the **View** menu, or by right-clicking it and clicking **Properties** on the shortcut menu. Pressing [F4] doesn't toggle the display of properties for data access pages as it does with other objects.

28 Click the **View** button to change to Page view.

29 Select the **Employee ID** number, and press [Tab] three times.

The order in which the insertion point moves through the fields is determined by the **TabIndex** property.

30 Switch back to Design view.

31 Click the navigation bar at the bottom of the data access page.

The entire bar is selected, and its properties appear in the **Properties** dialog box.

Delete

32 Click the **Delete** button on the navigation bar.

Now only that button is selected, and its properties are displayed.

33 In the **Properties** dialog box, click the **Format** tab to display the following properties:

Image : EmployeesNavDelete		
Format	Data	Other	All
Behavior	
BorderColor	rgb(0,0,0)
BorderStyle	none
BorderWidth	medium
Cursor	auto
Display	inline
Height	auto
Left	auto
Overflow	visible
Right	auto
Top	auto
Visibility	inherit
Width	auto

34 Click the **Visibility** property, and then select **hidden**.

This will prevent viewers from deleting records.

35 Click the **View** button on the toolbar to change to Page view.

The page is displayed, and the **Delete** button no longer appears on the navigation bar.

36 Click the **Save** button on the toolbar.

37 Return to Internet Explorer, and click the **Refresh** button.

When the browser reloads the Web page, the **Delete** button is no longer available.

38 Close the browser, close the **Employees** page, and close the **GardenCo** database.

Creating a Data Access Page with the Page Wizard

Ac2002-8-3
Ac2002e-6-1

Approved Courseware

Using AutoPage is a quick way to create a simple data access page in columnar format. But if you want more control over the content and layout, you should use the **Page Wizard**. With this wizard, you can select the initial fields to include on the data access page, create groups, and pick a theme from the dozens of those available. The theme you select is applied to the page when viewed in Access or Internet Explorer.

GardenCo

In this exercise, you will use the **Page Wizard** to create a data access page based on the Products by Category query in the GardenCo database. The working folder for this exercise is *SBS\Access\PgsMods\Wizard*. Follow these steps:

1 Open the **GardenCo** database located in the working folder.

2 Click **Pages** on the **Objects** bar.

3 Click the **New** button at the top of the database window.

4 In the **New Data Access Page** dialog box, click **Page Wizard**, select **Products by Category** from the list of tables and queries, and then click **OK**.

You then see the wizard, page shown on the next page, which is the same as the one displayed when you are creating a form or report.

5 Click the **>>** button to move all the fields to the **Selected Fields** list, and then click **Next** to display this page, in which you can set grouping levels:

6 Double-click **CategoryName**, and then click **Next**.

You use this page to set the order in which the records will initially be displayed.

7 Select **ProductName** in the first sort box, and click **Next**.

8 Select the **Do you want to apply a theme to your page** check box, and click **Finish**.

Access creates the page, opens it in Design view, and displays this **Theme** dialog box:

Theme	? X
Choose a Theme:	Sample of theme Straight Edge:

Layers
Level
Loose Gesture
Modern Shapes
Modular
Nature
Network
Network Blitz
Passport
Pie Charts
Pixel
Poetic
Profile
Quadrant
Radial
Radius
Refined
Rice Paper
Romanesque
Sandstone
Saturday TV Toons
Spiral
Straight Edge

Heading 1 style

▶Bullet 1
  ■ Bullet 2
     • Bullet 3

Horizontal Line:

_____

Heading 2 style

Regular Text Sample
Regular Hyperlink
Followed Hyperlink

☐ Vivid Colors
☑ Active Graphics
☑ Background Image

Set Default...

Button   Label: DATA

OK   Cancel

You can click the name of any theme to see a sample. You can also use the check boxes at the bottom of the dialog box to modify the theme, and you can set the selected theme as the default for all new pages.

9   Scroll to the bottom of the list, select **Willow**, and then click **OK**.

The new page appears in Design view.

10   If necessary, close the **Properties** dialog box, and then scroll to the top of the page.

11   Click the placeholder title text at the top of the page, and type **Products by Category**.

View

12   Click the **View** button to change to Page view, where the page looks like the graphic shown on the next page.

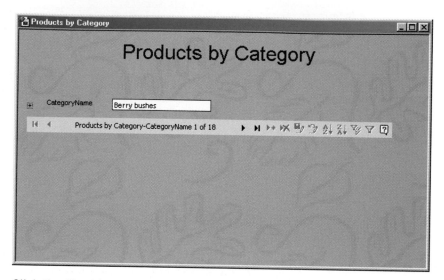

Next

13 Click the **Next** button on the navigation bar to move to the next category.

14 Click the **+** button to the left of **CategoryName**.

The display expands to show a product record under the category name, and a second navigation bar is displayed under the first, as shown here:

15 Click **Next** on the upper navigation bar to view the next product record in that category.

16 Click **Next** on the lower navigation bar to move to the next category.

The next category name is displayed, and the Products section disappears. You don't want to have to click the **+** button to display the section every time you move to a new category, so you need to make a change.

17 Switch to Design view, right-click the top header (**Products by Category-CategoryName**), and click **Group Level Properties** on the shortcut menu.

Access opens the **GroupLevel Properites** dialog box.

18 Double-click the **ExpandedByDefault** setting to change it to **True**.

19 Return to Page view, and click the **Next** button on the lower navigation bar several times.

The Product section now remains expanded as you move from category to category.

20 Close the page without saving it, and then close the **GardenCo** database.

Allowing Others to Analyze Data via the Web

PivotTables and Pivot-Charts
new for
OfficeXP

Ac2002e-6-2

Approved Courseware

A **PivotTable** is an interactive table that is linked to a database. Similarly, a **Pivot-Chart** is an intereactive chart that is linked to a database. If you add a PivotTable or a PivotChart to a data access page and publish it on the Web, people with the appropriate software can connect to it and analyze your data in various ways.

You use PivotTables to summarize the data in a database table or query in tabular format. You can rotate the columns and rows to summarize the data from different points of view. For example, you might want to use a PivotTable view of an order details table to see the total sales for a particular product or the total sales for all products in a particular month. Similarly, you use PivotCharts to summarize data visually so that it is easy to make data comparisons at a glance.

Important

Users must have Internet Explorer version 5.0 or later, Microsoft Office Web Components, and a valid Office XP license to work interactively with a PivotTable or Pivot-Chart on a data access page. Consider who your users will be before deciding to present information in this format.

GardenCo

In this exercise, you will create a data access page by hand and add a PivotTable to analyze product sales. The working folder for this exercise is *SBS\Access\PgsMods \Analyze*. Follow these steps:

1 Open the **GardenCo** database located in the working folder.

2 Click **Pages** on the **Objects** bar.

3 Double-click **Create data access page in Design view** to open a blank data access page.

Field List
4 If the Field List is not displayed, click the **Field List** button on the toolbar.

Toolbox

5 If the toolbox is not displayed, click the **Toolbox** button on the toolbar.

6 Size and arrange the page window, toolbox, and **Field List** so that you can see them all.

Office
PivotTable

7 In the toolbox, click the **Office PivotTable** tool, and then click in the upper left corner of the blank section on the page.

The Access window now looks something like this:

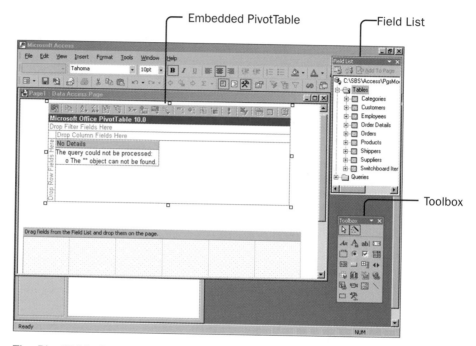

The PivotTable frame contains horizontal and vertical boxes labeled with the type of data they can hold: Filter Fields, Column Fields, Row Fields, and Details.

8 Click inside the PivotTable, and then double-click its frame to open the **Properties** dialog box.

Pressing F4 in a data access page does not open the **Properties** dialog box, as it does in other objects. The title of the **Properties** dialog box is **Object : PivotTable0**.

9 Click the **Other** tab, click the **DataMember** property, select **Product Sales for 2001** from the list, and close the **Properties** dialog box.

The PivotTable will now be based on the Product Sales for 2001 query in the GardenCo database.

10 In the **Field List**, click the plus sign to the left of **Queries**, and then click the plus sign to the left of **Product Sales for 2001.**

You can now see all the fields in this query.

11 Drag the **CategoryName** field from the **Field List** to the horizontal box labeled **Drop Filter Fields Here**.

12 Click the **CategoryName** down arrow to see a list of all the product categories in the database. Then clear the **All** check box, select the **Bonsai Supplies** check box, and click **OK**.

13 Now drag the **ProductName** field to the vertical box labeled **Drop Row Fields Here**.

You see all the products in the Bonsai Supplies category.

14 Drag the **ShippedQuarter** field to the horizontal box labeled **Drop Column Fields Here**.

15 Now drag the **ProductSales** field to the box labeled **Drop Totals or Detail Fields Here**.

View

16 Click the **View** button to switch to Page view, where your data access page looks like this:

Page1				
Microsoft Office PivotTable 10.0				
CategoryName ▾				
Bonsai Supplies				
		ShippedQuarter ▾		
		Qtr 1	Grand Total	
		+ –	+ –	
ProductName ▾		Product Sales ▾	No Totals	
Bonsai Mixed Garden		$50.00		
Bonsai Toolkit		$60.00		
Dward Jack Pine		$26.95		
Dwarf Ficus Benjamina		$32.00		
Dwarf Juniper		$16.50		
Dwarf Mugo Pine		$39.95		
Grand Total				

17 Experiment with the PivotTable by selecting different categories, products, and quarters from their drop-down lists.

18 Save the page as **Product Sales for 2001 DAP**.

Office Chart

19 Now you will chart the same data on the same data access page. Scroll the page all the way to the bottom, click the **Office Chart** button, and drag a rectangle below the PivotTable and about the same width and height as the table.

When you release the mouse button, you see a placeholder for the Office Chart Web component.

20 Click in the component to display the dialog box shown on the next page.

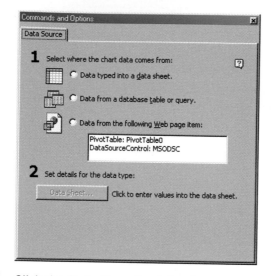

21 Click the **Data from the following Web page item** option, and then click **DataSourceControl:MSODSC**.

22 Click the **Data Details** tab, click the **Data member, table, view,** or **cube name** down arrow, and click **Product Sales for 2001** in the list.

23 Click the **Type** tab, click the upper left **Column** option, and then click the **Close** button to close the dialog box and see these results:

24 Drag **CategoryName** from the **Field List** to the **Drop Filter Fields Here** box. Then click the down arrow, clear the **All** check box, select the **Bonsai Supplied** check box, and click **OK**.

25 Drag **ProductName** to the **Drop Category Fields Here** box, drag **Shipped-Quarter** to the **Drop Series Fields Here** box, and drag **ProductSales** to the **Drop Data Fields Here** box.

26 Click the **View** button to see these results:

27 Experiment with the PivotChart by selecting different categories, products, and quarters from their drop-down lists.

28 Save the Product Sales for 2001 DAP page.

29 Close the page and the database.

30 Quit Access.

Quick Reference

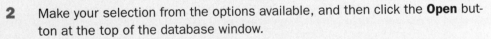

38 **To switch views of a database object**

View

- Click the **View** button on the toolbar.
- Click the **View** button's down arrow, and click an option in the drop-down list.

39 **To set the primary key field**

1 Display the table in Design view.
2 Select the field that you want to be the primary key field in the top portion of the window.
3 On the **Edit** menu, click **Primary Key**.

39 **To set a field's data type**

1 Display the table in Design view.
2 Click in the **Data Type** cell for the field you want to change, and then click the down arrow to display a list of all possible data types.
3 Click the type you want.

43 **To assign a caption (a column header that is different from the field name)**

1 Display the table in Design view.
2 Click the field to which you want to assign a caption.
3 Click the **Caption** box, and type the caption text.

44 **To set a text field's size**

1 Display the table in Design view.
2 Click the field whose size you want to change.
3 Click the **Field Size** box, and type the number of characters you want to allow in the field.

Chapter 3 Getting Information Into and Out of a Database
Page 52 **To import data from a delimited or fixed-width text file**

1 On the **File** menu, point to **Get External Data**, and then click **Import**.
2 In the **Files of type** list, click **Text Files**.
3 Navigate to the storage location of the file you want to import, click the file name, and then click **Import**.
4 Follow the instructions of the **Import Text Wizard**, click **Finish** on the wizard's last page to import the text file into the appropriate location, and then click **OK** to close the message box.

58   **To import data from an Access database**

1   On the **File** menu, point to **Get External Data**, and then click **Import**.

2   If necessary, select **Microsoft Access** in the **Files of type** list.

3   Navigate to the storage location of the file you want to import, click the database name, and then click **Import**.

4   Click the **Options** button to select any import options you want.

5   Select the objects you want to import, or click **Select All** to import all objects, and then click **OK**.

61   **To import data from an HTML file**

1   On the **File** menu, point to **Get External Data**, and then click **Import**.

2   In the **Files of type** list, click **HTML Documents**.

3   Navigate to the storage location of the file you want to import, click the file name, and then click **Import**.

4   Follow the instructions of the **Import HTML Wizard**, click **Finish** on the wizard's last page to import the data, and then click **OK** to close the message box that appears.

63   **To import XML data**

1   On the **File** menu, point to **Get External Data**, and then click **Import**.

2   In the **Files of type** list, click **XML Documents**.

3   Navigate to the storage location of the file you want to open, click the file name, and then click **Import.**

4   Click the **Options** button to select any import options you want, and then click **OK** twice.

65   **To export information to another application**

1   In the database window, click the object you want to export.

2   On the **File** menu, click **Export**.

3   Navigate to the folder where you want to store the exported file, select the appropriate **Save as type** option, type a name for the file, and click **Export**.

67   **To link a table in one database to another**

1   On the **File** menu, point to **Get External Data**, and then click **Link Tables**.

2   Navigate to the storage location of the file you want to link to, select the appropriate **Files of type** setting, select the file, and click **Link**.

3   Click the table you want to link to, and then click **OK**.

67   **To link to a named range in an Excel worksheet**

1   On the **File** menu, point to **Get External Data**, and then click **Link Tables**.

2   Navigate to the storage location of the file you want to link to, select **Microsoft Excel** in the **Files of type** list, select the file, and click **Link**.

3   Follow the instructions of the **Link Spreadsheet Wizard**, click **Finish** on the wizard's last page, and then click **OK**.

Chapter   4   Simplying Data Entry with Forms
Page   76   To edit form properties

1   Display the form in Design view.

2   Use the buttons and boxes on the Formatting toolbar to change the formatting of labels and controls.

3   To change the properties of a control, right-click the control, and click **Properties** on the shortcut menu.

4   Make your changes in the **Properties** dialog box.

83   **To rearrange form controls**

1   Display the form in Design view.

2   Select the control you want to move.

3   Drag the open-hand pointer in the direction you want to move the control and its label, or drag the pointing-finger pointer to move just the selected control.

84   **To fine-tune the size or position of a form control**

1   Display the form in Design view.

2   Select the control you want to change.

3   Move the pointer until it becomes the shape for the change you want, and then press the appropriate arrow key—⬆, ⬇, ⬅, or ➡—to move the control, in small increments, in a specific direction.

84   **To create a style based on a form**

1   Display the form in Design view.

2   On the **Format** menu, click **AutoFormat**.

3   Click **Customize**.

4   Click **Create a new AutoFormat based on the Form <form name>**, and then click **OK**.

5   Type a name for the new style, and then click **OK**.

6   Click **OK** to close the **AutoFormat** dialog box.

86 **To add a graphic to a form**

Toolbox

1 Display the form in Design view.

2 If necessary, click the **Toolbox** button to open the toolbox.

Image

3 Click the **Image** control in the toolbox, and then drag a rectangle the height and width that you want in the desired location on the form.

4 In the **Insert Picture** dialog box, navigate to the storage location of the file you want to use, and double-click it.

87 **To add a control to a form**

1 Display the form in Design view.

Toolbox

2 If necessary, click the **Toolbox** button to open the toolbox.

3 Click the appropriate control button in the toolbox, and then drag a rectangle in the desired location on the form.

4 If necessary, display the control's **Properties** dialog box, and make changes.

88 **To copy the formatting of one form control to another**

1 Display the form in Design view.

2 Click the control that contains the formatting you want to copy.

Format Painter

3 Click the **Format Painter** button on the toolbar, and then click the control to which you want to copy the formatting.

95 **To create a form using an AutoForm**

1 On the **Objects** bar, click **Forms**.

2 On the database window's toolbar, click the **New** button.

3 Click the option you want in the list, select the table on which you want to base the form, and then click **OK**.

Save

4 Click the **Save** button, enter the name you want for the form in the **Save As** dialog box, and click **OK**.

97 **To define a relationship between tables**

Relationships

1 With the database open, click the **Relationships** button on the toolbar to open the Relationships window.

Show Table

2 If the **Show Table** dialog box isn't displayed, click the **Show Table** button on the toolbar. Double-click the tables you want to work with in the list displayed, and then close the **Show Table** dialog box.

3 Drag a field from one table so that it is on top of the corresponding field in the other table.

4 Select the options you want in the **Edit Relationships** dialog box, and then click **Create**.

5 Close the Relationships window, clicking **Yes** when prompted to save its layout.

99 **To edit or delete a table relationship**

Relationships

1 With the database open, click the **Relationships** button on the toolbar to open the Relationships window.

2 Right-click the line representing the relationship you want to edit or delete, and click the appropriate command on the shortcut menu.

99 **To add a subform to a form**

Toolbox

1 Open the form in Design view.

2 If the toolbox isn't displayed, click the **Toolbox** button.

Control
Wizards

3 Make sure the **Control Wizards** button in the toolbox is active (has a border around it).

4 Click the **Subform/Subreport** button, and drag a rectangle in the desired location of the form.

Subform/
Subreport

5 Follow the instructions of the **Subform Wizard**, and click **Finish** on the wizard's last page to complete the process.

6 Adjust the size and location of the objects on your form as necessary.

102 **To adjust a subform's properties**

1 Display the form that contains the subform in Design view.

2 If necessary, open the **Properties** dialog box.

Form Selector

3 Click the **Form Selector** button in the upper left corner of the subform twice.

4 Make the changes you want in the **Properties** dialog box.

Chapter 5 **Locating Specific Information**

Page 108 **To sort information in a table**

Sort Ascending

1 With the table open in Datasheet view, click anywhere in the column of the field on which you want to base the sort, and then click the **Sort Ascending** button or the **Sort Descending** button. (To sort on more than one column of information, arrange them so they are side-by-side in the order you want to sort them, select the columns, and then use the **Sort** buttons.)

Sort
Descending

2 To reverse the sort order, click the opposite **Sort** button.

111 **To filter a table based on a selection**

1 Open the table in Datasheet view.

Filter By
Selection

2 Select the information you want to use as the filter criteria.

3 Click the **Filter By Selection** button.

4 If necessary, repeat steps 2 and 3 to filter the information further.

Remove Filter

5 Click the **Remove Filter** button to redisplay all of the table's records.

111 **To filter a table based on text you type**

1 Open the table in Datasheet view.

2 Right-click any field in the appropriate column, and click **Filter For** on the shortcut menu.

3 Type the criteria you want to use as the filter, and press `Enter`. (You can use wildcards and simple expressions as the filter criteria.)

111 **To filter a table excluding a selection**

1 Open the table in Datasheet view.

2 Right-click the appropriate field in any record, and click **Filter Excluding Selection** on the shortcut menu.

114 **To filter by form to locate information**

1 Open the table or form you want to work with in either Datasheet or Form view.

Filter By Form

2 Click the **Filter By Form** button on the toolbar.

3 Click the field box in which you want to create the filter, type the filter criteria you want, and press `Enter`; or select the criteria from the list of options. (Repeat this step for any other fields you want to filter.)

4 To add additional filter criteria for a particular field, click the **Or** tab and enter the criteria as necessary.

Apply Filter

5 Click the **Apply Filter** button.

116   **To save a query created in the Advanced Filter/Sort window**

   1   Click **Save As Query** on the **File** menu.

   2   Name the query, and click **OK**.

120   **To create a select query**

   1   On the **Objects** bar, click **Queries**.

   2   Double-click **Create query in Design view**.

   3   In the **Show Table** dialog box, double-click the tables you want to use in the query, and then close the dialog box.

   4   To include fields in the query, drag them from the lists at the top of the window to a column in the design grid. To copy all fields to the grid, double-click the title bar above the field list to select the entire list, and then drag the selection over the grid.

Run

   5   Click the **Run** button to run the query and display the results in Datasheet view.

122   **To add an expression to a query**

   1   With the query window displayed, right-click the appropriate cell in the design grid, and click **Build** on the shortcut menu.

   2   Double-click the **Functions** folder in the first column of the elements area, and then click **Built-In Functions**.

   3   Click the function type you want in the second column. Then double-click the function you want in the third column.

   4   Build the expression, and then click **OK**.

   5   Press [Enter] to move the insertion point out of the field, which completes the entry of the expression.

   6   To rename the expression, double-click **Expr1**, and then type the name you want.

128   **To turn off the display of a field in a query**

   1   Display the query in Design view.

   2   Clear the **Show** check box for any fields you don't want displayed.

   3   Switch to Datasheet view to see the results.

Chapter 6 **Keeping Your Information Accurate**

Page 135 **To create a table from scratch**

1 Click **Tables** on the **Objects** bar, and double-click **Create table in Design view**.

2 Click the first **Field Name** cell, type the field name you want, and press ⎄Tab to move to the **Data Type** cell.

3 Continue to fill in the necessary information for each field in the new table.

Save

4 Click the **Save** button, enter a name for the table, and click **OK**.

5 If necessary, assign a field as the primary key, or click **No** to have no primary key field.

139 **To set the Field Size property**

1 Open the table in Design view.

2 Select the field you want to change. Then click an insertion point in the **Field Size** property box. Enter the number of characters you want to allow in that field, or click the down arrow and select the option you want, and then save the table.

3 If the table contains data that doesn't fit this new criteria, click **Yes** in the message box to acknowledge the risk, and click **Yes** again to accept the deletion of the contents of any affected fields.

144 **To create a custom input mask**

1 Open the table in Design view.

2 Select the field to which you want to apply a special format.

3 In the **Field Properties** section, click **Input Mask**, type the mask you want, press ⎆Enter, and then save your changes.

145 **To create a field validation rule**

1 Open the table in Design view.

2 Select the field you want to add a rule to, and then click in the **Validation Rule** box.

3 Click the **...** button at the right end of the **Validation Rule** box to open the Expression Builder, or type an expression and press ⎆Enter.

4 To state the rule, type some explanatory text in the **Validation Text** box, and then save the table.

5 If Access warns you that data integrity rules have changed, click **Yes** to apply the rule or **No** to cancel it.

146   **To test validation rules for a table**

- Right-click the title bar of the table, and click **Test Validation Rules** on the shortcut menu.

147   **To create a table validation rule**

1   Open the table in Design view.

2   Right-click the table window, and click **Properties** on the shortcut menu.

3   Click in the **Validation Rule** box, type the expression for the rule you want, and press Enter.

4   In the **Validation Text** box, type the explanatory text, close the dialog box, and then save the table.

5   If Access warns you that data integrity rules have changed, click **Yes** to apply the rule or **No** to cancel it.

155   **To create an update query**

1   Use any method to create a query that displays the information you want.

2   In Design view, click **Update Query** on the **Query** menu.

3   In the **Update To** row of the field you want to update, type the text you want, or create an expression.

Run

4   Click the **Run** button, click **Yes** in the warning box, and then save the query.

156   **To create a backup copy of a table**

1   Click **Tables** on the **Objects** bar in the database window.

2   Click the table you want to back up, and then press Ctrl+C followed by Ctrl+V.

3   Type a name for the backup table, and click **OK**.

158   **To create a delete query**

1   Use any method to create a query that displays the information you want.

2   In Design view, click the **Query** menu, and click **Delete Query**.

3   Type the text you want in the **Criteria** row under the appropriate field.

Run

4   Click the **Run** button to run the delete query.

5   Click **Yes** in the warning box to delete the records, and then save the query, if necessary.

Chapter 7   Working with Reports

Page   167   **To modify a report**

View

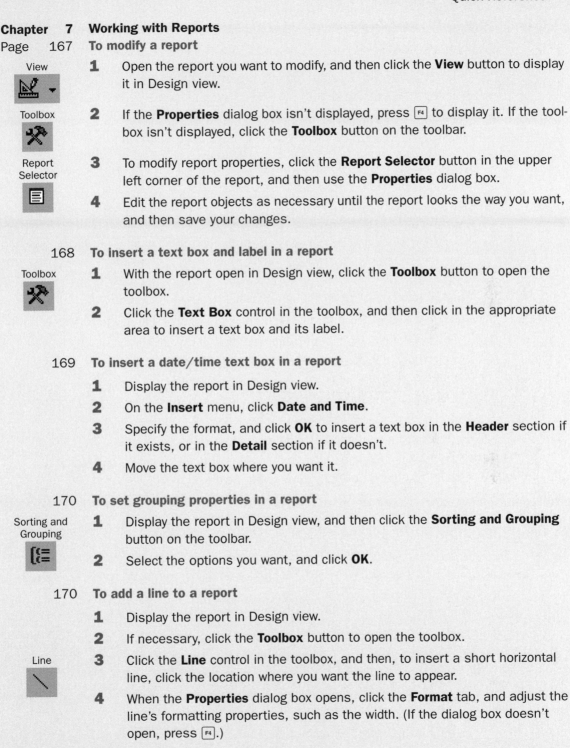

1   Open the report you want to modify, and then click the **View** button to display it in Design view.

Toolbox

2   If the **Properties** dialog box isn't displayed, press ⌨ to display it. If the toolbox isn't displayed, click the **Toolbox** button on the toolbar.

Report Selector

3   To modify report properties, click the **Report Selector** button in the upper left corner of the report, and then use the **Properties** dialog box.

4   Edit the report objects as necessary until the report looks the way you want, and then save your changes.

168   **To insert a text box and label in a report**

Toolbox

1   With the report open in Design view, click the **Toolbox** button to open the toolbox.

2   Click the **Text Box** control in the toolbox, and then click in the appropriate area to insert a text box and its label.

169   **To insert a date/time text box in a report**

1   Display the report in Design view.

2   On the **Insert** menu, click **Date and Time**.

3   Specify the format, and click **OK** to insert a text box in the **Header** section if it exists, or in the **Detail** section if it doesn't.

4   Move the text box where you want it.

170   **To set grouping properties in a report**

Sorting and Grouping

1   Display the report in Design view, and then click the **Sorting and Grouping** button on the toolbar.

2   Select the options you want, and click **OK**.

170   **To add a line to a report**

1   Display the report in Design view.

2   If necessary, click the **Toolbox** button to open the toolbox.

Line

3   Click the **Line** control in the toolbox, and then, to insert a short horizontal line, click the location where you want the line to appear.

4   When the **Properties** dialog box opens, click the **Format** tab, and adjust the line's formatting properties, such as the width. (If the dialog box doesn't open, press ⌨.)

171   **To create a report from scratch**

1   Select the table or query you want to base the new report on.

2   On the **Insert** menu, click **Report**.

3   Double-click **Design View**.

4   On the **View** menu, click **Report Header/Footer** to enclose the report in **Report Header** and **Report Footer** sections.

5   On the **View** menu, click **Sorting and Grouping**, and specify the fields that will be used to group the records in the report. Then click **OK**.

Save

6   Click the **Save** button, type the name of the report, and click **OK** to save the report as part of the open database.

172   **To modify grid properties in a report**

1   Open the report in Design view.

2   If the **Properties** dialog box isn't displayed, press ⌴ to display it.

Report Selector

3   Click the **Report Selector** button in the upper left corner of the report.

4   Click the **Format** tab in the **Properties** dialog box.

5   Set the **Grid X** and **Grid Y** properties to the number you want.

173   **To change the height of a report section**

1   Open the report in Design view.

2   If the **Properties** dialog box isn't displayed, press ⌴ to display it.

3   Click the section selector, and then set the **Height** property on the **Format** tab in the **Properties** dialog box to the height you want.

174   **To insert a label in a report**

Toolbox

1   Open the report in Design view.

2   If the **Properties** dialog box isn't displayed, press ⌴ to display it. If the toolbox isn't displayed, click the **Toolbox** button on the toolbar.

Label

3   Click the **Label** control in the toolbox, and then click where you want the label to appear.

4   Type the text you want for the label, and press ⏎.

5   Use the **Properties** dialog box to format the label as necessary.

176   **To insert a page number in a report**

1   Open the report in Design view.

2   On the **Insert** menu, click **Page Numbers**.

3   Select the options you want, and click **OK**.

177 **To add a subreport to a report**

Toolbox

Subform/
Subreport

1 Open the report to which you want to add a subreport in Design view.

2 If the toolbox isn't displayed, click the **Toolbox** button on the toolbar.

3 Click **Subform/Subreport** in the toolbox, and then click where you want the subreport to appear.

4 Follow the **SubReport Wizard's** instructions, and click **Finish** on the wizard's last page to see the subreport.

178 **To modify a subreport**

1 Display the report that contains the subreport you want to modify in Design view.

2 If the **Properties** dialog box isn't displayed, press [F4] to display it.

3 If necessary, select the subreport in the **Objects** list at the top of the **Properties** dialog box.

4 Use the options in the **Properties** dialog box to make the necessary changes.

5 Save your changes, and switch to Print Preview to see the results.

182 **To add a border to a subreport**

1 Display the report that contains the subreport you want to modify in Design view.

2 If the **Properties** dialog box isn't displayed, press [F4] to display it.

3 On the **Format** tab of the **Properties** dialog box, change the **Border Style** property to the option you want.

182 **To preview a report**

View

Next Page

Close

1 With the report open in Design view, click the **View** button to switch to Print Preview.

2 To move through the pages of the report, click the **Next Page** button on the navigation bar.

3 Click the **Close** button on the Print Preview toolbar.

184 **To preview the layout of a report**

1 With the report open in Design view, click the **View** button's down arrow, and click **Layout Preview**.

2 Click the **Close** button to return to Design view.

Chapter 8   **Making It Easy for Others to Use Your Database**

Page   192   **To open a switchboard**

- Click **Forms** on the **Objects** bar, and double-click **Switchboard** to open it in Form view. (Click the View button if you want to see it in other views.)

194   **To add a splash screen to a database**

1   With the database open, click **Forms** on the **Objects** bar, and then double-click **Create form in Design view**.

Save

2   Click the **Save** button, type a name for the form, and click **OK**.

3   If the **Properties** dialog box is not already displayed, press F4.

4   Set the form properties you want in the **Properties** dialog box.

Toolbox

5   Use the toolbox to insert any objects you want to include on your splash screen, and format them as necessary. (If necessary, click the **Toolbox** button to display the Toolbox.)

6   Save the design.

200   **To set startup options**

1   With the database open, click **Startup** on the **Tools** menu.

2   With the insertion point in the **Application Title** box, type the name you want to appear in the application's title bar, and press Tab.

3   Enter the text you want displayed in the Access title bar (it will replace the *Microsoft Access* title). You can also insert a graphic by clicking the **...** button at the end of the **Application Icon** box and browsing to the file you want.

4   Select any other desired options.

5   Click **OK** to close the **Startup** dialog box.

6   Close the database, and then open it again to see your changes in place.

205   **To display the properties of a database**

1   Open the database.

2   On the **File** menu, click **Database Properties**.

3   Click the **General** tab to note the size of the database, or click other tabs to view other information.

4   Click **OK** to close the dialog box.

205 **To compact and repair a database**

1 Open the database you want to compact and repair.

2 On the **Tools** menu, point to **Database Utilities**, and then click **Compact and Repair Database**.

206 **To run the performance analyzer on a database**

1 Open the database you want to analyze.

2 On the **Tools** menu, point to **Analyze**, and then click **Performance**.

3 To check the entire database, click the **All Object Types** tab.

4 Click **Select All**, and then click **OK** to start the analyzer.

5 Scroll through the list, click the entries, and read the analysis notes.

6 To fix a problem, click the entry, and then click the **Optimize** button.

7 Close the **Performance Analyzer** dialog box.

207 **To run performance documenter on a database**

1 Open the database you want to document.

2 On the **Tools** menu, point to **Analyze**, and then click **Documenter**.

3 Click the **All Object Types** tab.

4 Click **Select All**, and then click **OK** to start the documentation process.

209 **To export the performance documenter's report**

● After running performance documenter, click **Export** on the **File** menu, and then select a format.

Chapter 9 **Keeping Your Information Secure**

Page **212** **To encrypt a database**

1 With the database open, point to **Security** on the **Tools** menu, and then click **Encrypt/Decrypt Database**.

2 Browse to the folder where you want to store the encrypted database, type the name of the encrypted file you want to create, and click **Save**.

214 **To decrypt a database**

1 With the database closed, point to **Security** on the **Tools** menu, and then click **Encrypt/Decrypt Database**.

2 Browse to the folder where you want to store the decrypted database, type the name of the encrypted file you want to create, and click **Save**.

215   To assign a password to a database

Open

1   Click the **Open** button on the Access window's toolbar to display the **Open** dialog box.

2   Browse to the folder that contains the database you want to open, and click its file name.

3   In the dialog box, click the **Open** button's down arrow, and then click **Open Exclusive**.

4   On the **Tools** menu, point to **Security**, and click **Set Database Password**.

5   Type the password you want to use, and press [Tab] to move to the **Verify** box. Type the word again, and click **OK**.

216   To remove a database password

1   Open the database exclusively (you will have to enter the password).

2   On the **Tools** menu, point to **Security**, and then click **Unset Database Password**.

3   Type the password in the dialog box that appears, and press [Enter].

217   To share a database

1   With the database open, click **Options** on the **Tools** menu.

2   Click the **Advanced** tab.

3   In the **Default open mode** group, make sure that **Shared** is selected.

4   Select the options you want, and then click **OK** to close the dialog box.

218   To replicate a database

1   Open the database.

2   Point to **Replication** on the **Tools** menu, and click **Create Replica**.

224   To copy a database

1   Browse to the database in Windows Explorer.

2   Click the database file, and press [Ctrl]+[C] to copy it.

3   Press [Ctrl]+[V] to paste it in the same folder, or paste it in a different folder.

4   If necessary, rename the file.

224   To split a database

1   Open the database you want to split, point to **Database Utilities** on the **Tools** menu, and click **Database Splitter**.

2   Click **Split Database**.

3 Navigate to the folder in which you want to save the database, type the name you want, and click **Split**.

4 After the database is successfully split, click **OK** to return to the database window.

232 To join a workgroup

1 With Access open, point to **Security** on the **Tools** menu, and then click **Workgroup Administrator**.

2 Click **Join**.

3 Click **Browse**, browse to the database whose workgroup you want to join, click **Open**, and then click **OK**.

4 Click **OK** twice to close the alert box and the dialog box.

235 To change your account password

1 On the **Tools** menu, point to **Security**, and then click **User and Group Accounts**.

2 Click the **Change Logon Password** tab.

3 Click the **Old Password** box, type the current password, press [Tab], type the new password, press [Tab] again, and verify the new password by typing it again. Then click **OK**.

238 To secure VBA code in a database

1 With the database open, press [Alt]+[F11] to open the VBA Editor.

2 On the VBA Editor's **Tools** menu, click the **Properties** command for the database you have open.

3 Click the **Protection** tab, and click **Lock project for viewing**.

4 In the **Password** box, type the password you want, and press [Tab] to move to the **Confirm Password** box.

5 Type the password again, and then click **OK**.

6 Press [Alt]+[F11] to return to Access, and then close the database.

239 To remove a password from VBA code

1 With the database open, press [Ctrl]+[F11] to open the VBA Editor.

2 On the VBA Editor's **Tools** menu, click the **Properties** command for the database you have open.

3 On the **Protection** tab, clear the **Lock project for viewing** check box, remove the asterisks in the two password boxes, and click **OK**.

4 Close the database.

240 **To save a database as a distributable MDE file**

1 With Access open (but no databases open), point to **Database Utilities** on the **Tools** menu, and then click **Make MDE File**.

2 In the **Database To Save As MDE** dialog box, browse to the storage location of the database you want to save, select the file name, and then click **Make MDE**.

3 Type the name you want in the **Edit name** box, and click **Save**.

Chapter 10 **Working with Pages and Modules**

Page **245** **To export a database object to a static HTML page**

1 With the database open, select the object you want to export.

2 On the **File** menu, click **Export**.

3 Browse to the folder where you want to store the file, type the name you want in the **File name** box, select **HTML Documents** as the **Save as type** setting, click the **Autostart** check box, and then click **Export**.

4 In the **HTML Output Options** dialog box, make sure the **Select a HTML Template** check box is not selected, and then click **OK**.

5 If you don't see the HTML page, click the file name on the taskbar to display it. Click the **Next** hyperlink to scroll through the pages of the file.

262 **To use AutoPage to create a data access page**

1 With the database open, click **Pages** on the **Objects** bar.

2 Click the **New** button at the top of the database window.

3 Click the **AutoPage** option you want, display the list of tables and queries, click the table or query you want, and then click **OK**.

4 Click the **Save** button on the toolbar to save your new page.

5 In the **Save As Data Access Page** dialog box, browse to the folder where you want to save the file, type the name you want for the file, and click **Save**.

6 If Access warns that the connection string for this page uses an absolute page, click **OK** to dismiss the message. (A UNC path is appropriate if you are using a file on a network computer.)

7 Use the buttons on the navigation bar to view different records and perform other tasks.

264 **To update links when you move a data access page**

1 Try to open the data access page in Page view.

2 When you see the message that the file can't be found, click the **Update Link** button, and locate the HTM file.

3 When you get another error stating that the page can't find the database, switch to Design view, and open the **Page Properties** dialog box.

4 On the **Data** tab, click **ConnectionString**, and then click its **...** button.

5 Click the **Connection** tab, edit or browse to the correct path in the first box, and then click **OK**.

268 **To hide buttons on the navigation bar in a data access page**

1 Display the data access page in Design view.

2 Click the button on the navigation bar that you want to hide.

3 In the **Properties** dialog box, click the **Format** tab, click the **Visibility** property, and then select **hidden**.

269 **To create a data access page from scratch**

1 With the database open, click **Pages** on the **Objects** bar.

2 Double-click **Create data access page in Design view** to open a blank data access page.

Save

3 Click the **Save** button, browse to the folder where you want to save the file, type the name you want for the page, and click **Save**.

273 **To create a PivotTable**

Field List

1 Open a data access page.

2 If the Field List is not displayed, click the **Field List** button on the toolbar.

Toolbox

3 If the toolbox is not displayed, click the **Toolbox** button on the toolbar.

4 In the toolbox, click the **Office PivotTable** tool, and then click in the upper left corner of the blank section on the page.

Office
PivotTable

5 Click in the PivotTable, and then double-click its frame to open the **Properties** dialog box.

6 Click the **Other** tab, click the **DataMember** property, select the table or query on which the PivotTable will be based from the list, and close the **Properties** dialog box.

7 In the **Field List**, select the same table or query.

8 Drag a field from the Field List to the horizontal box labeled **Drop Filter Fields Here**.

9 Drag a field to the vertical box labeled **Drop Row Fields Here**.

10 Drag a field to the horizontal box labeled **Drop Column Fields Here**.

11 Drag a field to the box labeled **Drop Totals or Detail Fields Here**.

View

12 Click the **View** button to switch to Page view, and experiment with the Pivot-Table to make sure it works.

13 Save the page

275 **To create a PivotChart**

Field List

1 Open a data access page.

2 If the Field List is not displayed, click the **Field List** button on the toolbar.

Toolbox

3 If the toolbox is not displayed, click the **Toolbox** button on the toolbar.

4 Click the **Office Chart** button, and, on the page, drag a rectangle the size you want the chart to be.

Office Chart

5 Click in the component to display the **Commands and Options** dialog box.

6 Click the **Data from the following Web page item** option, and then click **DataSourceControl:MSODSC**.

7 Click the **Data Details** tab, click the **Data member, table, view, or cube name** down arrow, and click the name of the table or query you want to chart in the list.

8 Click the **Type** tab, click the upper left **Column** option, and then click the **Close** button to close the dialog box.

9 Drag a field from the Field List to the **Drop Filter Fields Here** box.

10 Drag fields to the **Drop Category Fields Here** box, the **Drop Series Fields Here** box, and the **Drop Data Fields Here** box.

View

11 Click the **View** button to see the results.

12 Save the data access page.

Glossary

action query   A type of query that updates or makes changes to multiple records in one operation.

Active Server Pages (ASP)   Pages stored on a server that generate different views of the data in response to choices users make on a Web page.

aggregate function   A function that groups and performs calculations on multiple fields.

arithmetic operator   An operator that performs an arithmetic operation: + (addition), - (subtraction), * (multiplication), or / (division).

ASCII   Acronym for *American Standard Code for Information Interchange*, a coding scheme for text characters developed in 1968. ASCII files have the extension *.asc*.

ASP   Acronym for *Active Server Pages*.

AutoForm   A feature that efficiently creates forms using all the available fields and minimal formatting.

back-end database   The part of a split database that is stored on a server for security reasons, and which usually consists of the tables and other objects that you don't want people to be able to modify. *See also* front-end database.

binary file   A file coded so that its data can be read by a computer.

Boolean   A data type that can hold either of two mutually exclusive values, often expressed as *yes/no, 1/10, on/off,* or *true/false.*

bound   Linked, as when a form used to view information in a table is linked to that table.

Briefcase   A replication folder that you use to keep files in sync when you work on different computers in different locations.

class module   One of two types of modules in Microsoft Visual Basic for Applications (VBA). A class module is associated with a specific form or report. *See also* standard module.

code   VBA programs; also called *procedures*, referred to in Access as modules. *See also* class module; standard module.

combo box   A control in which you can either select from a drop-down list or type an option.

comma-delimited text file   A data file consisting of fields and records, stored as text, in which the fields are separated from each other by commas.

command button   A control shaped like a button to which you can attach code that runs when the button is clicked.

comment   A note embedded in code that helps people reading the code understand its purpose.

comparison operator   An operator that compares values, such as < (less than), > (greater than), and = (equal to).

component   A part of a database that is used to store and organize information. Also known as a database object.

compression   A means of compacting information for more efficient means of transportation.

constant   A named item that retains a constant value throughout the execution of a program, as opposed to a variable, whose value can change during execution.

control   An object such as a label, text box, option button, or check box in a form or report that allows you to view or manipulate information stored in tables or queries.

control property   A setting that determines the appearance of a control, what data it displays, and how that data looks. A control's properties can be viewed and changed in its Properties dialog box.

control source   The source of a control's data—the field, table or query whose data will be displayed in the control.

criteria   The specifications you give to Access so that it can find matching fields and records. Criteria can be simple, such as all the records with a postal code of 98052, or complex, such as the phone numbers of all customers who have placed orders for over $500 worth of live plants within the last two weeks and who live in postal codes 98052, 98053, and 98054.

crosstab query   A query that calculates and restructures data for easier analysis. *See also* select query, parameter query, and action query.

data access page   A dynamic Web page that allows users to directly manipulate data in a database via the Internet.

data source   A database or file to which a data access page is connected.

data type   The type of data that can be entered in a field: text, memo, number, date/ time, currency, AutoNumber, Boolean (Yes/No), OLE object, and hyperlink. You set the data type by displaying the table in Design view.

data warehouse   A company that serves as a data repository for a variety of data and that may make use of replication to keep each database synchronized when more than one version of the database is updated in more than one remote location.

database application   A database that is refined and made simpler for the user by the sophisticated use of queries, forms, reports, a switchboard, and various other tools.

database program   A program that stores data. Programs range from those that can store one table per file (referred to as a flat database) to those that can store many related tables per file (referred to as a relational database).

database security   The protection of database information from accidental damage, destruction, or theft through the use of encryption, passwords, access permissions, replication, and other security measures.

database window   The window from which all database objects can be manipulated or accessed.

Datasheet view   The view in which the information in a table or query can be viewed and manipulated. *See also* views.

decrypting   "Unscrambling" a database that has been encrypted for security reasons.

delimited text file   A type of text file format in which each record and each field is separated from the next by a known character called a *delimiter*.

delimiter   A character such as a comma (,), semicolon (;), or backslash (\), or pairs of characters such as quotation marks (" ") or braces ({}), that are used to separate records and fields in a delimited text file.

design grid   The name given to the structure used in Design view to manually construct and modify advanced filters and queries.

Design Master   In replication, the term for the version of the database from which replicas are made and where changes made to replicas are copied and synchronized.

Design view   The view in which the structure of a table or query can be viewed and manipulated. *See also* views.

DHTML   Acronym for *Dynamic Hypertext Markup Language*.

Dynamic Hypertext Markup Language (DHTML)   A new version of the standard authoring language, HTML, that includes codes for dynamic Web page elements.

dynamic Web page A page whose content is created in response to some action on the part of a user who is viewing the page over the Internet. *See also* static HTML page.

encrypting "Scrambling" data for security reasons.

event An action performed by a user or by Access, to which a programmed response can be attached. Common user events include Click, Double Click, Mouse Down, Mouse Move, and Mouse Up. You can use macros or VBA modules to determine how Access responds when one of these events occurs.

exclusive use A setting used when you want to be the only person who currently has a database open. You must open a database for exclusive use when setting or removing a password that limits database access.

exporting The process of creating a file containing the information in a database table in a format that can be used by other programs.

expression A combination of functions, field values, constants, and operators that yield a result. Expressions can be simple, such as *>100*, or complex, such as *((ProductPrice*Quantity)*.90)+(Shipping+Handling)*.

Expression Builder A feature used to create formulas (expressions) used in query criteria, form and report properties, and table validation rules.

Extensible Markup Language (XML) A refined language developed for Web documents that describes document structure rather than appearance.

field An individual item of the information that is the same type across all records. Represented in Access as a column in a database table. *See also* record.

fixed-width text file A common text file format that is often used to transfer data from older applications. Each record is always the same number of characters long, and the same field within the records is always the same number of characters. In other words, the same field always starts the same number of characters from the beginning of each record, and any characters not occupied by real data are filled with zeros.

flag A marker that can be set to true or false to indicate the state of an object.

flat database A simple database consisting of one table. *See also* relational database.

form A database object used to enter, edit, and manipulate information in a database table. A form gives you a simple view of some or all of the fields of one record at a time.

Form view The view in which you can enter and modify the information in a record. *See also* views.

front-end database   The part of a split database that is distributed to the people who analyze and enter data. The actual data tables are stored on a server for security reasons. *See also* back-end database.

function   A named procedure or routine in a program, often used for mathematical or financial calculations.

function procedure   In VBA, a procedure that is enclosed in Function and End Function statements and returns a value. *See also* sub procedure.

group   One of four elements—the other three being object, permission, and user—on which the Access user-level security model is based.

grouping level   The level by which records are grouped in a report. For example, records might be grouped by state (first level), then by city (second level), and then by postal code (third level).

HTML   Acronym for *Hypertext Markup Language*.

HTML tag   An HTML command that determines how the tagged information looks and acts.

Hypertext Markup Language (HTML)   The authoring language used to create Web documents.

importing   The method whereby data is brought into an Access database from a different database or program. *See also* exporting.

input mask   A field property that determines what data can be entered in the field, how the data looks, and the format in which it is stored.

intranet   A secure, proprietary Web-based network used within a company or group and accessible only to its members.

keyword   A word that is part of the VBA programming language.

label control   An area on a form that contains text that appears on the form in Form view.

LAN   Acronym for *local area network*.

Layout Preview   A view of a report that shows you how each element will look but without all the detail of Print Preview.

linking   The process of connecting to data in other applications.

local area network (LAN)   A computer network that connects computers, printers, and other hardware to a server or group of servers.

logical operator   One of the Boolean operators: AND, OR and NOT.

Lookup Wizard   The wizard in Access that simplifies the creation of a Lookup list.

macro   A set of automated instructions that perform a sequence of simple tasks.

main form   One form that is linked to one or more tables. *See also* subform.

main report   One report that displays records from one or more tables. *See also* subreport.

many-to-many relationship   A relationship formed between two tables that each have a one-to-many relationship with a third table. *See also* one-to-many relationship; one-to-one relationship.

mapped network drive   A drive to which you have assigned a drive letter. Used for quickly accessing files stored in locations that are not likely to change. *See also* UNC path.

mask   A field property that determines what data can be entered in a field, how the data looks, and the format in which it is stored.

Microsoft Database Executable (MDE)   A compiled version of a database. Saving a database as an MDE file compiles all modules, removes all editable source code, and compacts the destination database.

Microsoft Visual Basic for Applications (VBA)   A high-level programming language developed for the purpose of creating Windows applications.

MDE   Acronym for *Microsoft Database Executable.*

module   A VBA program.

named range   A group of cells in an Excel spreadsheet.

native format   The file format an application uses to produce its own files.

navigation button   One of the buttons found on a form or navigation bar that helps users display specific records.

network server   A central computer that stores files and programs and manages system functions for a network.

object   One of the components of an Access database, such as a table, form, or report.

one-to-many relationship   A relationship formed between two tables in which each record in one table has more than one related record in the other table. *See also* many-to-many relationship; one-to-one relationship.

one-to-one relationship   A relationship formed between two tables in which each record in one table has only one related record in the other table. *See also* many-to-many relationship; one-to-many relationship.

operator   *See* arithmetic operator; comparison operator; logical operator.

optimistic locking   Locking a record only for the brief time that Access is saving changes to it.

option button   A control on a form that allows users to select preferred settings.

page   *See* data access page.

parameter query   A query that prompts for the information to be used in the query, such as a range of dates.

parsing   In Access, the process of analyzing a document and identifying anything that looks like structured data.

password   A secret sequence of letters and other symbols needed to log on to a database as an authorized user.

permission   An attribute that specifies how a user can access data or objects in a database.

pessimistic locking   Locking a record for the entire time it is being edited.

PivotChart   An interactive chart that is linked to a database.

PivotTable   An interactive table that is linked to a database.

populate   To fill a table or other object with data.

primary key   One or more fields that determine the uniqueness of each record in a database.

Print Preview   A view of a report that allows users to see exactly how the report will look when printed.

procedure   VBA code that performs a specific task or set of tasks.

property   A setting that determines the content and appearance of the object to which it applies.

query   A database object that locates information so that the information can be viewed, changed, or analyzed in various ways. The results of a query can be used as the basis for forms, reports, and data access pages.

record selector   The gray bar along the left edge of a table or form.

record source   The place from which information derives between two bound objects, such as a field that pulls information from a table. *See also* control source.

record   All the items of information (fields) that pertain to one particular entity, such as a customer, employee, or project. *See also* field.

referential integrity   The system of rules Access uses to ensure that relationships between tables are valid and that data cannot be changed in one table without also being changed in all related tables.

relational database   A sophisticated type of database in which data is organized in multiple related tables. Data can be pulled from the tables just as if they were stored in a single table.

relationship   An association between common fields in two tables.

replica   A copy of the Design Master of a database.

replicating   The process of creating a Design Master so that multiple copies of a database can be sent to multiple locations for editing. The copies can then be synchronized with the Design Master so that it reflects all the changes.

report   A database object used to display a table or tables in a formatted, easily accessible manner, either on the screen or on paper.

row selector   The gray box at the left end of a row in a table that, when clicked, selects all the cells in the row.

running a query   The process of telling Access to search the specified table or tables for records that match the criteria you have specified in the query and to display the designated fields from those records in a datasheet (table). *See also* criteria; query.

saving   The process of storing the current state of a database or database object for later retrieval. In Access, new records and changes to existing records are saved when you move to a different record; you don't have to do anything to save them. You do have to save new objects and changes to existing objects.

schema   A description of the structure of XML data, as opposed to the content of the data. Applications that export to XML might combine the content and schema in one .xml file or might create an .xml file to hold the content and an .xsd file to hold the schema.

select query   A query that retrieves data matching specified criteria from one or more tables and displays the results in a datasheet.

selector   A small box attached to an object that you click to select the object.

sharing a database   Providing access to a database so more that one person can access it to add or alter its information.

splash screen   An introductory screen containing useful or entertaining information. Often used to divert the user's attention while data is loading.

SQL   Acronym for *Structured Query Language*.

SQL database   A database that supports SQL and that can be accessed simultaneously by several users on a LAN.

standard module   A VBA program that contains general procedures that are not associated with any object.

static HTML page   A Web page that provides a snapshot of some portion of the database contents at one point in time.

string   A series of characters enclosed in quotation marks.

sub procedure   A series of VBA statements enclosed by Sub and End Sub statements.

subdatasheet   A datasheet that is embedded in another datasheet.

subform   A form inserted in a control that is embedded in another form.

subreport   A report inserted in a control that is embedded in another report.

switchboard   A form used to navigate among the objects of a database application so that users don't have to be familiar with the actual database.

synchronizing   The process of comparing the information in a database replica with the database's Design Master and merging any changes.

syntax   The format that expressions must conform to in order for Access to be able to process them.

table   Information organized in columns (records) and rows (fields).

Table Wizard   The Access tool that helps users construct tables.

tags   Codes in HTML that give instructions for formatting or other actions.

task pane   A pane that provides a quick and easy way of initiating common tasks.

template   A ready-made database application that users can tailor to fit their needs.

text box control   A control on a form or report where data from a table can be entered or edited.

transaction record   The written record of transactions.

unbound   Not linked, as when a control is used to calculate values from two or more fields and is therefore not bound to any particular field. *See also* bound.

UNC   Acronym for *universal naming convention.*

universal naming convention (UNC) path   A path format that includes the computer name, drive letter, and nested folder names. *See also* mapped network drive.

update query   A select query that changes the query's results in some way, such as by changing a field.

user   A person authorized to access a database but who generally is not involved in establishing its structure.

validation rule   A field property that tests entries to ensure that only the correct types of information become part of a table.

variable   A name or symbol that stands for a value that can change.

VBA   Acronym for *Microsoft Visual Basic for Applications.*

VBA procedure   A VBA program.

view   The display of information from a specific perspective.

Visual Basic Editor   The environment in which VBA code is written.

Visual Basic Integrated Development Environment (IDE)   *See* Visual Basic Editor.

Web browser   An application used to view Web pages on the World Wide Web.

WIF   Acronym for *workgroup information file.*

wildcard character   A placeholder for an unknown character or characters in search criteria.

wizard   A helpful tool that guides users through the steps for completing a specific task.

workgroup information file (WIF)   The file where information about the objects, permissions, users, and groups that comprise a specific workgroup is stored.

worksheet   A page in a Microsoft Excel spreadsheet.

XML   Acronym for *Extensible Markup Language.*

Index

A

Access. *See* Microsoft Access
Access objects
    data access pages (*see* data
        access pages)
    in expressions, 156
**access to VBA code, controlling,
    237**
action queries, 119
    converting select queries
        into, 156
    creating, 156
actions. *See* events
Active Server Pages (ASP), 244
advanced filtering, 116
aggregate functions, 128
aligning label text, 80
**analyzing performance,
    204, 206**
apostrophes in VBA, 93
append queries, 119
application title, renaming, 200
applying
    filters, 114
    form layout, 75
    startup options, 201
    styles, 28
    styles, to forms, 96
    themes, to data access
        pages, 271
**area codes, requiring for phone
    numbers, 143**
arithmetic operators, 118
ASCII, 53
ASP (Active Server Pages), 244
assigning
    passwords, 216
    permissions, 228
    users to groups, 230
authorizing database access.
    See user-level security;
    workgroups
**autocomplete, in Visual Basic
    Editor, 250**
AutoFormats, creating new, 85
AutoForms, 94
    background styles for, 96

automatically
    numbering, 39
    saving, 31
automating actions. *See*
    macros; modules
AutoNumber data type, 39
**AutoPage, creating data access
    pages with, 261**

B

back-end databases, 223–24
backgrounds
    AutoForm, styles for, 96
    form, 81
    form, resizing, 84
    label, 79
backing up
    before running update
        queries, 156
    databases, 224
    tables, 156
binary files, 212. *See also*
    databases
blank databases, creating, 34
Boolean data type, 135
    display options, 138
borders
    of controls, color of, 80
    subreport, transparent, 182
Briefcase
    folder, creating new, 219
    installing, 220
    renaming, 220
    replicating databases to, 219
    updating, 222
browsers. *See* Web browsers
building expressions, 123
business tables, 35

C

Calls form, 32
Caption property, 40
captions
    adding to form headers, 87

    for combo boxes, 89
    for fields, 40
    for labels, 80
changes, undoing, 31
changing. *See also* editing
    Access icon, 200
    data types, 41
    delimiters for delimited text
        files, 54
    field names, 40
    font, on form labels, 77
    passwords, 236
    primary key fields, 39
    query criteria, 155
characters
    in input masks, 141–42
    uniformly spaced (*see* fixed-
        width text files)
**check boxes, inserting in
    forms, 196**
checking
    variable spelling, 250
    VBA code syntax, 255
    wizard results, 30
class modules, 247
clearing design grids, 116
closing
    data type list, without making
        changes, 39
    databases, 6
    dialog boxes, 32
    switchboards, 6
    switchboards,
        automatically, 190
    tables, 10
**code, for tables in Web pages,
    viewing, 67**
code, VBA, 247
collapsing datasheets, 10
colors, 79
columns, 2
    adjacent, selecting, 46
    Data Type, 39
    Description, 39
    in Design view, 39
    Field Name, 39
    freezing, 47
    headings, setting, 51
    hiding, 46

Online Training Solutions, Inc. (OTSI)

OTSI is a traditional and electronic publishing company specializing in the creation, production, and delivery of computer software training. OTSI publishes the Quick Course® and Practical Business Skills™ series of computer and business training products. The principals of OTSI and authors of this book are:

Joyce Cox has 20 years' experience in writing about and editing technical subjects for non-technical audiences. For 12 of those years she was the principal author for Online Press. She was also the first managing editor of Microsoft Press, an editor for Sybex, and an editor for the University of California.

Steve Lambert started playing with computers in the mid-seventies. As computers evolved from wire-wrap and solder to consumer products, he evolved from hardware geek to programmer and writer. He has written 14 books and a wide variety of technical documentation and has produced training tools and help systems.

Gale Nelson honed her communication skills as a technical writer for a SQL Server training company. Her attention to detail soon led her into software testing and quality assurance management. She now divides her work time between writing and data conversion projects.

Joan Preppernau started working with computers as a PowerPoint slideshow production assistant. As a CD-ROM data-prep manager, she participated in the creation of training products for computer professionals. She now wears a variety of hats including operations manager, Webmaster, writer, and technical editor.

The OTSI team consists of the following outstanding publishing professionals:

Susie Bayers

Jan Bednarczuk

RJ Cadranell

Liz Clark

Nancy Depper

Leslie Eliel

Jon Kenoyer

Marlene Lambert

Robin Ludwig

Gabrielle Nonast

For more information about Online Training Solutions, Inc., visit *www.otsiweb.com*.

Get a **Free**
e-mail newsletter, updates,
special offers, links to related books,
and more when you

register on line!

Register your Microsoft Press® title on our Web site and you'll get a FREE subscription to our e-mail newsletter, *Microsoft Press Book Connections.* You'll find out about newly released and upcoming books and learning tools, online events, software downloads, special offers and coupons for Microsoft Press customers, and information about major Microsoft® product releases. You can also read useful additional information about all the titles we publish, such as detailed book descriptions, tables of contents and indexes, sample chapters, links to related books and book series, author biographies, and reviews by other customers.

Registration is easy. Just visit this Web page and fill in your information:

http://www.microsoft.com/mspress/register

Microsoft®

Proof of Purchase

Use this page as proof of purchase if participating in a promotion or rebate offer on this title. Proof of purchase must be used in conjunction with other proof(s) of payment such as your dated sales receipt—see offer details.

Microsoft® Access Version 2002 Step by Step
0-7356-1299-4

CUSTOMER NAME

Microsoft Press, PO Box 97017, Redmond, WA 98073-9830

MICROSOFT LICENSE AGREEMENT
Book Companion CD

IMPORTANT—READ CAREFULLY: This Microsoft End-User License Agreement ("EULA") is a legal agreement between you (either an individual or an entity) and Microsoft Corporation for the Microsoft product identified above, which includes computer software and may include associated media, printed materials, and "online" or electronic documentation ("SOFTWARE PRODUCT"). Any component included within the SOFTWARE PRODUCT that is accompanied by a separate End-User License Agreement shall be governed by such agreement and not the terms set forth below. By installing, copying, or otherwise using the SOFTWARE PRODUCT, you agree to be bound by the terms of this EULA. If you do not agree to the terms of this EULA, you are not authorized to install, copy, or otherwise use the SOFTWARE PRODUCT; you may, however, return the SOFTWARE PRODUCT, along with all printed materials and other items that form a part of the Microsoft product that includes the SOFTWARE PRODUCT, to the place you obtained them for a full refund.

SOFTWARE PRODUCT LICENSE

The SOFTWARE PRODUCT is protected by United States copyright laws and international copyright treaties, as well as other intellectual property laws and treaties. The SOFTWARE PRODUCT is licensed, not sold.

1. GRANT OF LICENSE. This EULA grants you the following rights:

    a. Software Product. You may install and use one copy of the SOFTWARE PRODUCT on a single computer. The primary user of the computer on which the SOFTWARE PRODUCT is installed may make a second copy for his or her exclusive use on a portable computer.

    b. Storage/Network Use. You may also store or install a copy of the SOFTWARE PRODUCT on a storage device, such as a network server, used only to install or run the SOFTWARE PRODUCT on your other computers over an internal network; however, you must acquire and dedicate a license for each separate computer on which the SOFTWARE PRODUCT is installed or run from the storage device. A license for the SOFTWARE PRODUCT may not be shared or used concurrently on different computers.

    c. License Pak. If you have acquired this EULA in a Microsoft License Pak, you may make the number of additional copies of the computer software portion of the SOFTWARE PRODUCT authorized on the printed copy of this EULA, and you may use each copy in the manner specified above. You are also entitled to make a corresponding number of secondary copies for portable computer use as specified above.

    d. Sample Code. Solely with respect to portions, if any, of the SOFTWARE PRODUCT that are identified within the SOFTWARE PRODUCT as sample code (the "SAMPLE CODE"):

        i. Use and Modification. Microsoft grants you the right to use and modify the source code version of the SAMPLE CODE, *provided* you comply with subsection (d)(iii) below. You may not distribute the SAMPLE CODE, or any modified version of the SAMPLE CODE, in source code form.

        ii. Redistributable Files. Provided you comply with subsection (d)(iii) below, Microsoft grants you a nonexclusive, royalty-free right to reproduce and distribute the object code version of the SAMPLE CODE and of any modified SAMPLE CODE, other than SAMPLE CODE, or any modified version thereof, designated as not redistributable in the Readme file that forms a part of the SOFTWARE PRODUCT (the "Non-Redistributable Sample Code"). All SAMPLE CODE other than the Non-Redistributable Sample Code is collectively referred to as the "REDISTRIBUTABLES."

        iii. Redistribution Requirements. If you redistribute the REDISTRIBUTABLES, you agree to: (i) distribute the REDISTRIBUTABLES in object code form only in conjunction with and as a part of your software application product; (ii) not use Microsoft's name, logo, or trademarks to market your software application product; (iii) include a valid copyright notice on your software application product; (iv) indemnify, hold harmless, and defend Microsoft from and against any claims or lawsuits, including attorney's fees, that arise or result from the use or distribution of your software application product; and (v) not permit further distribution of the REDISTRIBUTABLES by your end user. Contact Microsoft for the applicable royalties due and other licensing terms for all other uses and/or distribution of the REDISTRIBUTABLES.

2. DESCRIPTION OF OTHER RIGHTS AND LIMITATIONS.

    • **Limitations on Reverse Engineering, Decompilation, and Disassembly.** You may not reverse engineer, decompile, or disassemble the SOFTWARE PRODUCT, except and only to the extent that such activity is expressly permitted by applicable law notwithstanding this limitation.

    • **Separation of Components.** The SOFTWARE PRODUCT is licensed as a single product. Its component parts may not be separated for use on more than one computer.

    • **Rental.** You may not rent, lease, or lend the SOFTWARE PRODUCT.

    • **Support Services.** Microsoft may, but is not obligated to, provide you with support services related to the SOFTWARE PRODUCT ("Support Services"). Use of Support Services is governed by the Microsoft policies and programs described in the user manual, in "online" documentation, and/or in other Microsoft-provided materials. Any supplemental software code provided to you as part of the Support Services shall be considered part of the SOFTWARE PRODUCT and subject to the terms and conditions of this EULA. With respect to technical information you provide to Microsoft as part of the Support Services, Microsoft may use such information for its business purposes, including for product support and development. Microsoft will not utilize such technical information in a form that personally identifies you.

- **Software Transfer.** You may permanently transfer all of your rights under this EULA, provided you retain no copies, you transfer all of the SOFTWARE PRODUCT (including all component parts, the media and printed materials, any upgrades, this EULA, and, if applicable, the Certificate of Authenticity), **and** the recipient agrees to the terms of this EULA.

- **Termination.** Without prejudice to any other rights, Microsoft may terminate this EULA if you fail to comply with the terms and conditions of this EULA. In such event, you must destroy all copies of the SOFTWARE PRODUCT and all of its component parts.

3. **COPYRIGHT.** All title and copyrights in and to the SOFTWARE PRODUCT (including but not limited to any images, photographs, animations, video, audio, music, text, SAMPLE CODE, REDISTRIBUTABLES, and "applets" incorporated into the SOFTWARE PRODUCT) and any copies of the SOFTWARE PRODUCT are owned by Microsoft or its suppliers. The SOFTWARE PRODUCT is protected by copyright laws and international treaty provisions. Therefore, you must treat the SOFTWARE PRODUCT like any other copyrighted material **except** that you may install the SOFTWARE PRODUCT on a single computer provided you keep the original solely for backup or archival purposes. You may not copy the printed materials accompanying the SOFTWARE PRODUCT.

4. **U.S. GOVERNMENT RESTRICTED RIGHTS.** The SOFTWARE PRODUCT and documentation are provided with RESTRICTED RIGHTS. Use, duplication, or disclosure by the Government is subject to restrictions as set forth in subparagraph (c)(1)(ii) of the Rights in Technical Data and Computer Software clause at DFARS 252.227-7013 or subparagraphs (c)(1) and (2) of the Commercial Computer Software—Restricted Rights at 48 CFR 52.227-19, as applicable. Manufacturer is Microsoft Corporation/One Microsoft Way/Redmond, WA 98052-6399.

5. **EXPORT RESTRICTIONS.** You agree that you will not export or re-export the SOFTWARE PRODUCT, any part thereof, or any process or service that is the direct product of the SOFTWARE PRODUCT (the foregoing collectively referred to as the "Restricted Components"), to any country, person, entity, or end user subject to U.S. export restrictions. You specifically agree not to export or re-export any of the Restricted Components (i) to any country to which the U.S. has embargoed or restricted the export of goods or services, which currently include, but are not necessarily limited to, Cuba, Iran, Iraq, Libya, North Korea, Sudan, and Syria, or to any national of any such country, wherever located, who intends to transmit or transport the Restricted Components back to such country; (ii) to any end user who you know or have reason to know will utilize the Restricted Components in the design, development, or production of nuclear, chemical, or biological weapons; or (iii) to any end user who has been prohibited from participating in U.S. export transactions by any federal agency of the U.S. government. You warrant and represent that neither the BXA nor any other U.S. federal agency has suspended, revoked, or denied your export privileges.

DISCLAIMER OF WARRANTY

NO WARRANTIES OR CONDITIONS. MICROSOFT EXPRESSLY DISCLAIMS ANY WARRANTY OR CONDITION FOR THE SOFTWARE PRODUCT. THE SOFTWARE PRODUCT AND ANY RELATED DOCUMENTATION ARE PROVIDED "AS IS" WITHOUT WARRANTY OR CONDITION OF ANY KIND, EITHER EXPRESS OR IMPLIED, INCLUDING, WITHOUT LIMITATION, THE IMPLIED WARRANTIES OF MERCHANTABILITY, FITNESS FOR A PARTICULAR PURPOSE, OR NONINFRINGEMENT. THE ENTIRE RISK ARISING OUT OF USE OR PERFORMANCE OF THE SOFTWARE PRODUCT REMAINS WITH YOU.

LIMITATION OF LIABILITY. TO THE MAXIMUM EXTENT PERMITTED BY APPLICABLE LAW, IN NO EVENT SHALL MICROSOFT OR ITS SUPPLIERS BE LIABLE FOR ANY SPECIAL, INCIDENTAL, INDIRECT, OR CONSEQUENTIAL DAMAGES WHATSOEVER (INCLUDING, WITHOUT LIMITATION, DAMAGES FOR LOSS OF BUSINESS PROFITS, BUSINESS INTERRUPTION, LOSS OF BUSINESS INFORMATION, OR ANY OTHER PECUNIARY LOSS) ARISING OUT OF THE USE OF OR INABILITY TO USE THE SOFTWARE PRODUCT OR THE PROVISION OF OR FAILURE TO PROVIDE SUPPORT SERVICES, EVEN IF MICROSOFT HAS BEEN ADVISED OF THE POSSIBILITY OF SUCH DAMAGES. IN ANY CASE, MICROSOFT'S ENTIRE LIABILITY UNDER ANY PROVISION OF THIS EULA SHALL BE LIMITED TO THE GREATER OF THE AMOUNT ACTUALLY PAID BY YOU FOR THE SOFTWARE PRODUCT OR US$5.00; PROVIDED, HOWEVER, IF YOU HAVE ENTERED INTO A MICROSOFT SUPPORT SERVICES AGREEMENT, MICROSOFT'S ENTIRE LIABILITY REGARDING SUPPORT SERVICES SHALL BE GOVERNED BY THE TERMS OF THAT AGREEMENT. BECAUSE SOME STATES AND JURISDICTIONS DO NOT ALLOW THE EXCLUSION OR LIMITATION OF LIABILITY, THE ABOVE LIMITATION MAY NOT APPLY TO YOU.

MISCELLANEOUS

This EULA is governed by the laws of the State of Washington USA, except and only to the extent that applicable law mandates governing law of a different jurisdiction.

Should you have any questions concerning this EULA, or if you desire to contact Microsoft for any reason, please contact the Microsoft subsidiary serving your country, or write: Microsoft Sales Information Center/One Microsoft Way/Redmond, WA 98052-6399.

Key Elements of Access 2002

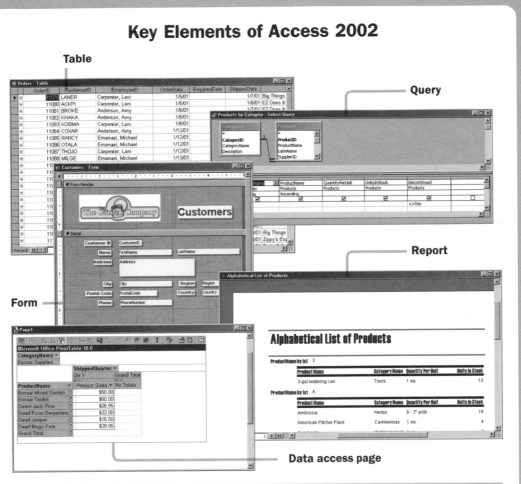

Table

Query

Form

Report

Data access page

Common Keyboard Shortcuts

Shortcut	Action
Ctrl + N	Create a new database
Alt + N	Create a new object of the type selected on the **Objects** bar
Ctrl + O	Open an existing database
Ctrl + P	Print the current or selected object
Shift + Enter	Add a control
Ctrl + ↑	Move the selected control in the direction of the arrow
Shift + ↑ or Shift + ↓	Increase or decrease the height or width of a control
F4	Open the **Properties** dialog box
F5	Switch from Form view to Design view
F11	Activate the database window
Ctrl + F6	Move among open windows
Shift + F10	Display the shortcut menu for the selected object

To set the primary key field

1. Display the table in Design view.
2. Select the field that you want to be the primary key field in the top portion of the window.
3. On the **Edit** menu, click **Primary Key**.

To create an input mask

1. Open the table in Design view.
2. Select the field to which you want to apply a special format.
3. In the **Field Properties** section, click **Input Mask**, type the mask you want, press [Enter], and then save your changes.

To import data from another Access database

1. On the **File** menu, point to **Get External Data**, and then click **Import**.
2. If necessary, click **Microsoft Access** in the **Files of type** list.
3. Navigate to the location of the file you want to import, click the database name, and then click **Import**.
4. Click the **Options** button to select any import options you want.
5. Select the objects you want to import, or click **Select All** to import all objects, and then click **OK**.

To define a relationship between tables

1. With the database open, click the **Relationships** button on the toolbar to open the Relationships window.
2. If the **Show Table** dialog box isn't displayed, click the **Show Table** button on the toolbar, and then double-click the tables you want to work with in the list displayed. Then close the **Show Table** dialog box.
3. Drag a field from one table and drop it on top of the corresponding field in the other table.
4. Select the options you want in the **Edit Relationships** dialog box, and then click **Create**.
5. Close the Relationships window, clicking **Yes** when prompted to save its layout.

To add a control to a form or report

1. Display the form or report in Design view.
2. If necessary, click the **Toolbox** button to open the toolbox.
3. Click the appropriate control button in the toolbox, and then drag a rectangle in the desired location on the form or report.

4. If necessary, display the control's **Properties** dialog box, and make changes.

To filter a table based on a selection

1. Open the table in Datasheet view.
2. Select the information you want to use as the filter criteria.
3. Click the **Filter By Selection** button.
4. If necessary, repeat steps 2 and 3 to filter the information further.
5. Click the **Remove Filter** button to redisplay all of the table's records.

To filter a form

1. Open the table or form in either Datasheet or Form view.
2. Click the **Filter By Form** button on the toolbar.
3. Click the field box in which you want to create the filter, type the filter criteria you want, and press [Enter]; or select the criteria from the list of options. (Repeat this step for any other fields you want to filter.)
4. To add the additional filter criteria for a particular field, click the **Or** tab and enter the criteria as necessary.
5. Click the **Apply Filter** button.

To create a select query

1. On the **Objects** bar, click **Queries**.
2. Double-click **Create query in Design view**.
3. With the **Tables** tab active, double-click the tables you want to use in the query. Then close the dialog box.
4. To include fields in the query, drag them from the lists at the top of the window to a column in the design grid. (To copy all fields to the grid, double-click the title bar above the field list, and drag the selection over the grid.)
5. Click the **Run** button to run the query and display the results in Datasheet view.

To create a data access page

1. With the database open, click **Pages** on the **Objects** bar.
2. Double-click **Create data access page in Design view** to open a blank data access page.
3. If the **Field List** is not displayed, click the **Field List** button on the toolbar.
4. If the toolbox is not displayed, click the **Toolbox** button on the toolbar.
5. Click the **Save** button, and type the name you want for the page.